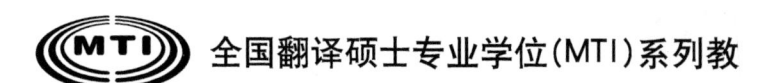

全国翻译硕士专业学位(MTI)系列教

总主编：何其莘 仲伟合 许 钧

商务口译

A Coursebook of Business Interpreting

主编：赵军峰
编者：赵军峰 张丽华 王丹
　　　梅传伟 赵丹

外语教学与研究出版社
FOREIGN LANGUAGE TEACHING AND RESEARCH PRESS
北京　BEIJING

图书在版编目(CIP)数据

商务口译 = A Coursebook of Business Interpreting / 赵军峰主编；赵军峰等编. — 北京：外语教学与研究出版社，2009.6 (2014.5 重印)
(全国翻译硕士专业学位 (MTI) 系列教材/何其莘, 仲伟合, 许钧主编)
ISBN 978-7-5600-8723-8

Ⅰ. 商… Ⅱ. ①赵… ②赵… Ⅲ. 商务—英语—口译—研究生—教材 Ⅳ. H315.9

中国版本图书馆 CIP 数据核字 (2009) 第 100758 号

出 版 人：蔡剑峰
项目负责：都帮森
责任编辑：骆　为　邓付华
封面设计：刘　冬
版式设计：付玉梅
出版发行：外语教学与研究出版社
社　　址：北京市西三环北路 19 号 (100089)
网　　址：http://www.fltrp.com
印　　刷：大恒数码印刷(北京)有限公司
开　　本：740×1000　1/16
印　　张：18.5
版　　次：2009 年 7 月第 1 版　2014 年 5 月第 6 次印刷
书　　号：ISBN 978-7-5600-8723-8
定　　价：32.90 元（附赠 MP3 光盘一张）
＊　　＊　　＊
购书咨询：(010)88819929　电子邮箱：club@fltrp.com
外研书店：http://www.fltrpstore.com
凡印刷、装订质量问题，请联系我社印制部
联系电话：(010)61207896　电子邮箱：zhijian@fltrp.com
凡侵权、盗版书籍线索，请联系我社法律事务部
举报电话：(010)88817519　电子邮箱：banquan@fltrp.com
法律顾问：立方律师事务所　刘旭东律师
　　　　　中咨律师事务所　殷　斌律师
物料号：187230001

全国翻译硕士专业学位（MTI）系列教材
编写委员会

总主编：
何其莘　　仲伟合　　许　钧

编　委：（以姓氏笔画为序）

文　军	王克非	王宏印	王维东
王斌华	仲伟合	任　文	孙致礼
许　钧	何　群	何刚强	何其莘
李　力	李长栓	陈宏薇	陈建平
姜秋霞	胡显耀	赵军峰	柴明颎
秦亚青	傅勇林	谢天振	詹　成
廖七一	穆　雷		

总 序

改革开放 30 年,助推中国翻译事业的大发展、大繁荣,勃勃生机,蔚为壮观。今天的翻译,无论在规模、范围上,还是在质量、水平上,以及对中国社会发展的贡献上都是史无前例的。随着我国经济持续、健康、快速的发展和改革开放的不断深入,我国综合国力不断增强,政治、经济、文化等各方面的国际交往日益频繁。作为服务于改革开放的先导力量和与世界沟通的桥梁,翻译的作用愈发突出。然而,在翻译需求不断攀升的同时,作为翻译人员主要培养阵地的高校,却日益暴露出其在翻译教学与实践之间的脱节问题。毕业生翻译技能不扎实,知识面狭窄,往往难以胜任不同专业领域所需的高层次翻译工作,致使翻译领域特别是高级翻译领域的供需矛盾日益突出,不能满足目前的经济和社会发展需要。这从数量上和质量上,都对高水平翻译人才的培养提出了迫切的要求。

为适应我国改革开放和社会主义现代化建设事业发展的需要,促进中外交流,培养高层次、应用型高级翻译专门人才,国务院学位委员会 2007 年 1 月 23 日第 23 次会议审议通过设置翻译硕士专业学位(MTI)。翻译硕士专业学位是我国第 18 个硕士层次的专业学位,其设立无疑是继 2006 年教育部批准试办翻译本科专业后我国翻译学科建设取得的又一里程碑式的成果,为我国培养高层次、应用型、职业化的翻译人才提供了重要途径,为我国翻译学的学科发展奠定了基础,同时也给我国的外语学科发展带来了机遇与挑战。

翻译硕士专业学位培养德、智、体全面发展,能适应全球经济一体化及提高国家国际竞争力的需要,适应国家经济、文化、社会建设需要的高层次、应用型、专业性口笔译人才。翻译硕士专业学位教育在培养目标、师资要求、教学内容以及教学方法和手段这四点上都与传统的翻译方向研究生教育有很大的不同。首先,翻译硕士专业学位教育注重对学生实践能力的培养,按口译或笔译方向训练学生的口笔译实际操作能力、跨文化交际能力,并为满足翻译实践积累所需要的百科知识。这一点与传统的外国语言文学学科中的翻译研究方向侧重培养学生的外国语言文学理论研究能力、学术研究能力以及就业为导向的教学能力的培养目标差别很大。第二,对学生实践能力的高要求和培养目标的应用型导向,也要求承担翻译硕士专业学位教学任务的教师必须具有丰富的口译或笔译实践经验,并了解翻译教学的原则。第三,翻译硕士专业学位教育中的翻译教学有别于外语教学中的教学翻译。翻译训练不是作为一种检测学生语言能力、水平的手段，而是建立在学生双语交际能力基础之上的职业技能训练，包括译前准备、笔记方法、分析方法、记忆方法、表达方法、术语库的建立等，专门训练学生借助语言知识、主题知识和百科知识对源语信息进行逻辑分析，并用另一种语言将理解的信息表达出来。最后，在教学方法和手段上，专业化的翻译教学需要的是双语交际环境、特定的交际对象和交际主题，还要考虑到翻译用人单位的需求等，要求学生不仅要具备扎实的中文基础和至少通晓一门外语，同时还要具备广博的其他学科（如经济、管理、法律、金融等）知识和实际翻译操作技能。另外，专业翻译人员培养还特别强调要忠实地表达讲话人/作者的想法或信息。因此，翻译作为一个职业（无论是兼职还是全职），专业化程度高，应用性和操作性都很强。要培养职业化高级翻译人才，现行外语教学体制是难以完成的。

职业化的翻译教育也因此需要专门化的教材。该教材体系应根据职业翻译人才的知识结构"双语知识、百科知识、翻译技能知识"三个部分来设计。专业翻译课程的设置也都是根据培养单位的师资特点及教学资源围绕上述三个板块安排的。因此，专业翻译教材应该至少包括口译技能类、笔译技能类、通识教育类、口笔译理论类等类别。正是在上述原则及《翻译硕士专业学位研究生指导性培养方案》的指导下，我们在2007年底组织国内多位了解翻译硕士专业学位并一直从事翻译教学与研究的专家、学者进行研讨，并着手编写国内第一套专门面向翻译硕士专业学位教育的系列教材。该套教材包括口译技能、笔译技能、翻译理论、通识教育及翻译工具书五个类别。整套教材以翻译职业技能训练为核心，以适当的应用型翻译理论为指导，配合不同学科领域的专题训练，旨在完善学生翻译学科知识结构，提高学生口笔译实践能力。在本系列教材全体编委的努力下，呈现在读者面前的这套"全国翻译硕士专业学位（MTI）系列教材"具备以下特点：

（1）口笔译训练的技能化。全面介绍翻译技能。以口译类教材为例，包括口译的记忆、笔记、数字口译、口译语篇分析、口译预测、语义识别、口译译前准备等技能；同声传译则介绍同声传译的概论、视译、应对策略等。

（2）口笔译训练的实战性。笔译的选材基本是社会、经济、文化、教育等领域的真实文本材料；口译则尽可能选用全真会议资料，而且题材范围涉及政治、外交、经济、文化、高科技、法律等多方面。

（3）口笔译训练的专业化。所介绍的口译技能、笔译技能等均为目前国内外口笔译质量评估及口笔译专业认证考试测试的主要方面，通过对本系列教材的学习可以了解职业化翻译培训的程序与内容。

（4）口笔译理论的指导性。对应用型的高水平翻译人才来说，树立正确的翻译观，掌握相关的翻译基础理论是非常重要的。本系列教材所涵盖的翻译基础知识和口笔译理论应努力领会和掌握。

（5）通识教育的融通化。口笔译实践要求掌握英汉两种语言的相关知识及跨文化交际知识，本系列教材中的通识类各分册对拓宽学生的知识面、提高其跨文化交际的意识和能力将起到重要的促进作用。

MTI 职业化人才培养的教学理念和面向实践的教学导向在目前的翻译教学界还是新事物，对其进行不断的探讨、丰富并开展教与学的交流是必要的，也将对翻译硕士专业学位发展大有裨益。外研社这套翻译硕士专业学位系列教材在开发之初就考虑到了这一点，在教材出版的同时，也将推出翻译硕士专业学位教学资源网，不仅指导系列教材的科学使用，也希望能够汇教学实时动态、集各方意见反馈、倡教学经验交流、促学科长远发展。

中国职业化翻译人才的培养才刚刚起步，需要译界、学界同仁"筚路蓝缕，以启山林"。教材建设是专业建设的核心任务之一，我们也希望借编写本套翻译硕士专业学位教材的机会为刚刚起步的中国职业翻译教育尽一份绵薄之力。本套教材的编写力求科学性、指导性和前瞻性，但内容等方面也难免有不尽完善的地方。希望通过本系列教材的编写，与关心中国翻译事业和从事翻译职业的同仁、同行一起关注我国翻译和翻译教学事业的发展现状，以及翻译硕士专业学位教育的实施和发展，进一步探讨高层次专业化翻译人才培养的模式和途径。

全国翻译硕士专业学位（MTI）系列教材编写委员会

2009 年 3 月

前 言

从词源角度看,"business"一词涉及的是个人或社会整体忙于从事商业上切实可行又有利可图的活动的一种状态。从广义上讲,它包括商品和服务供应商在商务社区所举行的各种活动。商务口译,即 Interpreting between Chinese and English in Business Settings,是在国际商务活动中专业性较强的口译行为。

本教材是针对翻译硕士专业学位(MTI)教育指导委员会所颁布的指导性教学大纲规定的选修课商务口译而开发的,凸显口译训练的专业化、高层次和应用型导向。本书主编系广东外语外贸大学高级翻译学院教授、博士、翻译学硕士生导师,具有 MBA 教育背景和各种商务口译实践经验,自 2000 年以来,曾出版多部经贸类、商务类口译教材,其中包括"十五"、"十一五"国家级规划教材。参编人员均有多年的商务口译教学、现场交传和同传实践背景。

考虑到与 MTI 系列的其他口译类教材要有一定的衔接和区别,本书更强调商务口译的专业针对性,在内容的编排上主要以商务知识专题为线索,不再对一般性的口译技巧做细致的讲解和归纳。但在编写时充分考虑到了语言的循序渐进性,遵循由简而繁的原则,并增加与主题知识相关的英汉对照语篇以及提纲挈领式的技巧点评。

在选材上,本书凸显口译的实践性、真实性、知识性和时效性,选取真实的语料和场景,既有最近几年来的商务谈判、访谈、陈述、演讲等既有文本,也有取之现场的新闻发布会、礼仪祝词和宣传"路演"等真实场景录音的转写。在商务大背景下,选材尽量涵盖具有代表意义的商务类专题,比如企业社会责任、企业文化、国际会展、政治与经济、市场营销、人力资源管理、战略管理、交通物流、金融证券、会计税收、国际经济组织以及 IT 产业等。在不同的商务专题下,各单元将依据口译实践的技巧规律进行选材和编排练习,兼顾英汉、汉英互译训练,由对话口译、段落口译向交替传译乃至同声传译过渡,穿插一些核心的口译技巧点评。本教材的突出特点在于内容的专题性和语料的真实性,书后所附的 MP3 光盘中有较大一部分由真实场景的现场录音组成。

根据 MTI 教学大纲的要求,选修课一般开课 15–18 周左右,本教材全书共 18 个单元,围绕 18 个商务专题展开。每单元由专题知识、热身练习、实战训练、口译指南和口译重点组成。专题知识由两篇精选的英汉对照短文构成,供学习者在口译训练之前认真阅读和对照学习；热身练习中的词汇、短语均选自专题知识和实战训练材料，答案提供在附录中；实战训练提供了2-4篇英语和汉语文章供学习者操练，选篇内容丰富，题材广泛，每篇文章的对应译文在与教材配套的MTI教学资源网（http://mti.fltrp.com）上呈现，读者可自查训练效果；口译指南主要是针对实训材料进行语篇分析，补充关键的主题背景知识，并就一些疑难点作出简要的点评和指导，建议可在训练之前先阅读这一部分，口译起来就会"有备无患"。每个单元最后的口译重点部分提供了若干个与主题相关的英、汉长句供读者精练。

本书的读者定位主要是已选修过基础口译和交替传译的MTI学员，此阶段的重点是进行商务主题内容的训练。此外，本书也可供商务英语高年级学生、英汉双语程度较高的商务、经贸专业毕业生以及对商务口译感兴趣的工商界从业人士使用。

本教材是国家级精品课程《英语口译》课程系列建设成果之一，也是广东省科技计划项目（2007B010400072）成果之一，并得到广东省高校人文社科重点研究基地广东外语外贸大学"翻译与研究中心"重大项目（07JDXM74002）以及广东外语外贸大学科研创新团队（GW2006-TB-007）的资助。本书在项目启动过程中得到了广东外语外贸大学副校长仲伟合教授、外语教学研究与出版社副社长徐建中先生、外研社高等英语教育出版分社社长常小玲女士以及祝文杰先生的鼓励和支持，在编写过程中得到了年轻能干的骆为编辑的支持，在此一并致谢。

由于时间仓促，本书在编写的过程中难免存在着不足，欢迎大家在使用时提出宝贵的建议。

编者谨识于广州白云山

2008年冬

目 录

第1单元	礼仪致词 Ceremonial Speeches 1
第2单元	商务谈判 Business Negotiation 15
第3单元	商务访谈 Business Interview 29
第4单元	广告宣传 Advertising & Publicity 43
第5单元	商务陈述 Business Presentation 55
第6单元	新闻发布会 Press Conference 71
第7单元	企业社会责任 Corporate Social Responsibility 83
第8单元	企业文化 Corporate Culture 99
第9单元	国际会展 International Exhibitions 115
第10单元	政治与经济 Political & Economic Issues 127

第11单元	营销与全球采购 Marketing & Global Sourcing	141
第12单元	人力资源管理 Human Resources Management	155
第13单元	战略管理 Strategic Management	169
第14单元	交通与物流 Transportation & Logistics	179
第15单元	金融与证券 Finance & Securities	195
第16单元	会计与税收 Accounting & Taxations	207
第17单元	国际经济组织 International Business Organization	221
第18单元	IT 产业 IT Industry	235
附录一	参考词汇表	249
附录二	主要参考书目	281

第1单元

礼仪致词

Ceremonial Speeches

I Background Knowledge

Directions: Read the following English passages and then compare them with their Chinese equivalents.

Passage 1

  A ceremonial speech is a speech of praise or blame, celebration or thanksgiving, condemnation or mourning. Ceremonial speaking stresses sharing of identities and values that unites people into communities. Eulogies, National Day orations, speeches of condemnation or commendation, farewell addresses, etc. are instances of epideictic discourse. Ceremonial speeches often serve to establish standards for action or provide the ethical and moral basis for future arguments. One should use language that is clear, vivid, inspiring and arousing. The style will be critical in the delivery of the epideictic speech; style is your word preference and syntax.

  Two major techniques of ceremonial speaking are identification and magnification. Identification creates the feeling of closeness, familiarity, and universality. Magnification expounds overcoming obstacles, exceeding the boundaries, shifting paradigms, achieving the unparalleled, benefiting humankind. The language you choose will influence how your audience will envision the subject. Words express an attitude toward the object, the idea, the event, or the person. Your words will convey a perspective or a reality.

  礼仪致词是一种用于表达赞美、指责、庆祝、感谢、谴责或者悲痛之情的致词。它强调的是听众身份和价值观的共享，以使人们结为团体。颂词、国庆演说、谴责词、赞扬词、告别演说等都是富于词藻的演讲。礼仪致词的目的通常是建立行动标准或者是为将来的讨论定下伦理和道德基准。其用语清晰生动，并且具有启发性和煽动性。在做词藻华丽的演讲时，风格是至关重要的，它体现在你的用词偏好和句法上。

认同和称赞是礼仪致词的两个主要手段。认同创造亲切感、熟悉感和共性。称赞旨在说明目前正在克服的障碍、创新的举措和新的计划是什么，如何取得卓越的成绩造福人类。礼仪致词的语言直接影响听众对该主题的想象。因为措辞反映出讲话者对事物、观点、事件或某人的态度。所以，你的言语会反映你的主观看法或者传达一个客观事实。

Passage 2

Ceremonial speeches mark special occasions—and if the speech is good, it will add to the occasion. There are a few general guidelines about how to make a good ceremonial speech:

Emphasize unity. Help audience members identify with each other, considering everyone as part of the whole. Focus on shared sentiments.

Show significance. Ceremonial speeches are given at special occasions, and that specialness should be emphasized. Discuss what is happening and why, and how it can make a difference in the lives of the audience.

Consider attitudes and expectations. Are you giving an award, for example? Consider the person receiving it. If they're rather somber, don't go overboard on the humor. On the other hand, if they're more jovial, be certain to have some fun!

礼仪致词是应景性语篇——如果讲得好，能令现场气氛增色。发表一篇成功的礼仪致词有以下几个指导原则：

强调一致性。帮助听众建立相互之间的认同感，把每个人都视为整体的一部分。重视大家共有的情感。

凸显重要性。礼仪祝辞是应景的演讲，必须强调该场景的特殊性。和听众探讨一下发生了什么，为什么会发生，以及它对听众的生活有什么影响。

考虑听众的态度和期望。比如，你是来颁奖的吗？如果是，那就要考虑领奖人的特点。如果他们是相当严肃的人物，就不要过于幽默。反过来，如果他们和蔼又快乐，那就一定得说得有趣些。

第1单元 礼仪致词

▮ Warm-up

1 Directions: Give the English equivalents of the following Chinese expressions.

坦诚交流	小康社会	招待会
集思广益	资源节约型	鸡尾酒会
以……的名义	环境友好型	茶话会
论坛	值此……之际	欢聚一堂
时代华纳集团	欢迎宴会	分论坛
源远流长	便宴	赞助人
博大精深	午宴	主办人
自强不息	便餐	承办
顽强奋进	工作午餐	协办
壮阔历程	自助餐	主持人
丧权辱国	答谢宴会	和谐社会
民不聊生	告别宴会	科学发展观
内忧外患	庆功宴	

2 Directions: Give the Chinese equivalents of the following English expressions.

commencement	Pixar
connecting the dots	pancreas
serif	biopsy
san serif	endoscope
typeface	dogma
typography	*The Whole Earth Catalog*
Macintosh	Stewart Brand
David Packard	Menlo Park
Bob Noyce	Stay Hungry. Stay Foolish.
NeXT	

商务口译

III Passages for Interpreting

Passage 1

Directions: Listen to the passage and interpret from Chinese into English at the end of each segment. Pay special attention to the numbers.

尊敬的各位领导，各位来宾，女士们，先生们：

经过紧张的筹备，泛珠三角区域渔业经济合作论坛第一次年会终于胜利召开了。在此，我谨代表广东省海洋渔业局对参加论坛的各位代表和嘉宾表示热烈的欢迎。//

今天我们共聚一堂，目的是探讨和拓展在泛珠三角区域合作框架下，渔业合作与发展的新路子，具体落实合作内容，推动泛珠三角区域渔业快速、协调可持续发展。// 同时，为进一步推进泛珠三角区域与东盟国家在渔业方面的合作，此次年会我们增加了与东盟的渔业合作内容。年会的举办得到了农业部和省政府的高度重视和大力支持。泛珠三角九省区、香港、澳门特别行政区渔业行政主管部门和东盟国家都派出代表参加这次年会。// 我相信通过大家的坦诚交流，集思广益，本次年会一定能取得丰硕的成果。借此机会，我向大家介绍一下广东省渔业的情况。//

广东是渔业大省。2006年预计全省水产品产量达到721.5万吨，比上年增长3.8%。渔业经济总产值1,200亿元，比上年增长17.8%。其中水产品产值548亿元，增长4.6%。// 今年1到9月份我省水产品出口量和出口额分别为29万吨、4.05亿美元，比去年同期增长了15.7%（和）21.7（%）。//

Passage 2

Directions: Listen to the passage and interpret from English into Chinese at the end of each segment.

Thank you.

I'm honored to be with you today for your commencement from one of the finest universities in the world. Truth be told, I never graduated from college, and this is the closest I've ever gotten to a college graduation. Today, I want to tell you three stories from my life. That's it. No big deal. Just three stories. //

The first story is about connecting the dots. I dropped out of Reed College after the first six months, but then stayed around as a drop-in for another 18 months or so before I really quit. So why did I drop out? //

It started before I was born. My biological mother was a young, unwed graduate student, and she decided to put me up for adoption. She felt very strongly that I should be adopted by college graduates, so everything was all set for me to be adopted at birth by a lawyer and his wife—except (that) when I popped out they decided at the last minute that they really wanted a girl. // So my parents, who were on a waiting list, got a call in the middle of the night asking, "We've got an unexpected baby boy; do you want him?" They said, "Of course." My biological mother found out later that my mother had never graduated from college and my father had never graduated from high school. She refused to sign the final adoption papers. // She only relented a few months later when my parents promised that I would go to college. This was the start in my life. //

And 17 years later I did go to college. But I naively chose a college that was almost as expensive as Stanford, and all of my working-class parents' savings were being spent on my college tuition. After six months, I couldn't see the value in it. I had no idea what I wanted to do with my life and no idea how college was going to help me figure it out. And here I was spending all of the money my parents had saved their entire life. //

So I decided to drop out and trust that it would all work out okay. // It was pretty scary at the time, but looking back it was one of the best decisions I ever made. The minute I dropped out I could stop taking the required classes that didn't interest me, and begin dropping in on the ones that looked far more interesting. //

It wasn't all romantic. I didn't have a dorm room, so I slept on the floor in friends' rooms. I returned Coke bottles for the five cent deposits to buy food with, and I would walk the seven miles across town every Sunday night to get one good meal a week at the Hare Krishna temple. I loved it. // And much of what I stumbled into by following my curiosity and intuition turned out to be priceless later on. Let me give you one example. Reed College at that time offered perhaps the best calligraphy instruction in the country. Throughout the campus, every poster, every label on every drawer was beautifully hand calligraphed. // Because I had dropped out and didn't have to take the normal classes, I decided to take a calligraphy class to learn how to do this. I learned about serif and san serif typefaces, about varying the amount of space between different letter combinations, about what makes great typography great. It was beautiful, historical, artistically subtle in a way that science can't capture, and I found it fascinating. //

None of this had even a hope of any practical application in my life. But 10 years later, when we were designing the first Macintosh computer, it all came back to me. And we designed it all into the Mac. // It was the first computer with beautiful typography. If I had never dropped in on that single course in college, the Mac would have never had multiple typefaces or proportionally spaced fonts. And since Windows just copied the Mac, it's likely that no personal computer would have them. // If I had never dropped out, I would have never dropped in on that calligraphy class, and personal computers might not have the wonderful typography that they do. Of course it was impossible to connect the dots looking forward when I was in college. But it was very, very clear looking backwards 10 years later. //

Again, you can't connect the dots looking forward; you can only connect them looking backwards. So you have to trust that the dots will somehow connect in your future. You have to trust in something—your gut, destiny, life, karma, whatever—because believing that the dots will connect down the road will give you the confidence to follow your heart, even when it leads you off the well-worn path, and that will make all the difference. //

My second story is about love and loss. // I was lucky—I found what I loved to do early in life. Woz and I started Apple in my parents' garage when I was 20. We worked hard, and in 10 years Apple had grown from just the two of us in a garage into a two-billion-dollar company with over 4,000 employees. // We (had) just released our finest creation—the Macintosh—a year earlier, and I (had) just turned 30. //

And then I got fired. // How can you get fired from a company you started? Well, as Apple grew we hired someone who I thought was very talented to run the company with me, and for the first year or so things went well. But then our visions of the future began to diverge and eventually we had a falling out. When we did, our Board of Directors sided with him. // And so at 30, I was out. And very publicly out. What had been the focus of my entire adult life was gone, and it was devastating. //

I really didn't know what to do for a few months. I felt that I had let the previous generation of entrepreneurs down—that I (had) dropped the baton as it was being passed to me. // I met with David Packard and Bob Noyce and tried to apologize for screwing up so badly. I was a very public failure, and I even thought about running away from the valley. But something slowly began to dawn on me: I still loved what I did. The turn of events at Apple had not changed that one bit. I had been rejected, but I was still in love. And so I decided to start over. // I didn't see it then, but it turned out that getting fired from Apple was the best thing that could have ever happened to me. The heaviness of being successful was replaced by the lightness of being a beginner again, less sure about everything. It freed me to enter one of the most creative periods of my life. //

During the next five years, I started a company named NeXT, another company named Pixar, and fell in love with an amazing woman who would become my wife. Pixar went on to create the world's first computer-animated feature film, *Toy Story*, and is now the most successful animation studio in the world. // In a remarkable turn of events, Apple bought NeXT, and I returned to Apple, and the technology we developed at NeXT is at the heart of Apple's current renaissance. And Laurene and I have a wonderful family together. //

I'm pretty sure none of this would have happened if I hadn't been fired from Apple. It was awful-tasting medicine, but I guess the patient needed it. Sometime life—sometimes life's gonna hit you in the head with a brick. Don't lose faith. // I'm convinced that the only thing that kept me going was that I loved what I did. You've got to find what you love. // And that is as true for work as it is for your lovers. Your work is going to fill a large part of your life, and the only way to be truly satisfied is to do what you believe is great work. And the only way to do great work is to love what you do. // If you haven't found it yet, keep looking—and don't settle. As with all matters of the heart, you'll know when you find it. And like any great relationship, it just gets better and better as the years roll on. So keep looking—don't settle. //

My third story is about death. When I was 17, I read a quote that went something like: "If you live each day as if it was your last, someday you'll most certainly be right." // It made an impression on me, and since then, for the past 33 years, I've looked in the mirror every morning and asked myself, "If today were the last day of my life, would I want to do what I am about to do today?" And whenever the answer has been "No" for too many days in a row, I know I need to change something. //

Remembering that I'll be dead soon is the most important tool I've ever encountered to help me make the big choices in life. Because almost everything—all external expectations, all pride, all fear of embarrassment or failure—these things just fall away in the face of death, leaving only what is truly important. // Remembering that you are going to die is the best way I know to avoid the trap of thinking you have something to lose. You are already naked. There is no reason not to follow your heart. //

About a year ago I was diagnosed with cancer. I had a scan at 7:30 in the morning, and it clearly showed a tumor on my pancreas. I didn't even know what a pancreas was. The doctors told me this was almost certainly a type of cancer that is incurable, and that I should expect to live no longer than three to six months. My doctor advised me to go home and get my affairs in order, which is doctor's code for "prepare to die". // It means to try and tell your kids everything you thought you'd have the next 10 years to tell them in just a few months. It means to make sure everything is buttoned up so that it will be as easy as possible for your family. It means to say your goodbyes. //

I lived with that diagnosis all day. Later that evening I had a biopsy, where they stuck an endoscope down my throat, through my stomach into my intestines, put a needle into my pancreas and got a few cells from the tumor. I was sedated, but my wife, who was there, told me that when they viewed the cells under a microscope the doctors started crying because it turned out to be a very rare form of pancreatic cancer that is curable with surgery. I had the surgery and, thankfully, I'm fine now. //

This was the closest I've been to facing death, and I hope it's the closest I get for a few more decades. Having lived through it, I can now say this to you with a bit more certainty than when death was a useful but purely intellectual concept: no one wants to die. //

Even people who want to go to heaven don't want to die to get there. And yet death is the destination we all share. No one has ever escaped it. And that is as it should be, because death is very likely the single best invention of life. It's life's change agent. It clears out the old to make way for the new. // Right now the new is you, but someday not too long from now, you will gradually become the old and be cleared away. Sorry to be so dramatic, but it's quite true. //

Your time is limited, so don't waste it living someone else's life. Don't be trapped by dogma, which is living with the results of other people's thinking. // Don't let the noise of others' opinions drown out your own inner voice. And most important, have the courage to follow your heart and intuition. They somehow already know what you truly want to become. Everything else is secondary. //

When I was young, there was an amazing publication called *The Whole Earth*

Catalog, which was one of the "bibles" of my generation. It was created by a fellow named Stewart Brand not far from here in Menlo Park, and he brought it to life with his poetic touch. // This was in the late (19) 60s, before personal computers and desktop publishing, so it was all made with typewriters, scissors, and Polaroid cameras. It was sort of like Google in paperback form, 35 years before Google came along. It was idealistic, overflowing with neat tools and great notions. //

Stewart and his team put out several issues of *The Whole Earth Catalog* and then when it had run its course, they put out a final issue. It was the mid-1970s, and I was your age. // On the back cover of their final issue was a photograph of an early morning country road, the kind you might find yourself hitchhiking on if you were so adventurous. Beneath it were the words: "Stay Hungry. Stay Foolish." It was their farewell message as they signed off. // Stay Hungry. Stay Foolish. And I've always wished that for myself. And now, as you graduate to begin anew, I wish that for you.

Stay Hungry. Stay Foolish. //

Thank you all very much. //

Passage 3

Directions: Listen to the passage and interpret from Chinese into English at the end of each segment.

尊敬的帕森斯先生，尊敬的各位贵宾，女士们、先生们：

晚上好！// 在这个美好的夜晚，我很高兴同大家在这里相聚，参加2005年北京《财富》全球论坛的开幕式。// 首先，我谨代表中国政府，并以我个人的名义，对各位朋友的到来表示诚挚的欢迎！向论坛主办方美国时代华纳集团表示衷心的祝贺！//

这次论坛确定以"中国和新的亚洲世纪"为主题，充分表达了大家对中国和亚洲发展前景的关注，表达了大家对中国及亚洲的发展对全球经济增长所发挥的作用的关注。// 这也充分说明，在经济全球化趋势深入发展的条件下，中国及亚洲的发展正在成为世界经济发展新的推动力量，世界经济发展也将给中国、给亚洲发展带来新的重要机遇。世界各国经济互利合作、相互依存的加深，必将给全球经济增长创造更加美好的前景。//

女士们、先生们！// 中国是一个有着五千多年悠久历史的文明古国。长期以来，中国人民以自己的勤劳智慧创造了灿烂的中华文明，为人类文明进步作出了重大贡献。// 北京就是一座有三千多年悠久历史的文明古城，八百多前北京开始建都。离今晚会场人民大会堂不远的地方，就是举世闻名的故宫。故宫始建于六百年前，是世界上现存最大最完整的古代宫殿建筑群。//

从历史悠久的北京和建筑精美的故宫这些缩影中，人们就能够生动地感受到中华文明源远流长、博大精深的深厚底蕴，感受到中华民族自强不息、顽强奋进的壮阔历程。//

19世纪中叶以后，由于列强的野蛮侵略和封建统治的腐败无能，中华民族陷入了丧权辱国、民不聊生的悲惨境地。面对内忧外患，中国人民不懈抗争，终于在中国共产党领导下建立了新中国。//

新中国建立以来，特别是1978年实行邓小平先生倡导的改革开放政策以来，中国发生了前所未有的深刻变革。//从1978年到2004年的26年间，中国国内生产总值从1,473亿美元增长到16,494亿美元，年均增长9.4%；进出口总额从206亿美元增长到11,548亿美元，年均增长超过16%；国家外汇储备从1亿6,700万美元增加到6,099亿美元；农村贫困人口从2亿5,000万人减少到2,600万人，中国的综合国力显著增强，人民生活不断改善。//中国人民在继承和发扬古老文明的基础上创造了新的历史。现在，13亿中国人民正万众一心地在中国特色社会主义道路上开拓前进。//

中国已经明确了本世纪头20年的奋斗目标，这就是紧紧抓住重要战略机遇期，全面建设惠及十几亿人口的更高水平的小康社会，到2020年实现国内生产总值比2000年翻两番，达到40,000亿美元左右，人均国内生产总值达到3,000美元左右，使经济更加发展、民主更加健全、科教更加进步、文化更加繁荣、社会更加和谐、人民生活更加殷实。//

我们深知，中国在相当长时期内仍然是发展中国家，从中国有13亿人口的国情出发，实现这个奋斗目标是很不容易的，需要我们继续进行长期的艰苦奋斗。//

为了实现这个目标，我们将坚持以科学发展观统领经济社会发展全局。我们将坚持以人为本，从最广大人民的根本利益出发，不断满足人民群众日益增长的物质、文化需求，努力促进人的全面发展。//

我们将坚持以经济建设为中心，把发展作为第一要务，推动经济建设、政治建设、文化建设与和谐社会建设全面发展。我们将坚持社会主义市场经济的改革方向，进一步推动制度创新，不断深化改革，激发全社会的创造活力，增强经济社会发展的内在动力。//

我们将坚持对外开放的基本国策，建立更加开放的市场体系，在更大范围、更广领域、更高层次上参与国际经济技术合作和竞争。//

我们将坚持走新型工业化道路，着力调整经济结构和加快转变经济增长方式，提高经济增长的质量和效益，大力发展循环经济，建设资源节约型、环境友好型社会，走生产发展、生活富裕、生态良好的文明发展道路。我们相信，只要坚定不移地走符合中国国情的发展道路，我们就一定能够实现既定的奋斗目标，为维护世界和平、促进共同发展发挥更大的建设性作用。//

女士们、先生们！中国的发展同亚洲及世界的发展紧密相关。中国的发展已经并将继续为亚洲及世界各国带来合作共赢的机遇。截至2004年底，中国累计实际利用外商直接投资额达到5,621亿美元，批准外商投资企业50多万个，并形成了年进口5,600多亿美元的大市场。//

目前，绝大多数国家和地区都有企业来华投资，《财富》500强企业中已有400多家在华投资，外商投资在华设立的研发中心达700多家。随着中国的不断发展，中国同世界各国和各类企业的合作必将进一步扩大。//

中国将继续稳步开放市场，创新引进外资的形式，完善有关鼓励和保护外商投资的法律法规，改革涉外经济管理体制，加强知识产权保护，努力为中国的对外经贸合作和外国来华投资提供一切便利，创造更好的环境。//

女士们，先生们。在座各位大企业的领导人是国际经济活动的重要参与者和推动者。长期以来，你们中的许多人及你们的企业，积极推动和开展与中国的经济技术合作，为中国经济的持续发展和中国有关产业技术水平的提高作出了重要贡献。//

实践证明，这种互利合作对双方都有利。我们欢迎各位继续扩大在中国的投资和贸易，加强同中国企业的经济技术合作。// 我相信，你们一定能够发挥各自的企业优势和丰富的经营经验，在推动国际经济技术合作、促进地区及世界经济发展方面发挥重要作用。让我们携手努力，为维护世界和平、促进共同发展作出更大的贡献。//

最后，我预祝2005年北京《财富》全球论坛取得圆满成功！//

谢谢大家。//

IV Guide to Interpreting

1. Passage 1 是2006年12月广东省海洋渔业局局长在"论珠三角区域渔业经济合作论坛"第一次年会上的祝词节选，节选内容强调会议的重要性和统计数字。在进行这类语篇的口译时，译员一定要注意熟悉礼仪场合的套语，分清礼仪场合的正式程度。对于这篇练习，译员还需要重点做到以下两点。首先，要养成良好的习惯，准备一份备忘录，放在随手可及的地方。上面用中英文列出：会议的名称、各有关单位的名称、主持人的名字和职位、出席会议的重要领导的名字和职位等。其次，做好心理准备，迎接数字的挑战。译员平时就要多练习数字转换，提高数字口译的能力。并且，在口译中记录数字的时候，千万不能忘记数字的背景。背景和数字是同等重要的，甚至背景还更为关键，因为如果实在来不及记下数字，可以抓住背景对数字进行概括，用"有显著提高"、"重大突破"、"反差很大"等表达补上，使信息损失最小化。

2. 史蒂夫·乔布斯（Steve Jobs）是一位非常优秀的演讲者。Passage 2是他在斯坦福大学毕业典礼上的演讲，生动有趣，极具鼓动性，是不可多得的一篇好演讲。要翻译好这个演讲，不仅要在内容上作到准确，更重要的是要注意语言的选择，配合现场气氛把乔布斯的幽默和煽情忠实地呈现给听众。首先，从主题的准备上，要抓住一条原则——尽可能地接近讲话者的知识体系。因此，要阅读乔布斯的简历，了解他主要的事迹。例如：他和谁创立了苹果公司？苹果机的名字是什么？他的领导力是怎样发展的？其次是语言的准备。除了书中给出的热身词汇以外，译员还要阅读他的相关资料，从中提取有用的语言点，找到中英对照的表达方法。最后是情绪的配合。现场的气氛非常热烈，掌声不断，译员要尽可能地传递演讲者的激情，以免译语听众产生心理落差。幽默的翻译需要靠译员的机智和平时的积累，挑战性比较大。

3. Passage 3 也是典型的礼仪祝词，是胡锦涛主席2005年在北京全球财富论坛上的致词，规格高，难度较大。致词行文非常正式，有很多官方语言。祝词中套语、四字格的表达方式所处可见。译员在平时要多阅读《中国日报》等主流报刊，经常浏览中国政府网，收集和积累中国英语（China English）的表达方法，建立自己的词汇库，例如"三个代表"、"和谐社会"、"小康社会"、"改革开放"和"科学发展观"等的权威英文表述。像这种类型的口译任务需要译员有充分的译前准备工作，力求准确无误。

V Highlight for Interpreting

Directions: Interpret the following sentences from English into Chinese or vice versa.

1. I'm honored to be with you today for your commencement from one of the finest universities in the world.

2. You have to trust in something—your gut, destiny, life, karma, whatever—because believing that the dots will connect down the road will give you the

confidence to follow your heart, even when it leads you off the well-worn path, and that will make all the difference.

3. If you live each day as if it was your last, someday you'll most certainly be right.
4. Right now the new is you, but someday not too long from now, you will gradually become the old and be cleared away. Sorry to be so dramatic, but it's quite true.
5. Don't let the noise of others' opinions drown out your own inner voice. And most important, have the courage to follow your heart and intuition. They somehow already know what you truly want to become. Everything else is secondary.
6. Stay Hungry. Stay Foolish.
7. 经过紧张的筹备，泛珠三角区域渔业经济合作论坛第一次年会终于胜利召开了。在此，我谨代表广东省海洋渔业局对参加论坛的各位代表和嘉宾表示热烈的欢迎。
8. 我相信通过大家的坦诚交流，集思广益，本次年会一定能取得丰硕的成果。
9. 首先，我谨代表中国政府，并以我个人的名义，对各位朋友的到来表示诚挚的欢迎！向论坛主办方美国时代华纳集团表示衷心的祝贺！
10. 从历史悠久的北京和建筑精美的故宫这些缩影中，人们就能够生动地感受到中华文明源远流长、博大精深的深厚底蕴，感受到中华民族自强不息、顽强奋进的壮阔历程。
11. 我们将坚持对外开放的基本国策，建立更加开放的市场体系，在更大范围、更广领域、更高层次上参与国际经济技术合作和竞争。
12. 在座各位大企业的领导人是国际经济活动的重要参与者和推动者。长期以来，你们中的许多人及你们的企业，积极推动和开展与中国的经济技术合作，为中国经济的持续发展和中国有关产业技术水平的提高作出了重要贡献。
13. 我相信，你们一定能够发挥各自的企业优势和丰富的经营经验，在推动国际经济技术合作、促进地区及世界经济发展方面发挥重要作用。让我们携手努力，为维护世界和平、促进共同发展作出更大的贡献。
14. 最后，我预祝2005年北京《财富》全球论坛取得圆满成功！

第2单元

商务谈判

Business Negotiation

I Background Knowledge

Directions: Read the following English passages and then compare them with their Chinese equivalents.

Passage 1

I want to introduce to you an idea called common interests. It is a special kind of interest. We will discuss what they are, and why they are so useful and why focus on them. First, the definition. A common interest is a shared goal or a mutual desire which the parties can achieve by working together. In other words, it's a single result that would please both of us. For example, Russia and America had a common interest in defeating Germany in World War II.

Common interests are not the same thing as competing interests. For example, it is not true when a car buyer and a car seller both want to get the best price from the other. That is not a common interest because they are fighting each other. The better one does, the worse the other does. They are not partners. They are competitors. That's a competing interest. Common interests mean something that makes us partners. It's not the same thing as where interests are different but not in conflict. That's called a complimentary set of interests. But now we are talking about a situation where we are partners side by side trying to get to the same place together.

现在我想介绍一个概念，叫做共同利益。这是一种特殊的利益。我们会讨论它是什么，为什么如此有用，以及为什么要关注它。首先，我们来看它的定义。共同利益指通过合作可以实现的共同目标或或共同愿望。换句话说，它是一个能让双方都满意的单一结果。比如，在第二次世界大战期间，美国和俄罗斯的共同利益就是打败德国。

共同利益与利益冲突是两个不同的概念。例如，当汽车销售员和买家都想拿到最好的价格时，他们之间就不是共同利益关系。因为他们在互相抗争，一方得利另一方则损失。他们不是合作关系而是竞争关系。这就叫做利益冲突。共同利益指的是使我们成为合作伙伴的东西。它也不同于互补性利益，即利益有所不同但不相冲突。而现在我们讲的是另一种情况，即利益的各方并肩作战以达成共同的目标。

Passage 2

Negotiation is something that we do all the time and is not only used for business purposes. For example, we use it in our social lives perhaps for deciding a time to meet, or where to go on a rainy day. Negotiation is usually considered as a compromise to settle an argument or issue to benefit ourselves as much as possible. Communication is always the link that will be used to negotiate the issue/argument whether it is face-to-face, on the telephone or in writing. Remember, negotiation is not always between two people: it can involve several members from two parties. There are many reasons why you may want to negotiate and there are several ways to approach it. The following is a few things that you may want to consider. If your reason for negotiation is seen as "beating" the opposition, it is known as "distributive negotiation". This way, you must be prepared to use persuasive tactics and you may not end up with maximum benefit.

This is because your agreement is not being directed to a certain compromise and both parties are looking for a different outcome. Should you feel your negotiation is much more "friendly" with both parties aiming to reach agreement, it is known as "integrative negotiation". This way usually brings an outcome where you will both benefit highly. Negotiation, in a business context, can be used for selling, purchasing, staff (e.g. contracts), borrowing (e.g. loans) and transactions, along with anything else that you feel are applicable for your business.

Before you decide to negotiate, it is a good idea to prepare. What is it exactly that you want to negotiate? Set out your objectives (e.g. I want more time to pay off the loan). You have to take into account how it will benefit the other party by offering some sort of reward or incentive (explained later). What is involved (money, sales, time, conditions, discounts, terms, etc.)? Know your extremes: how much extra can you afford to give to settle an agreement? Although you are not aiming to give out the maximum, it is worth knowing so that you will not go out of your limits. Know what your opposition is trying to achieve by their negotiation. This is useful information that could be used to your benefit and may well be used to reach a final agreement. Consider what is valuable to your business, not the costs. You may end up losing something in the negotiation that is more valuable to your business than money. It could be a reliable client or your company reputation.

It is important that you approach the other party directly to make an appointment to negotiate, should it be in person, writing or by phone (not through a phone operator, receptionist, assistant, etc.), as this will allow you to set the agenda in advance, and improve the prospects of the other party preparing sufficiently enough to make a decision on the day. Try to be fairly open about your reason for contact or they may lose interest instantly and not follow up on the appointment. Save all your comments for the actual appointment—don't give away anything that will give them a chance to prepare too thoroughly: it's not war, but it is business! So, it's time to negotiate and you've prepared well. What else must you have? Two things: confidence and power. Your power will come from your ability to influence. For example, you may be the buyer (but not always a strong position), or have something that the other party wants, or you may be able to give an intention to penalize if the other party fails to meet the agreement (as is the way with construction). As briefly mentioned above, you may be able to give a reward or an incentive. For example, you may be selling kitchen knives and as part of the package you are giving a knife sharpener and a storage unit away free as an incentive.

It is always important that you keep the negotiation in your control: this can mean within your price range, your delivery time or your profit margin. If you fail to do so, you will end up on the wrong side of the agreement, and with nothing more out of the deal other than maintaining trading relationships. When negotiating, aim as high as you feel necessary in order to gain the best deal for yourself. The other party may bring this down but it is a good tactic, as it is always easier to play down than to gain. Make sure that you remain flexible throughout the negotiation in case the opposition decides to change the direction of the agreement (they may want different incentives or even change their objectives). This is where your preparation comes to good use: knowing your limits and the other party's needs. If you're a quick thinker, then you've got an advantage. You'll need to turn it around quickly if things start to go against you without putting your objectives at risk. Confidence comes from knowing your business, your product, what its worth, and being able to communicate this well to the other party: these people are almost impossible to get the better of, as some of you will know only too well.

　　谈判是一种我们总在进行的活动，它并不仅限于商务用途。例如，我们也许会用它来决定见面的时间，或者下雨天该去哪儿。谈判通常被视为一种妥协手段来处理争端或问题，从而尽可能使双方都受惠。无论是采取面对面、打电话还是书面的形式，沟通总是被用作对问题/争端进行谈判的纽带。请记住，谈判不总是发生在两个人之间：它可能涉及双方的好几个成员。你想通过谈判来解决问题的原因有很多，要达到目的的方式也有好几个。下面的几个方式可供参考。如果谈判的目的是要"打败"对手，那这种谈判就叫做"分配式谈判"。这种方式必须采用说服性策略，而且最终有可能得不到利益的最大化。

　　那是因为双方达成的协议并没有导向某种妥协，双方所期待的结果也不一样。如果你会觉得双方都试图达成协议，谈判显得十分"友好"，这样的谈判就叫做"整合式谈判"。这种方式通常能给双方带来双赢的结果。在商务环境下的谈判行为，可以用于销售、采购、员工（如合同协议）、借入（如借贷）和交易，还有其他所有你认为适用的商务环节。

　　在决定谈判之前，最好先进行准备。首先要清楚谈判的确切目标是什么？因此，应先设定你的目标（例如，我希望争取到更多的时间来还贷）。接下来，考虑如果给予一些报酬或者激励措施，对方会得到怎样的好处（稍后再进行阐述）。谈判涉及哪些方面（金钱、销售、时间、条件、折扣、条款等）？了解自己的底线：为了达成协议，你能给得起多少额外的让步？即使你不准备做出最大限度的让步，但是清楚自己的底线也是必要的，这样你在日后的谈判中就不会超越底线。还要了解对方试图从谈判中得到什么。这是一个很有用的信息，既有利于争取你自身的利益，也有利于达成最终的协议。你需要考虑什么对你的企业来说是有价值的，当然这不是指金钱。因为在谈判中，你有可能最终失去对你的企业来说比金钱更有价值的东西。它可能是一个可靠的客户，或是你企业的信誉。

　　直接通过见面、书面或打电话（不应经过电话接线员、前台、助理等转述）的方式与对方接触来做一个谈判的预约是很重要的，因为这样一来，你就能提前设定好议程，并让对方充分准备从而能在预定的日期做出决定。而且要把你们为什么得联系的原因说明白，否则对方会立刻失去兴趣，或者不遵循约定。在实际的预约过程中，保留你所有的意见——不要透露可以使对方有机会做过于充分的准备的任何信息；这虽然不是战场，但也是商场！再接下来就是谈判了，而你已经做好了充分准备。除此之外，你还必须具备什么呢？两样东西：自信和强势。你的强势来自你施加影响的能力。例如，你可能是买家（但不总处在上风），或者你拥有对方想要的东西，又或者在对方不能达到协议要求的情况下，你能表现出惩罚的意图（像建筑工程一样）。前面已经简单地提到过，你需要给予对方一些报酬或者激励。例如，你在销售厨房刀具，作为一种促销手段，你可能会附赠磨刀器和储刀盒，和刀具一并打包销售。

把谈判掌控在自己的手中是一条金科玉律：这可能意味着谈判会在你的价格幅度以内、交货限期以前或保证在最小利润以上进行。如果你掌控不了，最终的协议会就对你不利，除了维持贸易关系以外，你不会从交易中得到任何好处。在谈判中，为了获取对你最有利的结果，你应该在必要的范围内把目标定高。对方可能会降低这个目标，但这也是一个很好的策略，因为降低总比获取容易。在整个谈判过程中，你必须确保留有余地，以防对方决定改变协议的方向（他们可能想要不同的激励措施，甚至改变初衷）。这时候，你的准备就派上用场了：你了解自身的底线和对方的需求。如果你才思够敏捷，就能拿下主动权。如果事情开始朝着对你不利的方向发展，你就需要在保证原定目标不受威胁的前提下迅速地把局面扭转过来。自信，来自对自己企业、产品和其价值的了解，并能在这些方面与对方很好地沟通；只要你们之中能有人非常清楚这些情况，对方是几乎不可能占上风的。

II Warm-up

1 **Directions:** Give the English equivalents of the following Chinese expressions.

提案	还盘	多听少说
发盘	让步	筹码
反提案	掌握主动	开放式问题

2 **Directions:** Give the Chinese equivalents of the following English expressions.

common interest	distributive negotiation
competing interest	integrative negotiation
complimentary interest	tax benefit

商务口译

telephone sales	political analyst
interest-based thinking	cultural differences
barter deal	broker
forward foreign exchange contract	liaison
economic turmoil	best alternative to an agreement
raw material supplier	

III Passages for Interpreting

Passage 1

Directions: Listen to the passage and interpret from Chinese into English at the end of each segment.

　　进出口商要想成功就得掌握谈判技巧。贸易谈判实际上是一种对话，在这个对话中双方说明自己的情况，陈述自己的观点，倾听对方的提案、发盘、并作反提案、还盘、互相让步，最后达成协议。掌握谈判技巧，就能在对话中掌握主动，获得满意的结果。我们应掌握以下几个重要的技巧：//

　　第一，多听少说。缺乏经验的谈判者的最大弱点是不能耐心地听对方发言，他们认为自己的任务就是谈自己的情况，说自己想说的话和反驳对方的反对意见。因此，在谈判中，他们总在心里想下面该说的话，不注意听对方发言，许多宝贵信息就这样失去了。// 他们错误地认为优秀的谈判员是因为说得多才掌握了谈判的主动。其实成功的谈判员在谈判时把50%以上的时间用来听。他们边听、边想、边分析，并不断向对方提出问题，以确保自己完全正确地理解对方。// 他们仔细听对方说的每一句话，而不仅是他们认为重要的或想听的话，因此而获得大量宝贵信息，增加了谈判的筹码。有效地倾听可以使我们了解进口商的需求，找到解决问题的新办法，修改我们的发盘或还盘。//"谈"是任务，而"听"则是一种能力，甚至可以说是一种天份。"会听"是任何一个成功的谈判员都必须具备的条件。在谈判中，我们要尽量鼓励对方多说，我们要向对方说"yes"、"please go on"，并提问题请对方回答，使对方多谈他们的情况，以达到尽量了解对方的目的。//

　　谈判的第二个重要技巧是巧提问题。通过提问我们不仅能获得平时无法得到的信息，而且还能证实我们以往的判断。出口商应用开放式的问题，即答复不是"是"或"不是",而是需要特别解释的问题,来了解进口商的需求,因为这类问题可以使进口商自由畅谈他们的需求。例如:Can you tell me more about your company? What do you think of our proposal ? 对于外商的回答,我们要把重点和关键问题记下来以备后用。//

发盘后,进口商常常会问:"Can not you do better than that?"对此发问,我们不要让步,而应反问:"What is meant by better?"或"Better than what?"这些问题可使进口商说明他们究竟在哪些方面不满意。// 例如,进口商会说:"Your competitor is offering better terms." 这时,我们可继续发问,直到完全了解竞争对手的发盘。然后,我们可以向对方说明我们的发盘是不同的,实际上要比竞争对手的更好。如果对方给我们的要求给予一个模糊的回答,如"no problem",我们不要接受,而应请他作具体回答。// 此外,在提问前,尤其在谈判初期,我们应征求对方同意,这样做有两个好处:一是若对方同意我方提问,就会在回答问题时更加合作;二是若对方的回答是"yes",这个肯定的答复会给谈判制造积极的气氛并带来一个良好的开端。//

Passage 2

Directions: Listen to the passage and interpret from English into Chinese at the end of each segment.

Let me tell you a story. A student of mine wrote that he was in his office one day when he got a phone call. It was his client and his client said, "Do you know that software project that your firm is working on for us?" "Yes, of course I do. We are working on it right now." The client said, "We want you to deliver it two weeks early." "Oh no," thinks [thought] my student, "we can't do that." And the student says [said], "I do not think that would be possible." And the client said, "Well, if you do not do it, we will not be able to work with you anymore. We need this!" "Well, Ok," says [said] my student, "I will check on it." And so he talks [talked] to his engineers and his engineers say [said], "No, we can not do this." // In fact, the reason we can not do it is because we are under great time pressure now, and there is no way we can do it faster. So the student calls [called] back the client, and he explains [explained], "I have checked with our engineers, and I am very sorry that we can not give you the software faster." Well the client said, "All right, I thank you for checking. That's Ok, goodbye! I think I understand, Ok." // So my student goes [went] back to his work. But a few minutes later, my student's boss calls [called] my student into his office. The clients, the client had called her boss and her boss had called my student's boss, and while my student was in the room, he heard on the speaker phone a very unhappy conversation. The boss of the client said, "If you do not get it to us two weeks sooner, that would be the end of our relationship." The student said that his boss was very upset. The student said to my... to his boss, "Tell her we will call her back shortly." So the boss told the client, "May we call you back?" "Yes, but you must call me back soon." "Ok. I will." The boss calls [called] an emergency meeting of the entire staff. And immediately, my student said, it was (a) disaster. The engineers kept saying, "We can not do this!" But my [the] boss and the other executives said, "We have to!" "We can not!" "We must!" "We can not!" " We must!" //

My student noticed, while this was... this argument was happening, oh my goodness, they are fighting over positions! Then the student said, "Wait a minute, let us take a moment." And he turned to the engineers and he said, "Why, tell me why we can not deliver this product so quickly?" And the engineers, for the first time, explained the underlying interest they had. "We are working hard," the engineers said, "to deliver a major feature that the client asked for. If we work on getting this project done quickly, that major feature will never happen. And the client said 'we want that major feature.' " Oh my goodness! That's the interest. We want to get the client the major feature. "Well, all right. Let's take a moment." My student said and asked, "why does the client want this software so quickly? " //

And they realized there was a specific reason. The client needed the software so that the client could have a group of telephone operators use the software immediately to receive telephone sales calls and to make telephone sales calls. In other words, the client needs the software so they can make telephone sales. "Wait a minute," says my student, "is there any way that we can help the client with that interest without rushing the software?" // And as soon as my student asked that question, his group started to think of creative options. They came up with several, including this one: what if we offered to work these... these telephone sales phones ourselves for two weeks? We have some extra staff, they are not busy. Why don't they handle the sales calls? Interesting! So the boss and my student called the client, calls [called] the client back, and they explain [explained], "We are sorry, we can not give you the software right away. But we want to make sure we understand your concern. And if we are right, we have an idea that may work for you instead." // And it turns out they were correct in their guess about what the client's interest was. "Yes, we want to sell this, use the telephone sales system quickly." "Well, " my student said, "what if we provided our own employees to handle the sales calls immediately?" The... the client said, "That is an excellent idea! We may very well use that! We bet it will work for us. If we think we need that, we will call you. But if you are willing to do that for us, we do not need the software right away. Thank you!" //

What was the result? The client decided they could live without the software after all for two weeks. And they did use just a little bit of this student's firm's assistance. In the process, the client found that this firm, my student's firm, was a much better company than they realized. "You have satisfied our need; you have shown us that you care about us; you have found a creative way to help us; you are willing to work with us even when it looks impossible. You are an excellent supplier. We want to do more business with you." // Now, wait a minute, did you see what just happened when this student received the phone call in the morning? It looked like it was the end of his career. It looked like it was the end of this relationship. It was a disaster. // But by the end of the afternoon, not only was the problem solved, but the relationship between the supplier and the company was much better, much stronger. The trust was much greater. How did my student do this? I will tell you how. // He used interest-based thinking. He asked why do you want this. He found creative options. And in the process, he built incredible trust and relationship. That is an example of how you can take your skill, your principle and turn it into a heroic solution. //

But now I want to go further. I want to show you that in international negotiation this creative idea can solve many problems that are common internationally. And I want to look with you at several common problems and how we can solve them with the same simple interest-based strategy. // One of the common problems you encounter in international negotiations is the problem of currency. Often there is some question—what currency will we use? For example, the American seller in this story says we must have a high price if you are going to pay us in Mexican currency. And the Mexican buyer says, "No, we must have a low price if we are going to pay in Mexican currency." Higher price, lower price, higher price, lower price, those are their positions, those are their demands. //

But why? What are their interests here? Well, the Americans are worried that if the Mexican currency goes down, the American seller will lose money. But why is the Mexican firm so worried? They are worried because they know that the Mexican government imposes a tax on the Mexican firm if the Mexican firm sends out too much currency outside Mexico. // Well those are their underlying interests. Is there a creative solution that can satisfy both sides' interests? Yes, there are several. One is to pay in dollars. Another is to pay in product instead of in currency, to do a barter deal. And a third is to use something called forward foreign exchange contracts to limit the risk. Those are three creative options. // And alone or together, they can help solve the currency issue. And they are used all the time when there is an issue of currency in international negotiations. //

Passage 3

Directions: Listen to the passage and interpret from English into Chinese at the end of each segment.

Let's take another example of interest-based solutions internationally. How do you satisfy government authorities who participate in negotiations? Internationally, governments of different countries often get involved in private business deals. // For example, in 1984, Toyota and General Motors wanted to build a factory together in the United States. But the American government said: "No. We do not want this to happen." "Yes, we want it to happen." "No, you can not!" "Yes!" "No!" "Yes!" "No!" Those were their demands. But why? What were the interests here? // In the case of Toyota and General Motors, their interest was the Toyota wanted access to US markets, and General Motors wanted to learn about Japanese management practice. Well what was the interest of the US government? The US government wanted to make sure that there is competition between big firms and it was afraid that if two big firms became partners, that would (be) lower competition, they wouldn't be competitors any more and customers would suffer. Is there a creative solution that can allow General Motors and Toyota to work together without putting them so close together that customers, consumers suffer? Yes, there is. // And this is the solution the two sides came to. You may build a factory together, General Motors and Toyota, that's Ok. But you can only talk to each other a little bit and what you do communicate you must disclose to the government so the government can see how close are you. Are you killing competition? And it turns out that was a success for everyone. // The factory that General Motors and Toyota created in Fremont, California in 1985 still exists today. It is one of the best manufacturing plants in the United States. But, as you know, Toyota and General Motors are still very much competitors. And right now, General Motors is losing and losing and losing. A creative solution satisfied the government as well as the parties. Another example of interest-based bargaining working. //

Let's take another one. Another, a third common international problem is that there can be drastic changes in circumstances and that is something we want to anticipate. How do we deal with sudden changes? That's an especially strong problem internationally because there can be so many surprises. // So for example, imagine a French buyer which is reluctant to invest in Africa. And now imagine an African seller which says: "Buyer from France, you must not just buy products from us, you must also invest!" "No investing!" "Yes investing!" "No investing!" "Yes investing!" Those are their positions, those are their demands. And it looks like they could never agree. // But now let's ask them each why do you want this? And if you ask the French investor, the French buyer will say: "We are worried about the risk of war, the risk of revolution, and the risk of economic turmoil." Let's ask the African seller why are you interested in investing? "Well," says the African seller, "because we and our government want to be more than a raw material supplier, we want our company and our country to develop." Well, is there a way to do both? Yes, there are several ways. // One is for the French company to buy insurance and the African firm can help pay for it. Another is to put clauses in the contract, which cancel or change the contract if terrible things occur. And the third possibility is for the buyer to hire a political analyst who can advise it about what changes are likely and what to do and the African seller can even help to pay for it. Three possible creative solutions that may make this... the buyer more confident to invest and may allow the seller to develop. //

How about cultural differences? Can interest-based bargaining help us with that problem? We have already seen an example of cultural differences hurting negotiators. In the first story I told you, can interest-based bargaining help there? Yes! // For example, consider an Asian negotiator who is reluctant to give a direct answer to a direct question. And now consider an Australian negotiator who says you must give me a direct answer to a direct question. And that is a very common problem where one side thinks the other is evasive, and the other side thinks the first is too direct. So they have very different communication styles. // But why, why did they speak this way? Well, the Asian negotiator may feel that a direct question makes it hard to save face, and the Australian negotiator may say a direct question helps me solve problems quickly. Those are their interests, saving face and solving problems. // Are there creative ways that we can do both? And the answer is yes, there are several, and you see them listed. Some of them are pretty simple and obvious like building the relationship, but others are more subtle. // For example, we can use signals, we can use hints, we can use unofficial private communication, we can use brokers, we can use liaisons. And as we will see later, there are other ways that we can bridge this communication gap creatively. So we have now seen four examples of problems that are common in international negotiations where creativity and a deep understanding of the problem can help us overcome. //

IV Guide to Interpreting

1. Passage 1是与专题知识部分相辅相成的一篇口译练习，就内容而言可以算作是商务谈判扫盲性质的。只要对商务谈判的内容较为熟悉，译起来就不会有太大的难度。建议将其与专题知识部分结合起来进行练习。
2. 本单元的练习没有选取具体谈判回合的交锋，而是选用专家讲座的语篇。Passage 2和Passage 3均取自美国教授塞思·弗里曼（Seth Freeman）国际商务谈判讲座的现场录音，极为口语化，通俗易懂，也不乏幽默风趣之处。弗里曼教授用生动的口吻阐述了许多谈判技巧。此外他还列举了大量的例子来讲解谈判的技巧。例子中也充满了对话内容，形象生动。口译时应注意讲话人的语气，再现原讲话的幽默风格。对于涉及到的具体案例，译者应该事先对讲话人的背景以及听众的构成有所了解，做到有的放矢。在做交传笔记时，译者应该从总体上把握信息点，并做有效的语义连接，不能受到过多短句的干扰。总之，无论是将这两个语篇用作交传训练还是同传训练，原讲话人的语言风格都是我们要关注的重点。

V Highlight for Interpreting

Directions: Interpret the following sentences from Chinese into English or vice versa.

1. 贸易谈判实际上是一种对话，在这个对话中双方说明自己的情况，陈述自己的观点，倾听对方的提案、发盘、并作反提案、还盘、互相让步，最后达成协议。
2. 缺乏经验的谈判者的最大弱点是不能耐心地听对方发言,他们认为自己的任务就是谈自己的情况,说自己想说的话和反驳对方的反对意见。因此,在谈判中,他们总在心里想下面该说的话,不注意听对方发言,许多宝贵信息就这样失去了。
3. 他们仔细听对方说的每一句话,而不仅是他们认为重要的或想听的话,因此而获得大量宝贵信息,增加了谈判的筹码。
4. 有效地倾听可以使我们了解进口商的需求,找到解决问题的新办法,修改我们的发盘或还盘。
5. 出口商应用开放式的问题,即答复不是"是"或"不是",而且需要特别解释的问题,来了解进口商的需求,因为这类问题可以使进口商自由畅谈他们的需求。
6. 这时,我们可继续发问,直到完全了解竞争对手的发盘。然后,我们可以向对方说明我们的发盘是不同的,实际上要比竞争对手的更好。
7. The client needed the software so that the client could have a group of telephone operators use the software immediately to receive telephone sales calls and to make telephone sales calls. In other words, the client needs the software so they can make telephone sales.
8. But by the end of the afternoon, not only was the problem solved, but the relationship between the supplier and the company was much better, much stronger. The trust was much greater.
9. I want to show you that in international negotiation this creative idea can solve many problems that are common internationally. And I want to look with you at several common problems and how we can solve them with the same simple interest-based strategy.
10. They are worried because they know that the Mexican government imposes a tax on the Mexican firm if the Mexican firm sends out too much currency outside Mexico.
11. The US government wanted to make sure that there is competition between big firms and it was afraid that if two big firms became partners, there would be lower competition, or they wouldn't be competitors any more and customers would suffer.
12. A third common international problem is that there can be drastic changes in circumstances and that is something we want to anticipate. How do we deal with

sudden changes? That's an especially strong problem internationally because there can be so many surprises.
13. And the third possibility is for the buyer to hire a political analyst who can advise it about what changes are likely and what to do and the African seller can even help to pay for it.
14. That is a very common problem where one side thinks the other is evasive, and the other side thinks the first is too direct. So they have very different communication styles.
15. We have now seen four examples of problems that are common in international negotiations where creativity and a deep understanding of the problem can help us overcome.

第3单元

商务访谈

Business Interview

I Background Knowledge

Directions: Read the following English passages and then compare them with their Chinese equivalents.

Passage 1

Commonly referred to as the Nobel Economics Prize or the Bank of Sweden Prize in Economic Sciences, the Nobel Economics Prize is short for the Bank of Sweden Prize in Economic Sciences in Memory of Alfred Nobel. It isn't involved in the five awarding fields mentioned in the will of Nobel but set up by the Bank of Sweden in 1968 in memory of Nobel with the same selection criteria as other awards. Its winners are selected by the Royal Swedish Academy of Sciences and Norwegian Ragnar Frisch and Dutch Jan Tinbergen shared the first award when the Bank celebrated its 30th anniversary in 1969.

诺贝尔经济学奖,全称是纪念阿尔弗雷德·诺贝尔瑞典银行经济学奖,通常称为诺贝尔经济学奖,也称瑞典银行经济学奖。诺贝尔经济学奖不属于诺贝尔遗嘱中所提到的五大奖励领域之一,而是由瑞典银行在1968年为纪念诺贝尔而增设的,其评选标准与其它奖项相同,获奖者由瑞典皇家科学院评选,1969年瑞士银行成立30周年庆典时第一次颁奖,由挪威人拉格纳·弗里希和荷兰人简·丁伯根共同获得。

Passage 2

What is the creative industry? Contemporary cultural creative industry derives from the discovery and invention of the creative industry—an innovative philosophy. Creative industry or creative economy is a newly-rising philosophy, thought or economic practice which has developed in the context of global consumption promotes innovation and personal creativity and emphasizes the support and promotion of culture and art to economics.

As for China, a major manufacturing and processing country in the world, which is transforming from manufacturing-based to creativity-based, it is of great significance to closely focus on and further study on the development of contemporary cultural creative industry in the world and precisely grasp the development trend of world industries.

The cultural creative industry in the future will be playing an increasing important role in the all-round and coordinated development of China's economy and further adjustment of industrial structuring. As for China with its secondary industry playing an important role in national economy, it is necessary to adjust industrial proportion at the right time and boost the development of tertiary industry, especially as those high-end industrial groups as high-tech cultural creative industry.

Creative industry is featured by intensive knowledge, high added value and deep integration, which exerts considerable influence on promoting our industrial development and optimizing our industrial structure.

什么是创意产业？当代文化创意产业的兴起源于创意产业这一创新理念的发现和发明。创意产业或创意经济是一种新兴理念、想法或经济活动，它是在全球化的消费背景中发展起来的，推崇创新、个人创造力、强调文化艺术对经济的支持与推动的新兴的理念、思潮和经济实践。

对于中国这个正在从制造型向创意型转变的世界制造业、加工业大国来说，密切关注和深入研究当代世界文化创意产业的发展，准确把握世界产业发展的动向，具有重要意义。

未来的文化创意产业对中国经济的全面协调发展和产业结构的进一步调整将具有越来越重要的作用。对于第二产业在国民经济中占据重要地位的中国来说，适时地调整产业比重，进一步推动第三产业特别是高科技支持的文化创意产业类高端产业群的发展，是十分必要的。

创意产业是知识密集型、高附加值、高整合性的产业，对于提升我国产业发展水平，优化产业结构有相当大的影响。

II Warm-up

1 **Directions:** Give the English equivalents of the following Chinese expressions.

万有引力	无聊	大力发展
灵感	创意产业	优势
最高成就	传统产业	劣势
尖锐	点石成金	成本控制

2 **Directions:** Give the Chinese equivalents of the following English expressions.

get preoccupied	mind-set
equilibrium	Hollywood studio
information asymmetry	bailout program
Information Technology	distressed mortgage
gain some insight	American International Group
Silicon Valley	Bear Stearns
Internet bubble	JPMorgan Chase
venture capitalist	Fannie Mae
recruit faculty	Freddie Mac
computer animation	soybean futures
put the photograph on end	Capitol Hill
R&D	foreclosure
conventional service	savings portfolio

III Passages for Interpreting

Passage 1

Directions: Listen to the dialog and interpret alternatively from Chinese into English or vice versa at the end of each segment.

I= Interviewer   H= Spence   A= Audience

商务口译

I: 您在生活当中是不是痴迷于自己的专业？//

S: I think all of us who love what we do as scholars and researchers get preoccupied, and I think that's actually pretty common among people who do that kind of thing after that. //

I: 我想在他们的日常生活当中可能更多的是观察，更多的是思考。比如说牛顿当年发现万有引力的时候就是看到苹果是从树上往下掉的，而不是往上掉的。我们想知道这个，迈克尔·斯宾塞先生，他在1972年写他这篇博士论文的时候，您看到了什么苹果？哪件事触动了您，写论文的灵感到底是什么？//

S: That's a very good question. Economists, particular economists who are interested in what's going on in the world usually see something that they can't understand. And what I saw that I couldn't understand was job market. And I saw job market as... as informationally flood in the sense that there were enormous gaps between the knowledge that employers had of the people they are trying to employ and the knowledge that the individuals who are trying to be employed had. // And I started to ask myself, how can a market like this work? And that led me in the direction of trying to find the information flows in the market and I came to call those information flows signal and developed the theory of how market settling the equilibrium with information being transferred in the market. So that's what got me started, I was simply, I just couldn't understand how a market with information asymmetry that was that big could actually function. // And I pick job market. You could set to look at me as a potential employee of yours for 10 hours. And you wouldn't know anything interesting about me in the job that you try to assess me for in your organization. So that's (to) give you some sense of what the initial informational gap is and why. My purpose wasn't just to collect the experience but to write (it) into the economic theory as precisely as I could what actually went on in the market place. //

I: 我们想问一下，您个人觉得说，您1972年这篇到今天得奖的论文是不是也是您在学术领域当中的一个最高的成就。//

S: If I stand back from it and pretend not to be myself, I have to say that the work that George Akerlof, and Joseph Stiglitz and I probably did change parts of macro economics more than anything else I did. //

I: 30年前，您在写这篇论文的时候其实还非常的年轻，还不到30岁。//

S: I remember thinking at the time was a wonderful moment. For me, it was. I wrote down a model that just—and I worried it's a much more abstract version of the model than many people read. There was a 30 second period while I suddenly realized what the equilibrium was, and what its properties were, because I knew them from differential equations and I also knew that it made sense and it was really different from another kind of equilibrium, so I thought this was properly pretty important when I did it, because it was so clear and clean and so easy to see the property once the equilibrium was specified in a certain way. So that was a wonderful moment for me. // But people often ask "why do you do what you do". I think you do them actually for those moments and for the same moment that students have when they all of a sudden see something that either they didn't understand before or even that you didn't understand. Those are the absolute highpoints for teachers and researchers in my experience. //

A: 我想请问您，怎么样把您的经济理论和企业的实际结合起来？既在理论上有贡献，而且又对现实经济生活起到了积极作用？谢谢。//

S: That's a very nice question. I wanted to see what business did in market, so I would understand how market works better. It's very interesting to look in detail at what the role looks like (in) somebody else's eye. What I want to bring together is (to) apply theory with the understanding of business strategy and increasingly now and understanding of Information Technology. // What I am trying to do as a number of other people is (to) understand what it does to market and economy and business processes, and things like that. And I hope to gain some insight in that area and to be helpful. The reason Silicon Valley shakes when I speak is that they are worried I'll say something stupid. //

A: 我想问一个尖锐的问题，对于（以）互联网为代表的信息技术，特别是互联网的泡沫的破灭，那么，经济学家应当担负什么样的责任。//

S: I think that there is a lot of guilt to be hanging around the Internet bubble. We are in an totally uncharted territory with respect to the impact of the Information Technology. I think economists particularly failed in remembering that no matter how revolutionary something is, people don't change their behavior and organizations don't change their behavior overnight. // If you really look at what happened in the Internet bubble and in companies, say in the business to business side of thing which could be very large in the future, and (there are) a bunch of really smart people, look at, gee, can do the thing a whole new way, you know. And it's much more efficient. And then without really thinking about it, they thought this will happen tomorrow. // They are entrepreneurs, the venture capitalists, you know, the investment bankers, everybody. That is wrong. It's gonna take decades to get these all done. We should be held responsible for not doing our part to prevent some of the damages that went with this Internet bubble. //

A: 我想问斯宾塞先生一个问题，在您这些年的职业生涯中，您曾经有过的最大的挑战是什么？您曾经有过的最大的挫折是什么？//

S: Good question. And it's easy to answer. You know, I always say in a university there's [are] only four things that happen that are very important every year. One is research, two is teaching, three is recruiting faculty and four is recruiting students. // And if you do all four those well, you could do everything else badly, and it won't make a bit of difference. So the things I am proudest of are recruiting great faculty and when we succeeded in doing that. And the things I feel the most badly about is when [that] we lost some young person who is really important. And when you lose one, it's the greatest failing, at least that's how I saw. //

Passage 2

Directions: Listen to the dialog and interpret alternatively from Chinese into English or vice versa at the end of each segment.

I= Interviewer   H= John Hawkins

I: 欢迎您。霍金斯先生。今天的话题会围绕着创意而展开，是不是可以在今天节目的现场请您用特别创意的方式来给我们大家做一个自我介绍？//

H: Good evening! You're creative. I've been... I walked to the studio past three of other TV studios. I've seen people. I've seen dancers. I've seen actors and I've seen the cameramen. The television studio is probably as much as a theater or an art gallery where you see creativity almost coming out of the walls, it's in the air. I've been interested in creative economy now for about 10 years. But before that I was a journalist and photographer and film producer. So really, from the age of about 15 I've always been involved in creative economy. //

I: 我知道约翰·霍金斯先生从(19)79年就来到了中国，后面有多次访问中国的经历，在每一次访问的过程当中我想知道有什么样最让你觉得有创意的东西，给你留下印象很深，能不能在今天的现场告诉我们大家。//

H: I saw a wonderful thing just two days ago at Shanghai Theater Academy. There were theater producers from nine countries who have to work together and been together directors, and performers and musicians on the same stage, but they were doing at a distance. And what they did was to create a computer animation of the entire performance. So that everybody, whatever country they were in, or indeed if they were traveling somewhere else, and the directors and the lighting people and the sound people of that performances, could see as if they were there themselves. It was wonderful. //

I: 之前我们看到过一些媒体对您的专访，包括您说过的一句话，说创意来自于无聊，我们当时都觉得是不是记者写错了，这个创意怎么可能来自于无聊呢？这句话真的是您说的吗？ //

H: There is [was] a man who was an advertising director from Germany and he interviewed a number of people about why they were creative. And the overwhelming answer that they gave—if they were a musician or a writer or an actor—was that it was the only way they could live their life. There was never alternative. They have to be creative in order to be alive. And one of the answers was if I'm not creative, then I'm not alive. I'm not living. I get bored. One person said: I get sad. I get lonely. I have to be creative. //

I: 创意产业跟我们大家所熟知的传统产业它最大的区别在哪里呢？ //

H: The biggest difference, I think, is the creativity starts in oneself. We could be creative in the studio. We could be creative in the office. But [And] we can be creative at home. We could be creative on the street, in a cafe. We could be creative anywhere, because we are using our brains which are portable. Our brains go with us. And we can use them wherever we are. We don't depend upon land. We don't depend upon financial capital. We don't depend upon factories, and machinery and equipment. We only depend upon our imagination. That is the difference. //

I: 在您的研究领域还有没有更好的、更能说明创意能够点石成金的例子？ //

H: I was looking a few days ago at a photograph of an envelope with a letter inside. And it was to sell for 4,000 pounds, 4,000 pounds. This is a photograph of an envelope with a letter inside by an artist. She takes, she puts the photograph on end, so it's like that. And she slits it. And you see inside the letter. And out of the shape of the envelope, the letter inside, she creates an astonishingly beautiful image. She takes a photograph of that. And she prints it out. So it's about four foot [feet] high. I think that's a very good example of creativity. To take something which is commonplace in front of this and to give it a twist, and in her case to produce photographs. She prints and (for) each print she sells for 4,000 pounds. //

I: 就中国现在的产业结构和产业基础来讲，在中国现阶段我们就大力地来发展创意产业，究竟是优势更大一点还是劣势可能更大一点？//

H: I'm talking... I'm talking quite long-time scales. And I think there is an interest... I've noticed an interesting [interest] in China in developing your own R&D, your own education, your own design, your own creativity innovation. And I think that if people want to be creative'and they want to explore their imaginations, then they should be allowed to do so. I think it's good for the individual. And I think it's good for the society. If I live in a country, I want that country to be in control of its own ideas, its own knowledge, its own brands, its own designs and not simply to be someone manufacturing for other people. The films that I see in England should come from China as well as from America. So it's both. You must manufacture. But I hope you will also increase your creative knowledge (and) design industries. So they work together. //

I: 我们用什么样的办法来控制我们在创意产业当中的这份成本呢？//

H: I think there's an important difference that conventional manufactory, conventional services worry almost entirely about the cost, because they know the price is fixed. They know the price. They know the revenue. With most creative products, you don't know the revenue. I could produce a film for five million dollars. I could produce a film for ten million dollars. I could produce a film for fifty million dollars. It doesn't mean... the ticket price would be the same, the ticket price would be the same. // So in the creative industries, we worry much more about controlling cost. We worry much more about increasing the revenue. We worry much more about increasing the revenue. It's a different mind-set. // And when we talk about the management of creativity, which is a question new(ly) raised, it is really about managing those creative geniuses who come up with a wonderful idea that we all think "yes, thank you, let's do it". And then the production lines starts [start]. Productivity doesn't really operate as a criteria in this business. // Some artists produce good work every year. Some artists produce a wonderful piece of work and then produce nothing for a few years. And one can't control that. One can't manage that. One can't analyze that and try and order it to suit oneself. It's up to the individual. They work differently. // We all know that each Hollywood studio produces about twenty (to) twenty five films a year. It hopes to be really successful on two. It hopes it breaks even on another two. And they lose money on the eighteen. In order to succeed in many industries in a creative economy, you have to have a high level of output. You can't succeed on one product a year. //

Passage 3

Directions: Listen to the dialog and interpret from English into Chinese at the end of each segment.

Q= Correspondent from *New York Times* A= White House Spokesman

Q: The bailout program being negotiated by the Bush administration and Congressional leaders calls for the government to spend up to $700 billion to buy distressed mortgages. How did the politicians come up with that number, and could it go higher? //

A: The recovery package cannot go higher than $700 billion without additional legislation. As for that figure, it lies between the optimistic estimate of $500 billion and the pessimistic guess of $1 trillion about the cost of fixing the financial mess. But the $700 billion is in addition to an $85 billion agreement on a bailout of the insurance giant American International Group, plus $29 billion in support that the government pledged in the marriage of Bear Stearns and JPMorgan Chase. On top of all that, the Congressional Budget Office says the federal bailout of the mortgage finance companies Fannie Mae and Freddie Mac could cost $25 billion. //

Q: Who, really, is going to come up with the $700 billion? //

A: American taxpayers will come up with the money, although if you are bullish on America in the long run, there is reason to hope that the tab will be less than $700 billion. After the Treasury buys up those troubled mortgages, it will try to resell them to investors. The Treasury's involvement in the crisis and the speed with which Congress is responding could generate long-range optimism and raise the value of those mortgages, although it is impossible to say by how much. //

So it would not be correct to think of the federal government as simply writing a check for $700 billion. It is just committing itself to spend that much, if necessary. But the bottom line is, yes, this bailout could cost American taxpayers a lot of money. //

Q: So is it fair to say that Americans who are neither rich nor reckless are being asked to rescue people who are unknown? What is in this package for responsible homeowners of modest means who might be forced out of their homes, perhaps for reasons beyond their control? //

A: Yes, you could argue that people who cannot tell soybean futures from puts, calls and options are being asked to clean up the costly mess left by Wall Street. To make the bailout palatable to the public, it is being described as far better than inaction, which administration officials and members of Congress say could imperil the retirement savings and other investments of Americans who are anything but rich. //

But it is a good bet that the negotiations between the administration and Capitol Hill will include ideas about ways to help middle-class home-owners avoid foreclosure and perhaps some limits on pay for executives. And it should be noted that neither party is solely responsible for whatever neglect led the country to the brink of disaster. //

Q: How is it that the administration and Congress, which have not tried to find huge amounts of money to, say, improve the nation's health insurance system or repair bridges and tunnels, can now be ready to come up with $700 billion to rescue the financial system? And is it realistic to think that the parties can reach agreement and get legislation passed in a hurry? //

A: The first question will surely come up again, involving as it does not just issues of spending policy but also more profound questions about national aspirations. As for rescuing the financial system, elected officials in both parties became convinced that, while a couple of venerable investment banks could fade into oblivion or be absorbed by mergers, the entire financial system could not be allowed to collapse. //

And, yes, the parties are likely to reach an accord. Many members of Congress are eager to leave Washington to go home and campaign for the November elections and no one wants to face the voters without having done something to protect modest savings portfolios as well as giant investors. //

IV Guide to Interpreting

1. 对于专业性较强的访谈类语篇的口译任务来说，了解采访对象的专业背景至关重要。三位美国学者乔治·阿克尔洛夫（George Akerlof）、迈克尔·斯宾塞（Michael Spence）和约瑟夫·斯蒂格利茨（Joseph Stiglitz）因为在"对充满不对称信息市场进行分析"领域作出了重要贡献，而分享2001年诺贝尔经济学奖。这三名获奖者在20世纪70年代奠定了"对充满不对称信息市场进行分析"的理论基础。Passage 1的采访对象斯宾塞教授，1943年出生于新泽西州的蒙特卡莱，是哈佛大学和斯坦福大学研究生院的教授，同时也是两所大学的院长。他的贡献在于揭示了人们应如何利用所掌握的更多信息来谋取更大收益方面的有关理论。阿克尔洛夫、斯宾塞和斯蒂格利茨的分析理论用途广泛，既适用于对传统的农业市场的分析研究，也适用于对现代金融市场的分析研究。同时，他们的理论还构成了现代信息经济的核心。斯宾塞一直致力于研究就业市场中的代理人问题。斯宾塞认为，假如雇主不能区分劳动能力的高低，那么就会导致劳动力市场以低工资雇用低能力者，形成劳动力市场上"劣币驱逐良币"的现象。斯宾塞还发现一个现象，即高能力的男性会被预期获得比同等能力的妇女更高的学历。在这种均衡下，男女之间的教育回报由于教育方面投资的不同而不同。另外，斯宾塞信号发送模型还对博弈论产生了深远的影响，他的专业竞争下的市场均衡模型已经影响到其他领域，比如增长理论和国际贸易。

2. Passage 2的采访对象约翰·霍金斯（John Howkins）教授是来自英国林肯大学的经济学家，他是国际创意经济的领军人物，《知识产权宪章》的负责人和英国创意集团的主席及创始人之一。2001年，他在《创意经济》一书中首次提出"创意产业"这一概念，被称为"创意产业之父"。在创意产业比重逐年增加的今天，我们对"创意经济"早已不陌生，教授关于创意经济有三点基本看法。第一点，人人都是有创意的。在创意面前，人人都是平等的，每个人都有均等的机会来表达自己有创意的观点。第二点，创意需要有非常自由的空间，自由的空间才能让创意的观点得到有效成长。第三点，创造力必须要有社会性的或者经济性的市场，否则无法形成创意经济。本单元的两篇采访内容均取自现场录音，有时原讲话人可能会出现语误或信息的冗余和重复，译员除了要充分了解受采访对象的专业知识背景之外，还要注意讲话人的主要意图，要根据他们讲话的内容筛选出主要的信息予以传译。Passage 1和Passage 2属于交替传译，英译汉和汉译英交替出现，译员在转译训练时应注意把握英汉两种语言的区

商务口译

别和思维的转变。
3. Passage 3取自《纽约时报》的记者访谈，谈论的是美国政府针对2008年席卷全球的金融海啸的一项高达7,000亿美元的政府救援计划。进行口译训练之前，译员应该对此次金融危机的形成原因和危害性有所了解，可以在网络上搜索有关以下名词的相关专题知识，比如"次贷危机"、"房利美"和"房地美"、"投资银行"以及"大豆期货"等。具备充分的专业背景知识才能正确译出专题内容的逻辑架构，才能理解政府财政援助计划的实施与国会参众两院的关系，以及此计划与广大纳税人的利害关系。

V Highlight for Interpreting

Directions: Interpret the following sentences from Chinese into English or vice versa.

1. 我们想知道这个，迈克尔·斯宾塞先生，他在1972年写他这篇博士论文的时候，您看到了什么苹果？哪件事触动了您，写论文的灵感到底是什么？
2. 我们想问一下，您个人觉得说，您1972年这篇到今天得奖的论文是不是也是您在学术领域当中的一个最高的成就。
3. 我想请问您，怎么样把您的经济理论和企业的实际结合起来？既在理论上有贡献，而且又对现实经济生活起到了积极作用？
4. 我想问一个尖锐的问题，对于（以）互联网为代表的信息技术，特别是互联网的泡沫的破灭，那么，经济学家应当担负什么样的责任。
5. 今天的话题会围绕着创意而展开，是不是在今天节目的现场请您用特别创意的方式来给我们大家做一个自我介绍？
6. 我知道约翰·霍金斯先生从1979年就来到了中国，后面有多次访问中国的经历，在每一次访问的过程当中我想知道有什么样最让你觉得有创意的东西，给你留下印象很深，能不能在今天的现场告诉我们大家。
7. 之前我们看到过一些媒体对您的专访，包括您说过的一句话，说创意来自于无聊，我们当时都觉得是不是记者写错了，这个创意怎么可能来自于无聊呢？这句话真的是您说的吗？
8. 就中国现在的产业结构和产业基础来讲，在中国现阶段我们就大力地来发展创意产业，究竟是优势更大一点还是劣势可能更大一点？
9. Economists, particular economists who are interested in what's going on in the world usually see something that they can't understand.

10. That's a very nice question. I wanted to see what business did in market, so I would understand how market works better. It's very interesting to look in detail at what the role looks like (in) somebody else's eye.
11. I think economists particularly failed in remembering that no matter how revolutionary something is, people don't change their behavior and organizations don't change their behavior overnight.
12. And what they did was to create a computer animation of the entire performance. So that everybody, whatever country they were in, or indeed if they were traveling somewhere else, and the directors and the lighting people and sound people of that performances, could see as if they were there themselves.
13. They have to be creative in order to be alive. And one of the answers was if I'm not creative, then I'm not alive. I'm not living. I get bored. One person said: I get sad. I get lonely. I have to be creative.
14. The $700 billion is in addition to an $85 billion agreement on a bailout of the insurance giant American International Group, plus $29 billion in support that the government pledged in the marriage of Bear Stearns and JPMorgan Chase. On top of all that, the Congressional Budget Office says the federal bailout of the mortgage finance companies Fannie Mae and Freddie Mac could cost $25 billion.
15. But it is a good bet that the negotiations between the administration and Capitol Hill will include ideas about ways to help middle-class home-owners avoid foreclosure and perhaps some limits on pay for executives. And it should be noted that neither party is solely responsible for whatever neglect led the country to the brink of disaster.

第4单元

广告宣传

Advertising & Publicity

I Background Knowledge

Directions: Read the following English passages and then compare them with their Chinese equivalents.

Passage 1

Advertising is a form of communicating a message by the use of various media. It is persuasive, informative, and designed to influence purchasing behavior or thought patterns. Advertising is a mass-mediated communication, it must be characterized by:

1) paid for;
2) delivered to an consumer via mass media; and
3) be attempting to persuade.

Advertising is a two way communication process. Not only must the advertisement effectively communicate the message, but the individual consumer must be willing to "buy into" the message. In other words, for the advertisement to be effective, the communication must be sent and received. Meanwhile, consumers are capable of interpreting the advertisement any way he/she wants. They can either accept the message, ignore the message or rally against the message. As a matter of fact, the consumer has power to dictate what is communicated and what is not.

广告是通过使用各种媒体进行信息传递的一种方式,它具有说服力和信息性,专为影响购买行为和思维模式而设计。广告是一种以大众为媒介的交际,必须具备以下特点：
1）有偿性；
2）通过大众媒体向消费者传递信息；
3）说服性

广告是一个双向交际过程。广告不仅要有效地传递信息，而且消费者必须愿意来"买进"这些信息。换句话说，要使广告起作用，就必须发送信息并使信息得到接受。同时，消费者也能够按照他/她自己的方式理解广告的含义，他们可以接受这条信息，也可以忽略这条信息，还可以共同来抵制这条信息。实际上，消费者能够决定传递哪些信息、不传递哪些信息。

Passage 2

China Import and Export Fair, also called the Canton Fair, is held twice a year in Spring and Autumn since it was inaugurated in the Spring of 1957. It is China's largest trade fair of the highest level, of the most complete varieties and of the largest attendance and business turnover. Preserving its traditions, the Fair is a comprehensive and multi-functional event of international importance.

Forty eight trading delegations, being composed of thousands of China's best foreign trade corporations (enterprises) with good credibility and sound financial capabilities, take part in the Fair, including foreign trade companies, factories, scientific research institutions, foreign invested enterprises, wholly foreign-owned enterprises, private enterprises, etc.

Besides traditional way of negotiating against samples, the Fair holds Canton Fair online. The Fair leans to export trade, though import business is also done here. Apart from the above-mentioned, various types of business activities such as economic and technical cooperations and exchanges, commodity inspection, insurance, transportation, advertising, consultation, etc. are also carried out in flexible ways. Business people from all over the world are gathering in Guangzhou, exchanging business information and developing friendship.

中国进出口商品交易会，又称广交会，创办于1957年春季，每年春秋两季在广州举办。广交会是中国目前规模最大、层次最高、商品种类最全、到会客商最多、成交效果最好的贸易盛会。秉承多年传统，广交会是在国际上享有重要地位的综合性、多功能展览会。

有由数千家中国最好的外贸企业组成的48个贸易代表团参展，它们资信

第4单元 广告宣传

良好、实力雄厚,包括外贸公司、生产企业、科研院所、外商投资企业、外商独资企业、私营企业等。

广交会贸易方式灵活多样,除传统的看样成交外,此次还举办网上交易会。广交会以出口贸易为主,也做进口生意,还可以开展多种形式的经济技术合作与交流,以及商品检验、保险、运输、广告、咨询等业务活动。来自世界各地的客商云集广州,互通商情,增进友谊。

II Warm-up

1 **Directions:** Give the English equivalents of the following Chinese expressions.

广交会	重要平台	新闻发布会
一地一馆两期	历史见证	各界朋友
琶洲一期展馆	友谊纽带	万商云集
两地两馆两期	贸易桥梁	亲身体验
专业展区	合作共赢	勃勃生机
采购商	共同发展	建言献策

2 **Directions:** Give the Chinese equivalents of the following English expressions.

Ultra HVDC	creative cooperation
corporate activity	business operation
self-drive	hard disk drive
various restraints	automotive equipment
groundwork	business collaboration
diversification of products	semiconductor
technological innovation	personnel training
business affair	in-house education system
research institute	invention incentive system
push forward	perpendicular magnetic disk
cutting-edge	finger vein authentication
joint research	μ-chip
industry-university cooperation	energy saving technology
intellectual property strategy	social value

商务口译

III Passages for Interpreting

Passage 1

Directions: Listen to the passage and interpret from Chinese into English at the end of each segment.

女士们、先生们，新闻界的朋友们：

大家上午好！// 首先，请允许我对今天出席第104届中国进出口商品交易会——也就是大家熟悉的广交会——新闻发布会的各位朋友表示感谢！我想还是直入主题，向大家介绍拥有悠久历史、50多年来从未间断的广交会的一些新情况。//

第一届广交会从1957年开始举办，在经过两次展馆变迁之后，1974年开始启用大家熟悉的广州流花路展馆。// 随着近30年中国对外贸易的发展和广交会自身的成长，从2002年春第91届广交会开始，广交会由一期15天改为两期共12天，可以说是"一地一馆两期"。// 2004年第95届广交会，随着琶洲一期展馆正式启用，广交会开始"两地两馆两期"的运行模式。即将于今年10月15号开幕的第104届广交会，将进行又一次重大改革，简单地说就是"一地一馆三期"。// 所谓"一地一馆"，就是从第104届起，我们的广交会将全部在新落成的现代化的琶洲展馆举办；所谓"三期"，就是广交会将按照专业化的要求，分三期各五天举办。//

相对于第103届广交会，第104届有许多不同的特点：一是专业化程度更高，进一步细分了专业展区。二是展出面积、参展企业规模创下新的记录。三是每期展览的时间缩短，但总的时间跨度延长。四是广交会全部集中在琶洲新馆，告别了分地举办给采购商带来的不便。//

广交会是我国对外贸易的重要平台，是中国经济发展和对世界开放的历史见证。50多年来，一直保持着中国展会历史最长、规模最大、到会采购商最多且国别范围最广、商品种类最齐全、成交效果最好的声誉，成为联系中外工商贸易界的"友谊纽带、贸易桥梁"。// 第104届广交会的改革，将使她成为规模更大、更加开放、更加专业、服务更优、成效更好的国际贸易平台，为来自世界各国和地区的参展客商提供更多的商机，促进中外企业合作共赢、共同发展。//

女士们、先生们。// 今天，我们选择在香港地区召开新闻发布会，与香港工商贸易界同仁共同交流广交会分三期改革的情况，表明商务部高度重视港澳地区工商贸易界对广交会的重要作用。// 香港各界朋友一直以来对广交会给予了高度的关注、积极的参与和支持，成就了广交会"万商云集"的美誉。我谨代表商务部对大家长久以来对广交会的关注表示衷心的感谢。//

最后，我诚挚地欢迎在座的各位来宾和记者朋友在今秋10月莅临琶洲参观、采访，亲身体验我们焕发着勃勃生机的第104届盛会，为广交会的发展建言献策，共同创造广交会新的辉煌。//

谢谢各位！//

Passage 2

Directions: Listen to the passage and interpret from English into Chinese at the end of each segment.

ABB[1] has maintained its leadership position in HVDC[2] transmission through careful, customer-focused innovation that expands the usefulness of our existing technology. // We are currently cooperating with customers in China on studies for ultra high-voltage electricity transmission, to meet their need for a technology that makes it economically viable to transport bulk power over very long distances—for example, from the west of China to Guangdong or Shanghai—distances of 2,000 kilometers or more. The newest Ultra HVDC technology makes it possible to transmit 6,400 megawatts over a single power line, with minimum costs and losses. //

Successful companies that want to stay at the leading edge of their industry know that innovation is not a department but a mind-set of the entire organization. // It starts with a vision, determined and promoted from the top, which creates a focus on winning. The Apollo space program in the US, for example, triggered a decade of innovation after declaring that its strategic goal was to put a man on the moon by the end of the 1960s. //

A strategic goal cannot be divorced from reality, however. Before setting a target, an organization needs to develop a point of view regarding the evolution of the industry it is in and to consider how competitors are positioning themselves. It must also be based on an analysis of an organization's core competencies, which are typi-

---

1 ABB集团，全球500强企业，是电力和自动化技术领域的全球领导厂商，集团总部位于瑞士苏黎世。

2 High Voltage Direct Current.

cally a combination of core technologies and customer knowledge. //

ABB went through such an exercise several years ago during a financial crisis. The management at that time made two key decisions that laid the foundation for ABB's current success. It decided to concentrate on two businesses, power and automation, where it had the longest experience and the deepest customer knowledge. // These businesses expected strong demand because of a global need to strengthen power grids, raise productivity and cut energy consumption. //

It also decided to maintain investment in R&D, knowing that the company needed to retain its technological advantage in these businesses to survive and prosper in the longer term. A comprehensive review of this strategy in 2007 has confirmed that it remains appropriate for the coming years. //

Finally, a strategic goal needs to be backed by the right structure. Our experience at ABB, supported by research and employee surveys, is that innovation is as much about successful implementation as it is about generating ideas. It depends on all parts of the organization working as a team, sharing information across business units and functions, and this requires a culture of transparency and trust. //

Once a promising idea is identified, a clear structure is needed to bring it to fruition as an innovative new product. // For this, ABB has a model with seven project phases. At each stage critical questions are addressed which will determine whether the idea progresses to the next. Customers are involved at key stages so that their feedback can be taken into account. Successful innovation is the entire process, not just the idea at the beginning. //

But the generation of innovative ideas cannot be ordered and is best developed through a supportive culture. In China, as in Europe or North America, skilled employees are in short supply and have no difficulty finding good jobs. They are looking for more than just good pay. //

Once recruited, promising employees must be encouraged to stay by rewarding them with the right work environment and offering them opportunities for personal growth. // Researchers at ABB are encouraged to explore their own ideas and given time to brainstorm with colleagues or external partners about them before they are channeled toward development and tangible products in a structured process. Organizations that are overly rigid and bureaucratic are not conducive to innovation and the really creative people won't stay. //

第4单元 广告宣传

Passage 3

Directions: Listen to the passage and interpret from English into Chinese at the end of each segment.

Ladies and Gentlemen,

Today's Hitachi Group is a corporation boasting sales of 10 trillion *yen*; however, its corporate activities started with making a domestic 5hp motor for the first time in Japan in 1910. // Namihei Odaira, the company's founder, thought that "in heavy industry, sales are directly related to production and so we must not be separated from the field. Hitachi's basic idea is to sell products that we have designed and produced by ourselves, by our own hands. If we lack self-drive then we will not be a leader, and under various restraints the company will not develop and it will be extremely difficult to succeed". //

Strong involvement in domestic production as well as the company's own development of technology became the groundwork for the current Hitachi's growth and the source of its subsequent exports and diversification of products. The idea is that technological innovation enables expansion of business affairs by structural change of business. //

Currently, Hitachi has research institutes in six locations in Japan and four locations overseas (China, USA, Singapore and Europe), pushing forward cutting-edge research in a wide range of fields ranging from parts and materials to hardware, systems and services. // Also, while leading the world in international joint research with overseas universities and research institutes, we are striving to improve our technical capabilities and personnel training through domestic and overseas industry-university cooperation. //

To proceed with research and development, the speed at which it is carried out, intellectual property strategies, and personnel training are important. Although Hitachi has placed importance on research and development since its foundation and has strengthened the group's research and development capabilities, the development of modern technology is now progressing at such a speed and in such a wide range of fields that it cannot be supported by a single corporation. // Accordingly, the Hitachi Group has been changing to an organization that develops products and technologies useful for the society through creative cooperation with various external institutions including customers, corporations and universities. We aim to promote efficient business operations, including technological development, and one of the ways we are doing this is by purchasing items such as next generation hard disk drives and automotive equipment from other companies for business collaborations, and by running businesses jointly with other companies for products such as semiconductors, ATMs and mobile phones. //

In personnel training, we provide various systems including friendly in-house education systems and invention incentive systems in order to increase researchers' confidence in innovation. Providing invention incentive systems has contributed to the excellent creation of inventions. We promote activities to strategically take out patents for technology we have created, aiming to provide it to outside parties and utilize it effectively. //

Through the above-mentioned commitment, we have recently created many innovative practical businesses including those related to perpendicular magnetic disks, finger vein authentication, μ-chips, and environmental and energy saving technology, which have contributed to the creation of social value. //

IV Guide to Interpreting

1. 从总体上讲，广告宣传的目的是向客户传递一定的信息，它的翻译有别于政治、经济类语言的翻译，因此译员在翻译时应以准确传递原文信息为主。Passage 1是对广交会有关知识的介绍，有明显的广告宣传的风格。在这篇练习中，原文中的"一地一馆三期"因为在其前后都做出了解释，所以在翻译时可以直接按照字面意思译成"one location, one complex and three phases"；在翻译"一直保持着中国展会历史最长、规模最大、到会采购商最多且国别范围最广、商品种类最齐全、成交效果最好的声誉"这样复杂的句子时，应注意首先翻译其主干成分，即先译成"the Fair has always kept the reputation as a grand exhibition"，然后再用介词短语进行补充说明；"'万商云集'的美誉"中的"万商云集"在此没有必要逐字翻译，翻译出来反而有些累赘，鉴于口译时间极短，所以此处可采用意译，译成"high prestige for its great number of participants"，这不失为口译时的一个策略；另外，还要关注一些会展专有词汇的翻译，如"展馆"翻译为"complex"，"展览会"、"博览会"翻译为"fair"、"event"或"exhibition"。"complex"本意为结合体、复合体，因展馆由多个展位共同组成，所以译为"complex"较为合适。例如："流花展馆"译为"Liuhua Complex"，"运动展馆"译为"Sports Complex"。

第4单元 广告宣传

2. Passage 2的英文稿选自著名跨国公司ABB的总裁在广东经济发展国际咨询会上的发言。在口译之前，译员要做充分准备，须上网对该公司的业务尤其是在中国的业务有所了解。就具体口译处理方法而言，要注意英汉两种语言之间的区别。英语通常结果在前，原因在后，而汉语则相反，所以在翻译"ABB has maintained its leadership position in HVDC transmission through careful, customer-focused innovation that expands the usefulness of our existing technology."时，译员可采用由后往前的翻译策略，这种方法在连续传译中较为普遍；在"It decided to concentrate on two businesses, power and automation, where it had the longest experience and the deepest customer knowledge."这句话的翻译中，为了与上文的"two key decisions"相照应，译员可以在翻译时增加"决定之一"并在下文增加"另一个决定"，在口译过程中适当增加一些过渡词可以使上下文更加连贯、清楚；在翻译"Successful innovation is the entire process, not just the idea at the beginning."时，应注意在英译汉中，要使翻译出来的汉语更加符合表达习惯。为此，不宜把这句话直接翻译成"整个过程"，而应译为"成功的创新是整个过程的成功"，并且把英语中的名词"idea"译为动词短语"想法被成功地提出"；"Once recruited, promising employees must be encouraged to stay by rewarding them with the right work environment and offering them opportunities for personal growth."这句话比较长，翻译成一句比较困难，这时可以采用拆分法，把介词"by"后的部分单独翻译为一句话，使表达更加流畅。

3. Passage 3节选自日立电器公司的广告宣传。和Passage 2的练习类似，在做Passage 3的口译之前，译员同样要准备充分。在口译中，有一些具体的技巧点评如下：由"before"引导的句子多数会出现在句子后一部分，因此译员在一开始难以把握。在这种情况下，我们多采用"顺句驱动"的策略，即按照原文句子顺序进行翻译，对原文的句子顺序尽可能地少调整或不调整，因此在口译中通常会把"before"译为"然后"；"self-drive"本意为"自己驾驶"，但这里的"drive"是"动力"的意思，因此，译员可采取意译的策略，译为"自主独立的精神"，也可译为"自我勉励"或"自我激励"；在"the company will not develop and it will be extremely difficult to succeed"这句话的翻译中，译员可采用汉语中的四字表达，译为"停滞不前，难成气候"，意思明了，言简意赅，更加符合汉语的表达习惯；译员在翻译时，不应拘泥于原文的句子形式，在不违背原文意思的前提下，可以适当调整句子结构。例如，在"cutting-edge research in a wide range of fields..."

51

商务口译

的翻译中，译员就巧妙地将其译为"尖端而广泛的研究"，意思未变，但更加简洁流畅。

V Highlight for Interpreting

Directions: Interpret the following sentences from Chinese into English or vice versa.

1. 随着近30年中国对外贸易的发展和广交会自身的成长，从2002年春第91届广交会开始，广交会由一期15天改为两期共12天，可以说是"一地一馆两期"。

2. 所谓"一地一馆"，就是从第104届起，我们的广交会将全部在新落成的现代化的琶洲展馆举办；所谓"三期"，就是广交会将按照专业化的要求，分三期各五天举办。

3. 50多年来，一直保持着中国展会历史最长、规模最大、到会采购商最多且国别范围最广、商品种类最齐全、成交效果最好的声誉，成为联系中外工商贸易界的"友谊纽带、贸易桥梁"。

4. 第104届广交会的改革，将使她成为规模更大、更加开放、更加专业、服务更优、成效更好的国际贸易平台，为来自世界各国和地区的参展客商提供更多的商机，促进中外企业合作共赢、共同发展。

5. 香港各界朋友一直以来对广交会给予了高度的关注、积极的参与和支持，成就了广交会"万商云集"的美誉。我谨代表商务部对大家长久以来对广交会的关注表示衷心的感谢。

6. 最后，我诚挚地欢迎在座的各位来宾和记者朋友在今秋10月莅临琶洲参观、采访，亲身体验我们焕发着勃勃生机的第104届盛会，为广交会的发展建言献策，共同创造广交会新的辉煌。

7. We are currently cooperating with customers in China on studies for ultra high-voltage electricity transmission, to meet their need for a technology that makes it economically viable to transport bulk power over very long distances—for example, from the west of China to Guangdong or Shanghai—distances of 2,000 kilometers or more.

8. Researchers at ABB are encouraged to explore their own ideas and given time to brainstorm with colleagues or external partners about them before they are channeled toward development and tangible products in a structured process.

9. Today's Hitachi Group is a corporation boasting sales of 10 trillion *yen*;

however, its corporate activities started with making a domestic 5hp motor for the first time in Japan in 1910.
10. Strong involvement in domestic production as well as the Company's own development of technology became the groundwork for the current Hitachi's growth and the source of its subsequent exports and diversification of products.
11. Currently, Hitachi has research institutes in six locations in Japan and four locations overseas (China, USA, Singapore and Europe), pushing forward cutting-edge research in a wide range of fields ranging from parts and materials to hardware, systems and services.
12. Although Hitachi has placed importance on research and development since its foundation and has strengthened the group's research and development capabilities, the development of modern technology is now progressing at such a speed and in such a wide range of fields that it cannot be supported by a single corporation.
13. In personnel training, we provide various systems including friendly in-house education systems and invention incentive systems in order to increase researchers' confidence in innovation.
14. Providing invention incentive systems has contributed to the excellent creation of inventions. We promote activities to strategically take out patents for technology we have created, aiming to provide it to outside parties and utilize it effectively.

第5单元

商务陈述

Business Presentation

I Background Knowledge

Directions: Read the following English passages and then compare them with their Chinese equivalents.

Passage 1

A business (also called a firm or an enterprise) is a legally recognized organizational entity designed to provide goods and/or services to consumers or corporate entities such as governments, charities or other businesses. Businesses are predominant in capitalist economies, most being privately owned and formed to earn profit to increase the wealth of owners. The owners and operators of a business have as one of their main objectives the receipt or generation of a financial return in exchange for work and acceptance of risk. Notable exceptions include cooperative businesses and state-owned enterprises. Socialistic systems involve either government, public, or worker ownership of most sizable businesses.

The etymology of "business" relates to the state of being busy either as an individual or society as a whole, doing commercially viable and profitable work. The term "business" has at least three usages, depending on the scope—the singular usage (above) to mean a particular company or corporation, the generalized usage to refer to a particular market sector, such as "the music business" and compound forms such as "agribusiness", or the broadest meaning to include all activity by the community of suppliers of goods and services. However, the exact definition of business, like much else in the philosophy of business, is a matter of debate.

商业机构（又称公司或企业）是法律上认可的有组织的实体，旨在为消费者或诸如政府、慈善机构或其他企业之类的法人实体提供商品和/或服务。在资本主义经济体中，商业机构占主导地位。其中大部分都归私人所有，目的是赚取利润，增加所有者财富。这类商业机构的所有者和经营者的主要目的之一就是，以付出劳动和承担风险为条件，换取金融回馈。与此类商业机构明显不同的企业包括合作企业和国有企业。在社会主义体制下，大多数规模化企业要么是政府所有，要么是公共所有，或者是劳动者所有。

从词源角度看，"商业"一词所涉及的是个人或社会整体忙于从事商业上切实可行又有利可图的活动的一种状态。"商业"这个术语根据其使用范围的不同至少有三种用法。用作单数时（如上），它指的是某个特定的公司或法人团体，更普遍的用法是指某个特定的市场行业，比如说"音乐行业"，而用作像"农业综合企业"这种复合形式时，或取其最广泛的含义时，它则包括商品和服务供应商团体所举行的所有活动。然而，对商业一词如何进行确切定义，就像商业哲学里的其他许多问题一样，却是有争议的。

Passage 2

Good presentation skills are essential in today's workplace. Even those workers who aren't required to make presentations regularly as part of their job may be expected to present information occasionally at meetings. Public speaking, even in a business setting among co-workers you see every day, can be stressful for many people. The three skills listed below can help you present well during any type of business presentation:

Communicating with the Audience

The first step in your business presentation should be to form your message to meet the needs and expectations of your audience. Ask yourself what the purpose of your presentation is and what your audience is supposed to gain from it. Write this into a timed script and ask yourself if it's something that you would find appropriate if you were an audience member hearing it from someone else. Check to make sure the information you need to convey is logical and complete, yet also interesting to hear. Tone is one of the most important presentation skills. Make sure your prepared script is natural-sounding and isn't pompous or insulting to anyone in any way. Practice your script a few times a day and then make simple bullet points of key words from the script on an index card. You can then begin practicing your presentation using the bullet points to prompt you if you get stuck. Having the card beside you on the actual presentation day can be a real confidence booster.

Using Presentation Tools Effectively

Whether you'll be using something like PowerPoint or just large charts, these visual tools can enhance your presentation skills in several ways. They can help take some of the visual focus off you and this can make you feel more relaxed. Visual tools can also make the contents of your presentation easier for your audience to understand. Even a handout with bullets outlining your main points can help your audience gain clarity on what you're saying. Taking cues from respected higher ups at your company about which types of presentation tools to use can also enhance your corporate professionalism.

Anticipating Audience Questions

Thinking like your audience can really improve your presentation skills. Anticipate the questions the audience could ask at the end of your presentation and have good answers ready. It's also very important to prepare yourself for how you'll answer any unexpected questions by practicing how you'll respond to questions you may feel are irrelevant or impossible to answer. Again, when you attend presentations by respected higher ups in your company, take cues from them. Notice how they deal with difficult questions and apply their techniques to suit your own position and style.

掌握良好的陈述技巧在当今的工作场合是很必要的。即便是那些没被要求在工作中做常规性陈述的员工也可能偶尔需要在开会时陈述信息。公众演说对很多人来说都是很有压力的，即便是在一个由你每天都能见到的同事组成的商务环境中亦是如此。以下列出的三大技能能帮助你在任何场合的商务陈述中都有好的表现：

与听众交流

在商务陈述中，第一步就是要组织一下你的信息，使其满足听众的需求和期望。问问自己陈述的目的是什么，以及听众从中应该能获取什么信息。 将这一点写进一份有时限的讲稿中，并问问自己如果是你在听另外一个人做这个陈述的话，这样的讲稿是否合适。检查一下以确保你所要传递的信息是有逻辑的、完整的，而且听起来不枯燥。正确运用语调是最重要的陈述技巧之一。要确保你准备的讲稿听起来自然、不夸张，也不会给任何人带来任何形式的侮辱。每天把你的讲稿演练几次，然后从中抽取一些关键词作为提纲写在索引卡上。之后你便可以开始练习陈述了，如果在哪里卡住了，你可以用提纲来提示自己。

商务口译

在实际陈述的时候,旁边放一张索引卡会增长你的信心。

有效利用陈述工具

无论你是用幻灯片这样的工具还是仅仅采用大图表,这些视觉工具都能从几个方面提升你的陈述技能。它们能转移听众放在你身上的部分注意力,这会让你更加轻松。视觉工具也能够使你的陈述内容更容易被听众理解。甚至是一份列出了关键点的核心讲义也能帮助听众清楚地了解你要讲的内容。此外,从你们公司那些受人敬重的上层领导那里找线索,看看他们都用哪些类型的陈述工具,这也能提升你在公司的职业形象。

预测听众提问

从听众角度考虑问题能真正提高你的陈述技能。预测一下在你做完陈述时听众可能会提的问题并想好应对方式。练习如何回答那些在你看来与主题不相关的或是无法回答的问题,用这种方式让自己做好准备以应对那些意想不到的问题,这也是非常重要的。此外,在听公司那些受人敬重的上层领导做陈述时,试着从他们那里找线索。留意一下他们是如何应对困难问题的,并正确应用他们的技巧,使其符合你自己的身份和风格。

II Warm-up

1 **Directions:** Give the English equivalents of the following Chinese expressions.

天津滨海新区	全程代办
"共赢奥运、传播奥运"	一站式服务
夏季达沃斯世界经济论坛	人才支撑
"10+3 媒体合作研讨会"	摩托罗拉
亚欧大陆桥	奥的斯电梯
服务外包	丰田汽车
保税港区	三星电子
综合保税区	盐碱荒地
保税物流园区	天然气储量
天津经济技术开发区	开采
首问负责	地热

2 **Directions:** Give the Chinese equivalents of the following English expressions.

corporate entity	sandwich of innovation
etymology	leapfrogging technology
agribusiness	S.M.A.R.T. innovation
pompous	Green Village Program
bullet point	innovation-driven economy
confidence booster	critical engine
Transrapid	low-end processing
portfolio	high-quality talent pool
megatrend	management know-how
cross-functional business unit	legal framework
high-end market	winning combination

III Passages for Interpreting

Passage 1

Directions: Listen to the passage and interpret from Chinese into English at the end of each segment. Pay special attention to the numbers.

各位来宾，女士们、先生们： //

在即将迎来北京奥运会之际，来自东盟10国和中日韩主流媒体的各位朋友，又一次相聚天津滨海新区，以"共赢奥运、传播奥运"为主题，进一步扩大合作友谊。// 在此我谨代表天津市人民政府和滨海新区管委会对大家表示热烈的欢迎，对长期以来各位给予天津和滨海新区的支持表示衷心的感谢！//

2008年是天津发展的关键一年。作为北京奥运会的协办城市，我们正在全力以赴做好各项准备工作。// 今年9月，天津滨海新区还将举办夏季达沃斯世界经济论坛。天津和滨海新区日益受到国内外媒体的广泛关注。这次"10+3媒体合作研讨会"将"走近滨海、感知天津"作为议题，具有十分重要的意义。// 下面，我主要介绍一下天津滨海新区的有关情况。//

天津是环渤海地区的经济中心，是中国北方最大的沿海开放城市。2007年，天津市人均生产总值6,050美元，将逐步建设成为经济繁荣、社会文明、科教

59

发达、设施完善、环境优美的国际港口城市、北方经济中心和生态城市。// 滨海新区位于天津东部沿海地带，规划面积2,270平方公里，海岸线153公里，人口152万，是中国最有潜力、最具活力、最富魅力的现代化经济新区。//

一是区位优势明显。滨海新区拥有世界吞吐量第六的综合性港口，内陆腹地广阔，遍及中国北方12个省市区，是亚欧大陆桥最近的东部起点，是蒙古、哈萨克斯坦等邻近内陆国家的重要出海口。// 今年8月北京奥运会之前，京津两市之间的第二条高速公路将正式通车，时速350公里的京津城际高速铁路也将建成运营，届时从北京到滨海新区仅需40分钟左右。//

第二是产业基础比较雄厚。滨海新区现在已经形成了电子信息、汽车和装备制造、石油和海洋化工、现代冶金、绿色食品、生物医药、新材料新能源七个主导产业。航空航天、金融物流、服务外包（等）新的优势产业正在崛起。// 2007年，滨海新区实现工业总产值6,283亿，高新技术产值占总量的比重达到47%。//

三是功能区域集中。滨海新区聚集了国家级开发区、保税区、高新区、出口加工区、保税港区、综合保税区、保税物流园区。// 其中，天津经济技术开发区（TEDA）连续10年保持全国开发区投资环境最好。东疆保税港区是中国面积最大、政策最优惠、功能最齐全的海关特殊监管区域，将建成符合国际通行惯例的自由贸易港区。//

四是对外开放度高。滨海新区率先实行首问负责、全程代办的一站式服务，建立了符合国际惯例的投资环境，开通了24小时服务专网96667。// 现有15,000多家外资企业，包括摩托罗拉、奥的斯电梯、丰田汽车、三星电子等89家世界500强企业，到2007年底累计实际利用外资231亿美元，是国内投资条件最好、经营成本最低、回报率最高的地区之一。//

五是科技资源密集。滨海新区所处的京津冀地区集中了约占全国27%的科技人才。现有国家级和省部级工程中心31家，企业技术研发中心70家，外商投资研发中心41家，博士后工作站52家。// 滨海新区作为全国职业教育改革试验区，与德国、西班牙合作培养了一大批高素质技术工人，形成了多层次的人才支撑。//

六是发展前景广阔。滨海新区面积是浦东新区的四倍，是香港的两倍，比深圳大300多平方公里，有1,214平方公里可供开发利用的盐碱荒地，这在国内外大中城市中是很少见的。// 已探明渤海海域石油资源总量100多亿吨，天然气储量1,937亿立方米，年可开采地热2,000万立方米，原盐年产量240多万吨。//

女士们、先生们、朋友们，天津滨海新区的开发开放，为包括东盟各国和日本、韩国在内的广大投资者提供了巨大商机。// 我们真诚欢迎更多中外企业和有识之士抓住难得机遇，积极参与天津滨海新区的开发建设，实现互利共赢。希望新闻界的各位朋友，更多地关注天津、了解天津，积极宣传推介滨海新区，为我们提出建设性的意见。//

最后，祝大家在天津滨海新区工作愉快。谢谢！//

Passage 2

Directions: Listen to the passage and interpret from English into Chinese at the end of each segment.

Respected Vice Governor Tong Xing, Ladies and Gentlemen,

Good morning! // When talking about innovation and company growth—I think Siemens is an excellent example. We just celebrated our 160th birthday about a month ago. And for all that time, innovation has driven our growth and made major contributions to the world. We have radically changed the way societies work and the way people live. //

(*Slide 2: Siemens innovations have changed the world*)

In the field of energy alone—Siemens invented the dynamo and formed the basis for the entire power industry. You might say we invented electrical engineering itself. And many of our countless applications have been spectacular, from the world's first electric railway to the 310-mph Transrapid operating in Shanghai. We have also been pioneers in healthcare—providing everything from the first X-ray systems to the most precise 3-D body scans available on the market today. //

(*Slide 3: Innovation is our lifeblood*)

All along the way—innovation has been our lifeblood. And it is our major strength in all our businesses. To keep at the cutting edge in our industry, we invest nearly six billion euros a year in R&D. And all this pays off—with thousands of inventions every year, with top worldwide patent positions and with a steady stream of technical breakthroughs. //

(*Slide 4: Siemens conducts R&D at 150 locations*)

Our research and development reflects our global reach: we work on the future in all parts of the world. Our nearly 50,000 R&D employees work at 150 locations in over 30 countries around the globe. And as you can see here—China is an important center for our R&D activities. We know it is essential to provide local products for all market sectors—from low-end to high-end—and our China facilities serve the country, the region and the world. //

(Slide 5: Global megatrends)

Our portfolio focuses on providing answers to the challenges of the global megatrends. Demographic change, urbanization and climate change are altering our world at an ever faster pace. Growing numbers of people need access to clean water. They require energy. They need mobility. They demand greater environmental protection. They worry about scarcer natural resources. And they demand better security and healthcare. // As the world population soars, these challenges will grow. Many major Chinese cities like Guangzhou and Shenzhen are rapidly emerging as megacities—and must master these challenges if they want to remain economically viable and livable. //

(Slide 6: In times of change and challenges...)

Companies like Siemens also face a changing world. New markets open up. New competitors arrive on the scene. National monopolies end. The pace of innovation accelerates. Industries are privatized. Markets are deregulated. And companies must adapt to these changes. //

We are currently preparing a new organizational set-up at Siemens as the basis for greater innovation and stronger growth. Starting next year, our business will be organized in three sectors: Energy, Industry and Healthcare. We will also have cross-functional business units serving the entire company. // And why are we doing this? Because we need to focus our businesses even stronger on the challenges of the megatrends. We need to be less complex, and faster. And—in the end—we need to better leverage all our strengths to be even more innovative. //

(Slide 7: Sandwich of innovation)

In China, for example, we are pursuing a so-called sandwich of innovation strategy. This not only helps us safeguard our leading position in high-end markets but helps us expand in middle [mid]- and low-end markets. //

For the high-end market, we are concentrating on five crucial points to sustain our leading position. First, focus on key leapfrogging technologies—such as science, nanotechnology, renewable energy and biotechnology. // Second, target innovations based on know-how unique to China, such as combining traditional Chinese medicine and western medicine for new medical treatments. // Third, use new business models—such as working with Chinese partners to provide Internet-based machine maintenance and monitoring. // Fourth, work on innovations for leading markets in China, like 3G or post-3G wireless communications. // And fifth, offer extreme innovations or advanced technologies and solutions not previously available. //

To operate in the highly competitive mid- and low-end markets, we eliminate unnecessary features, use local materials and manufacture locally. In emerging markets, the goal of innovation is to find new ways to do old things. Such as continuously improving existing products and moving up into high-end segments. //

We push S.M.A.R.T. innovation to achieve this goal. It stands for: simple, maintenance-friendly, affordable, reliable and timely to market. Since most companies in Guangdong are small or medium-sized with limited capital, S.M.A.R.T. innovation is the best way for them to serve the market. //

(Slide 8: Challenges in Guangdong)

Innovation does not come easily. For anyone! We see four major challenges that apply in general and specifically to Guangdong. One needs talent—in particular experienced innovation coaches. One needs the right mechanisms to transfer ideas to the market. One needs to improve the efficiency of R&D investment. And one needs better human resources policies to focus on innovation. //

(Slide 9: Investment alone does not guarantee...)

Most people think money is the key to success. But investments alone are not the answer. China has huge advantages but needs defined strategies and processes and something else: innovation coaches. They are trained and experienced in solving real problems—and can adjust strategies dynamically. And that is essential in a rapidly changing business environment! //

(Slide 10: Siemens innovation strategy)

And where do these innovation coaches come from? They must be cultivated. At Siemens, we train people worldwide by giving them practical experience in solving real-life problems. And we give them international working exposure. Here in China, for example, Siemens Corporate Technology brought in experienced coaches from Germany and other countries to work with Chinese colleagues. //

(Slide 11: Partnerships are the key)

Partnerships between the private sector and the government are the most effective way to boost innovation. We offer our expertise, while governments provide the infrastructure and financial support. One example is Singapore, where we are working to create a regional hub for water treatment technologies. //

商务口译

(*Slide 12: Siemens Green Village Program*)

Clean water is crucial for sustainable economic growth and a good quality of life. As one example of how the private sector can work with the government—we have just launched the Siemens Green Village Program. It will provide innovative solutions for environmental care in Guangdong. The pilot project will deliver safe water in a rural village of Guangdong. We will study the situation, work out an innovative solution, implement the work—then transfer skills and know-how to a local partner so people can continue to help themselves. //

(*Slide 13: Thank you*)

Ladies and gentlemen. Guangdong is transforming itself into an innovation-driven economy. And I believe this can best be achieved by combining the systematic innovation structures of international partners with the great talents, vast resources and enormous market of China. Close partnership is the answer to sustained innovation! //

Thank you! //

Passage 3

Directions: Listen to the passage and interpret from English into Chinese at the end of each segment.

Respected Vice Governor Tong, Distinguished Guests, Ladies and Gentlemen, //

On behalf of Emerson, I would like to thank you for this opportunity to share our thoughts with you on how innovation helps to change economic development and investment in Guangdong Province. For many years, Emerson has participated in this important conference and I am delighted to be here addressing this gathering today—it's a tremendous honor. //

Emerson's business philosophy includes a commitment to doing business without borders—we are a global company. We applaud Guangdong government's decision to organize an international consultative conference as an investment in its ongoing successful economic development, and as a means of promoting international trade and investment. //

Guangdong is perceived by many as the pioneer of economic reform in China. Since 1978, when China began to open up, Guangdong, especially the Pearl River Delta (PRD), rapidly developed its economy. After more than two decades of substantial economic and social development, Guangdong has reached new heights in terms of overall economic strength. The province is a critical engine in China's economic development and it is a provincial leader in many fields. //

At Emerson, we have witnessed the rapid development of Guangdong. We first entered China in the late 1970s through a technology transfer in industrial pressure transmitters and were one of the first foreign companies to conduct business in China since the beginning of its economic reform. Today Emerson has more than 40 local enterprises, including manufacturing, engineering and sales offices throughout China. Emerson's relationship with China and her people has been long and rewarding for us. //

In the 1980s and early 1990s, Guangdong's economic development benefited from labor intensive, low-end processing and light industries. These industries created vast job opportunities, and greatly improved living standards. // Guangdong's success is impressive and a model for other provinces in China; yet, after more than two decades of development, there are still many issues facing the province that present both opportunities and challenges. //

For example, the cost of land, labor and materials has risen rapidly in recent years, making the low value-added processing industries model unsustainable over the long-term. These industries also have low-profit margins while creating heavy pressures on energy consumption and the environment. //

However, many foreign firms that utilized China's inexpensive labor and land are now seeing China as an important market for business growth. By investing in R&D in China, they can develop high-quality and localized products and solutions that meet customer demands. The abundant, relatively low-cost and high-quality talent pool in China is the main factor that attracts foreign R&D investment. //

It's now a critical moment for Guangdong to take advantage of global trends and move to innovative, high value-added technology and capital intensive industries in order to maintain a healthy mix of industries and ensure sustainable economic growth. Emerson is committed to partner with Guangdong and China to achieve this goal. //

Emerson is a broad global technology and engineering leader in developing and delivering innovative solutions to our customers with over $22 billion in sales in 2007. We serve the process industry, electronics and electronic equipment manufacturers, computer and telecom companies, a wide range of industrial manufacturers, power and energy industries and much more. // We employ more than 136,000 people, operate in 274 manufacturing locations worldwide and market our products in 150 countries. We are truly a global technology and innovation company—touching most parts of the manufacturing world. //

Our growth in China and around the globe is the result of our continued efforts to develop innovative new technologies and products that our customers want. In fact, in the last three years, we introduced over 600 major new products. // Over the years, new products as a percent of sales have grown steadily. This year, new products introduced in the past five years are expected to represent 35 percent of our sales. Our goal is to take that key measurement to 40 percent. //

A significant amount of our innovation focus in China deals with the energy efficiency and improving the environment. // For example, we designed our next-generation digital scroll technology in China and it can be used for both cooling and heating. // A Suzhou-based engineering team that included 14 local engineers developed a compressor design that can save around 70 percent of energy used in heating compared to other methods. // Additionally, Emerson also participated in the formulation and issuance of three Chinese national energy efficiency standards and marking systems for air-conditioning products in August 2004. These standards help to raise energy efficiency, reduce energy consumption, and improve the overall technological level of China's air-conditioning products. //

We see a huge potential for Guangdong to be the destination of high value-added innovative industries, and utilize these industries to sustain its economic growth into the next decade. // Today, we have more than 30,000 employees working in China—more in this country than any other outside North America. Many of them are in Guangdong Province. // We also established engineering centers in six cities including Shenzhen. In recent years, both Emerson and China have cooperated closely on many technologies and new product innovations and both parties have grown tremendously. //

However, Guangdong is facing fierce competition from other regions and countries to attract quality foreign and domestic investment, as well as overseas and local talent. // From Emerson's perspective, when we evaluate investment opportunities anywhere around the world, we have several considerations in mind, including:

- Ease of doing business;
- The quality of infrastructure;

- The education level and skill base of the labor force;
- The structure of the labor laws;
- The cost of labor, material and logistics; //

Favorable policies toward overseas and local R&D investment are definitely a crucial factor. Acquiring a large quantity of high-quality workers is important for Guangdong province to win this game. Emerson sees that a quality workforce is essential for technology innovations. There is an immediate need to educate, bring in and retain high-quality workers so that the province will be more attractive to high value-added companies. //

We believe that people are our most important asset, and we mean it. That's why we are especially proud that Emerson has been recognized as one of China's top employers for 2007 in the Shanghai region for our highly regarded operating environment in which people can, and do, make a positive difference. //

We see the benefits of training and promoting Chinese employees to senior management level. Chinese managers usually have strong technical knowledge and a better understanding of the Chinese market and culture. //

For example, Emerson Network Power has a program to identify core staff and provide them with Executive MBA and MBA education. The company also provides annual management training programs that cover topics like leadership, professional techniques, English and management skills. // As a result of this program, dozens of senior executives have been promoted from local staff. Emerson Network Power is also one of the first multinational companies to fully utilize the local workforce in global R&D and manufacturing in China. //

International partnership and cooperation are another way to benefit Chinese enterprises and their workforces. Emerson helps the industries we serve to grow and increasingly adapt their operations to meet international standards. // We frequently work side by side with our manufacturing partners and suppliers to develop new systems, overcome engineering challenges and deliver world-class service to customers. By accumulating knowledge in advanced technologies and management know-how, Chinese enterprises become more capable to compete in overseas markets. //

After two decades of rapid development, Guangdong Province, possesses one of the best transportation and communications infrastructures in China, enabling the province to attract significant investment. // A predictable and consistent government policy and legal framework are also critical for multinational companies to commit long-term investment in Guangdong. The development of a service sector also has significant potential for future growth. // Because of rapid business development in China, Emerson has recently built a new e-Resource center in Xi'an. This facility will not only help us better serve our customers by providing accounting, logistics, a helpdesk and other back-office activities but it will also include technical support engineers as well as design engineers to support our divisions. //

Looking ahead, we clearly see challenges and opportunities in front of Guangdong province. Emerson remains very positive about Guangdong's and China's economic growth prospects, its abilities to adapt to the latest technologies, and its efforts to continue to educate a strong pool of local talent. // Emerson will continue to bring our established management processes, our technological know-how and strong ethical value system that is both robust and highly successful. Together, Emerson and Guangdong Province will continue to innovate, and will continue to be a winning combination. //

Once again, I would like to thank the government of Guangdong Province for giving me the opportunity to talk to you today. Thank you. //

IV Guide to Interpreting

1. Passage 1是自天津某地方领导的商务介绍节选，重点介绍天津滨海新区的投资环境。和很多中文演讲类似，这篇商务陈述也是先礼节性地致意，再总说，然后分成六个方面进行陈述，一条条说得简洁明了。译员需要注意，每一条的第一句话，一般都是一个小标题，是对后续内容的提纲挈领的总结。译员在记交传笔记时一定要注意不能漏掉这个最重要的信息点，否则即使其他信息记得再全，也不免"捡了芝麻，丢了西瓜"。另外一个值得注意的地方是，本篇练习中出现了大量的数字以及专有名词。译员在翻译之前必须对天津滨海新区的人文地理和社会文化有所了解，做到有备无患。
2. 广东经济发展国际咨询会，又称"洋顾问思维旋风"，始于1999年，每年11月份举办，聘请全球500强国际企业的高管来广东省出谋献策。Passage 2和Passage 3的商务陈述均节选自2007年的"洋顾问"演讲，讲话人分别是西门子公司和艾默生公司的的重要领导。当然，在口译练习之前要上网了解一下广东经济发展国际咨询会的背景和介绍，以及西门子和艾默生公司的简介和业务，尤其是与广东省的合作内容。在做口译练习之前，要尽可能多查阅和掌握这两个公司在业务中所涉及的专业词汇，功课做足了，译起来就不会太难了。

3. 现今的商务陈述一般都配有多媒体视听手段，如PPT或投影。Passage 2的文本来自全真的演讲现场，演讲稿中间夹有幻灯片的出现。译员除了要听译演讲者的讲话内容，还要注意幻灯片上的内容，当然更要注意幻灯片的转换时间，要将口译与演讲者的声音以及幻灯片的播放节奏协调起来。

V Highlight for Interpreting

Directions: Interpret the following sentences from Chinese into English or vice versa.

1. 在此我谨代表天津市人民政府和滨海新区管委会对大家表示热烈的欢迎，对长期以来各位给予天津和滨海新区的支持表示衷心的感谢！
2. 滨海新区位于天津东部沿海地带，规划面积2,270平方公里，海岸线153公里，人口152万，是中国最有潜力、最具活力、最富魅力的现代化经济新区。
3. 滨海新区现在已经形成了电子信息、汽车和装备制造、石油和海洋化工、现代冶金、绿色食品、生物医药、新材料新能源七个主导产业。航空航天、金融物流、服务外包（等）新的优势产业正在崛起。
4. 东疆保税港区是中国面积最大、政策最优惠、功能最齐全的海关特殊监管区域，将建成符合国际通行惯例的自由贸易港区。
5. 已探明渤海海域石油资源总量100多亿吨，天然气储量1,937亿立方米，年可开采地热2,000万立方米，原盐年产量240多万吨。
6. All along the way—innovation has been our lifeblood. And it is our major strength in all our businesses. To keep at the cutting edge in our industry, we invest nearly six billion euros a year in R&D. And all this pays off—with thousands of inventions every year, with top worldwide patent positions and with a steady stream of technical breakthroughs.
7. At Siemens, we train people worldwide by giving them practical experience in solving real-life problems. And we give them international working exposure. Here in China, for example, Siemens Corporate Technology brought in experienced coaches from Germany and other countries to work with Chinese colleagues.
8. Emerson's business philosophy includes a commitment to doing business without

borders—we are a global company. We applaud Guangdong government's decision to organize an international consultative conference as an investment in its ongoing successful economic development, and as a means of promoting international trade and investment.

9. Over the years, new products as a percent of sales have grown steadily. This year, new products introduced in the past five years are expected to represent 35 percent of our sales. Our goal is to take that key measurement to 40 percent.

10. We believe that people are our most important asset, and we mean it. That's why we are especially proud that Emerson has been recognized as one of China's top employers for 2007 in the Shanghai region for our highly regarded operating environment in which people can, and do, make a positive difference.

11. Emerson will continue to bring our established management processes, our technological know-how and strong ethical value system that is both robust and highly successful. Together, Emerson and Guangdong Province will continue to innovate, and will continue to be a winning combination.

第6单元

新闻发布会

Press Conference

I Background Knowledge

Directions: Read the following English passages and then compare them with their Chinese equivalents.

Passage 1

A press conference is a voluntary presentation of information to the media. In a press conference, you decide what information is presented, how it is presented, and who presents it. It is an opportunity to get your story on TV, radio or in the paper.

To hold a press conference you contact the media, pick a time and place, make a presentation and respond to reporters' questions. Whatever your organizational goals are, remember that you have to have something newsworthy to announce, reveal, or talk about at your press conference.

The characteristics of the press conference are, formal and solemn, communicative with superior methods.

新闻发布会是一种自发向新闻界发布有关信息的活动。在新闻发布会上，组织者决定发布什么信息、如何发布信息以及由谁来发布。这样，组织者就能通过电视、电台或者报纸向公众发布信息。

要举办一场新闻发布会，组织者要联系媒体，选择合适的时间和地点，作出陈述并回答记者的问题。无论组织这场发布会的目的是什么，切记你所宣布、揭露或谈到的信息是具有新闻价值的。

新闻发布会通常具有正规隆重、妙想高论畅所欲言等特点。

商务口译

Passage 2

Major steps for setting up a press conference:

• Clearly state a good reason for holding a press conference: the news you are going to reveal has not been covered in the press yet, or there is an emergency, or an important new issue.

• Decide what message you want to deliver through the media.

• Work out the location of the press conference. Find an appropriate place that is convenient and has the facilities you need.

• Set the date and time of the press conference.

• Invite the media.

• Invite guests.

• Prepare your spokesperson(s) to deliver your message.

• Prepare background materials.

• Prepare visual aids. Charts, big maps, or pictures will help get your message across.

举行一场记者招待会的主要步骤有:

• 明确声明召开记者招待会的原因：将要发布的新闻尚未被披露，或者有突发事件或重大事件发生。

• 确定你要通过媒体向外发布的信息。

• 选定举行记者招待会的地点。选择的地点要便利，并能提供你要的各种设施。

• 确定记者招待会的时间与地点。

• 邀请媒体。

• 邀请嘉宾。

• 选择好发布信息的发言人。

• 准备好背景材料。

• 准备好直观道具，如表格、大地图、图片等，这样可以帮助你传达信息。

II Warm-up

1 Directions: Give the English equivalents of the following Chinese expressions.

收支平衡	逃税漏税	外交部
贸易顺差	代理国库	发改委
外汇投资	拆借市场	工业和信息化部
存款准备金率	债券市场	公安部
再贷款利率	中国外汇交易中心	财政部
外包	农村信用社	人力资源和社会
扩大内需	中国银监会	保障部
发展服务业	邮政储蓄	农业部
监管机构	抵押担保	中国海关总署
"三农"	权威性	质检总局
支付清算系统	股份制改革	民航总局
残旧币	趋势性变化	食品药品监督管
反洗钱	财政赤字	理局
走私	适当收缩	进出口银行
贩毒	流动性过剩	互利双赢
贪污受贿	股权分置	贸易摩擦
金融诈骗	商务部	

2 Directions: Give the Chinese equivalents of the following English expressions.

stock market	JCCT
average Chinese investor	comment on
cool down	civilian nuclear cooperation
diversification	military trade
foreign exchange reserves	

商务口译

III Passages for Interpreting

Passage 1

Directions: Listen to the dialog and interpret from Chinese into English at the end of each segment.

香港记者： 谢谢您，周行长，我注意到你们在2004年已经提出我国国际收支平衡的问题，但这些年来，贸易顺差仍然突飞猛进，这会导致哪些问题？// 对这个问题您有什么对策？国家外汇管理局已经缩减短期外债，国家正在组建国家外汇投资公司，行长能否给我们提供更多的信息？// 香港作为国际金融中心，我们可以做什么？我们也注意到，香港提出资金自由流通的200多个建议中有80多个是关于金融的，请问今年之内有哪些可以付诸实施的？//

周小川： 首先，我前一段时间已经说到，中央银行有若干个手段来压延市场上过多的流动性，包括公开市场业务操作、存款准备金率、再贷款利率以及其他一些手段，我们还会继续使用。//
至于进出口贸易不平衡，贸易顺差还在继续扩大，首先取决于国内需求的大小和国际市场对中国产品需求的大小，它决定了进出口的增长速度。进口和出口，其实两个都是在增长的，就像两个人赛跑，看谁跑得更快一些。// 有助于出口增长的因素，比如说国内新的投资形成的新生产能力，还有外商直接投资也十分踊跃，不断形成新的生产能力。正如薄部长所说的，外商直接投资对出口发挥了很大作用。// 另外，全球信息化的发展，使得信息非常灵敏，出口厂商很容易捕捉到全球的机会。现在流行一本书叫《世界是平的》，就是描述这种现象。包括服务业，现在外包也越来越多。// 有助于中国进口增长的因素，（还有）比如说汇率的调整。另外，中国也进口了比较多的原材料。在中国出口方面，我们也面临着成本逐渐上升、劳动工资的提高、社会保障的完善等（问题）。这些因素都在综合影响着进出口平衡。综合下来的结果，当前还存在贸易不平衡的趋势，这需要一定的时间来慢慢加以调节和解决。//
从中国政府调节国际收支不平衡的政策来讲，前不久召开的中央金融工作会议对这个问题作了说明。// 首先，最重要的是，调节国际收支不平衡最有效的手段是实行经济结构性调整政策。首先是扩大内需，其中特别是扩大消费内需和发展服务业，服务业是（能使）将来内需有很大增长

第6单元　新闻发布会

空间的重要环节。// 此外结构性调整政策还包括扩大进口，这需要解除一些政策上的障碍。此外还包括支持中国企业走出去，到外面去投资建厂。但经济结构性调整政策出效果的时间可能会长一些，但它是非常重要的，是为主的政策。//

作为辅助性政策，汇率政策作为价格杠杆也能起到一定作用，能够调节进出口之间的平衡。另外就是外汇管理可以配合上面提到的结构性政策和汇率政策来进行转变，比如给对外投资提供方便，（给）经常项目用汇提供方便。//

刚才香港记者提到缩减短期外债的问题，现在借短期外债的必要性已经不大，主要是过去有些体制方面的限制，导致外资银行和外商投资企业借的短期外债比较多，现在在这方面的需求已经不太必要了，所以要收缩一下。上面这些做法都有助于促进国际收支平衡。//

大家可能已经注意到，三个监管机构，银行、证券和保险方面都对如何更好地发挥内地和香港金融之间的合作，提出了一些政策和考虑。// 从中国人民银行的角度来讲，我们在1月份发布了将进一步扩大香港人民币业务，具体是指在香港发行人民币债券，这项工作正在紧密准备之中，估计较快可以出台。//

中央电视台记者：请问周行长，在市场上有些企业可能会有各种不良记录，比如环保不达标。// 目前人民银行把这些不良记录都纳入到企业诚信数据库，如果企业再向银行申请贷款有可能通不过审核，类似这样的金融服务央行还做了哪些？金融在支持"三农"方面还有哪些考虑呢？//

周小川：央行的金融服务有广义和狭义之分。您刚才谈到的诚信服务就是中央银行服务的一个内容。// 中央银行提供服务的有支付清算系统。凡是跨银行的支付，一般都是靠中央银行的支付清算系统来提供清算。现在支付清算系统的大额系统，每天大约有50万笔交易，总交易金额是1万亿（元）人民币左右，可见这项金融服务很重要。//

在小额系统中也有很多服务品种，其中一项和大家比较密切的就是银行卡跨行交易，通过中央银行和商业银行的相互合作，提供了跨行交易的清算服务和其他服务，包括对信用卡的标准、互联互通、支付保障的服务。// 中央银行提供的另外一个服务是印钞造币。大家手里用的纸币硬币，都是要制造的，这里面要进行一版一版的更新，要防伪，同时还要反假币。钞票还要有运输、保管，（要掌握）哪个地方有需要，哪个地方可以提取，哪个地方有残旧币，哪个地方要回收销毁。//

还有就是反洗钱服务，这不是一个正面服务，但是为了保证金融稳定，主

商务口译

要是防止社会上出现不良现象，防止走私、贩毒、贪污受贿、金融诈骗、逃税漏税等。//

此外，人民银行的金融服务还有一项叫代理国库，国库的收入支出都由人民银行代理。这些服务大家一般不太容易看得到，因为大家打交道的都是商业银行的营业网点，但正是中央银行这些背后的服务，才保证了国民经济健康有效的发展。//

央行广义的金融服务可以把金融市场的建设放在里面。金融市场是由中央银行、商业银行和其他金融机构共同建立的。// 人民银行在金融市场方面，主要负责银行间市场的发展和自律完善，其中包括资金的拆借市场、债券市场，也包括其他一些产品市场。还有外汇市场，大家都知道有个中国外汇交易中心，还有黄金市场。这些市场也可以理解成是为市场参与者提供的一种服务。//

提到为"三农"服务，中央银行在本届政府和银行及其他金融机构一起做了几件事，也还有几件事没有做完，正在推进。//

第一，和银监会共同推进农村信用社的改革，并取得一定进展，使得农村信用社贷款能力有了很大提高。//

第二，要完善农民在贷款时抵押担保的做法。过去存在着抵押难、担保难的问题。目前还在探索进行小额贷款，现在叫微小贷款。//

第三，今年中央1号文件在农业问题上提到，经过试点以后要大力推进发展农业保险。//

第四，关于邮政储蓄的改革。过去邮政储蓄对农村提供了很好的支付方面的服务，但是吸收的存款有时候不能回流到农村进行使用。// 邮政储蓄改革中有一部分内容包括在金融改革中。通过邮政储蓄改革，将来能使邮政系统，特别是邮政系统吸收的存款能够更好地为"三农"服务。//

第五，今年要开展农业银行股份制改革，包括财务重组、股份制改革，今后还要择机上市。这个改革会加强对县域经济和"三农"的服务。//

此外有两件事已经做得差不多了，一个是对"三农"贷款，即农村信用社和其他农村金融机构贷款的利率市场化方面的改革。二是通过央行实行差别准备金率对农村信用社给予正向鼓励，提升他们的贷款能力。//

前面提到的一、二、三、四、五都已经起步了，但推进程度不一样，今年以及今后还要进一步向前推进。这是我们在"三农"方面的想法。//

日本《朝日新闻》记者：我想问周行长，2月末，全球股市同时出现大跌，很多人感觉是上海市场引起了这次调整。您怎么看这样的说法？// 怎么分析全球，包括中国一直在波动的市场。在全球股市越来越密切的情况下，中

国金融市场，包括股市，需要什么样的改善？//

周小川： 关于股市变化，通常有不同的原因，有时是市场自身的原因，有时可能是由于宏观经济方面出了问题，有时也可能是微观方面，比如说某几间公司出了问题，这有多种可能性。//

对于前不久发生的股市价格波动的问题，我看外界，不管是媒体也好，经济学家也好，市场人士也好，都有很多的评论。我个人觉得，这还不是宏观层面的问题，应该不会造成重大的趋势性变化。//

这次股市波动在全球都有一定的相互关联影响，这说明全球化在逐步进展。过去中国认为自己的市场是一个相对比较小型的市场，也是一个正在建设中的、比较幼年的市场，或者说是在转轨经济中逐步发展的新兴市场。// 由于全球经济一体化的进展，股市波动相互之间关联密切，这也说明中国的市场还需要加速发展，我们要进一步提高直接融资的比重，进一步把资本市场建设得更好、更快、更加国际化。// 这样，不管是外部对我们的影响，还是我们对外部的影响，就会使大家感觉是在大致相近的条件和规律下运作，就能更好地应对市场变化。同时也应该看到，市场总是在不断调整、不断变化的，市场不会像池塘里的静水，总会有各种各样的波涛存在。//

关于流动性过剩问题。流动性偏多是全球的现象，中国也存在流动性偏多的问题。美国财政赤字那么大，它那儿的流动性也很丰富。// 因此，资金面上的宽松是全球一体化之下相互影响的现象。宏观调控当局都应该重视这个问题，做好自己的工作，对于过剩的流动性应该采取稳健的、适当收缩的政策。//

从分析角度也要分析得更透一些，不见得流动性过剩会直接对某一个或者某一天的资产市场，包括股票市场和房地产市场，产生直接冲击和影响。要看到市场是非常复杂的，波动的原因也是多种多样的。//

Passage 2

Directions: Interpret the following dialog alternatively from English into Chinese or vice versa at the end of each segment.

***Wall Street Journal* journalist:** *Xiexie*, I'm... with the *Wall Street Journal*. International investors are now very interested in China's stock market. // Do you think the rise of the stock market over the past two years went too far, too fast? And the average Chinese investors might be risking too much? What measures is your government considering to further cool down or regulate the stock market? // And another topic related to investment—the government has announced plans for a new agency to manage the diversification of China's foreign exchange reserves. Can you tell us what kind of assets this agency will invest in? //

温家宝：谢谢你。我关注股市的发展，但更关注股市市场的健康（发展）。// 去年以来，我们加强了资本市场的基础制度建设，特别是成功地推进了股权分置改革，解决了历史上的遗留问题。我们的目标是建立一个成熟的资本市场。// 这就需要：第一，提高上市公司的质量；第二，要建立一个公开、公正、透明的市场体系；第三，要加强资本市场的监管，特别是完善法制。最后，就是要加强股市市场情况的信息的及时披露，使股民增强防范风险的意识。//

你谈到中国的外汇储备如何使用，这确实是我们面临的一个大的问题。其实从我的经历来看，外汇少的时候，有少的难处。//（上世纪）90年代的时候，我们因缺少外汇，曾经向国际货币基金组织借，他们只借（给）我们八亿美元。现在外汇多了，超过一万亿（美元）了，怎么把它们使用好？（这）又成为我们一个新的难题。//

……我们是要组建一个外汇投资机构，这个机构是超脱任何部门的，依照国家的法律来经营外汇，有偿使用，接受监管，保值增值。//

中国对外投资时间还短，我们十分缺乏经验。我最近查了一下资料，现在非金融类的对外投资，截至2005年底，只有733亿美元，去年一年新增160亿美元。这同发达国家比起来，简直是微乎其微。//

我知道女士想提出的问题，就是我们成立这个公司开展对外投资会不会影响美元资产。在中国的外汇储备当中，美元资产占多数，这是个事实。// 中国购买美元资产是互利的，中国组建外汇储备的投资公司，不会影响美元资产。谢谢你。//

Passage 3

Directions: Listen to the dialog and interpret alternatively from English into Chinese or vice versa at the end of each segment.

Q: The 19th China-US JCCT meeting will be held next week in the US. Which Chinese departments will attend? // What is your expectation? And how would you comment on the current China-US trade relations? //

第6单元　新闻发布会

A: 第19届中美商贸联委会将于16号在美国洛杉矶举行。中国国务院副总理王岐山将与美国商务部长古铁雷斯、贸易谈判代表施瓦布共同主持此次会议。// 随王岐山副总理访美的中方代表团成员包括国务院有关部门、商务部、外交部、发改委、工业和信息化部、公安部、财政部、人力资源和社会保障部、农业部、海关总署、质检总局、民航总局、食品药品监督管理局和进出口银行等部门的十几位副部级以上官员。按照惯例，周文重大使和雷德大使也将出席。//

今年是中美建立商贸联委会机制25周年，该机制对促进和深化中美双边经贸关系，拓展双方经贸合作领域发挥了不可替代的重要作用。// 我们相信此次联委会将对扩大双方经贸合作，妥善处理中美经贸问题，推动中美经贸关系健康稳定发展发挥积极的作用。//

中美经贸关系的主要特征是互利双赢。中美现在互为第二大贸易伙伴，去年的双边贸易额达到3,021亿美元，是建交当初的120多倍。中美经贸合作给两国人民带来实实在在的好处，也为促进世界经济的增长作出了贡献。//

中美经贸关系发展迅速，规模大，在发展过程中出现一些问题和摩擦也是正常的。我们希望双方能够以战略的眼光，从大局出发，坚持通过坦诚对话、平等协商和扩大合作解决问题。事实证明，对话协商是解决中美贸易摩擦的有效途径。//

Q: It is understood that the newly elected Pakistani President Zardari will visit China next week, and Venezuelan President Chavez shall follow. Is it fair to assume that they want to talk about civilian nuclear cooperation or military trade? //

A: 我们欢迎扎尔达里总统和查韦斯总统方便时访华。双方可以通过外交渠道保持沟通，目前我还没有这方面的消息发布。//

至于你提到的核能合作，我们的立场是一贯的。我们认为，各国在履行核不扩散国际义务的前提下，享有和平利用核能并为此开展国际合作的权利。// 中方也将根据自己的国际义务，在平等互利的基础上，继续与有关国家在和平利用核能领域开展合作。//

关于你提到的军品贸易，我没有这方面的具体信息。但是我们的政策是明确的。中国对军品出口一直采取非常慎重和负责的态度，实行严格的管理。//

IV Guide to Interpreting

1. 新闻发布的形式有主动发布和被动发布、正式和非正式之分。主动发布新闻就是主动对外发布消息，如发表政府声明、外交部声明、外交部发言人谈话等；被动发布主要指应询回答记者提问。正式发布新闻指通过一种正规的方式传达信息，方式主要有：新闻发布会、记者招待会、网上发布新闻和网上在线交流、冷餐会或酒会、接受记者单独专访或多家联合采访、发送新闻稿等；非正式发布新闻的方式主要有公开场合交谈、背景吹风会、向个别记者提供重要信息、请记者用餐等。

2. 新闻发布会与记者招待会是有区别的，但现在国内对两者的称呼上有些混用。外交部每周举行两次新闻发布会，这种新闻发布会也常被称为外交部记者招待会。实际上，新闻发布会，顾名思义，是发布新闻的活动。一般由发言人先发布新闻，再回答记者提问。而记者招待会往往不先发布新闻，只立足于回答记者提问。新闻发布会一般指政府或部门发言人举行的定期、不定期或临时的新闻发布活动。这种发布会规格较低，活动时间较短，一般在半小时至一小时左右，如外交部新闻发布会、国台办新闻发布会等。记者招待会更适用于中央领导、部长或部门领导人，如总统记者招待会、总理记者招待会、部长记者招待会或大使记者招待会等。

3. Passage 1 节选自 2007 年"两会"期间中国人民银行行长周小川答中外记者提问。现在的记者提问，因为机会难得，通常一口气问好几个问题，而在口译时，译员一定要记清楚问题的数目，了然于胸，然后还要在从宏观上关注领导人回答问题的针对性。这篇练习选取了三个不同的记者提出的数量不同的问题以及周小川作出的回答。要注意的是，周行长回答问题的重点也不一样，有的回答得详细，并且分列成若干条内容，有的只作简单的答复。但无论如何，译前了解中国央行的一些机构特征和业务功能，熟悉金融市场和银行方面的有关术语，根据《中国日报》等报刊的相关表达做出自己的词汇表十分必要。

4. Passage 2 节选自国务院总理温家宝在 2007 年两会之后例行的规模最大、最正式的记者招待会，内容上选取了与金融市场尤其是股市有关的专题问答，记者用英语问，总理用汉语回答，这是典型的交传训练内容。结合 Passage 1 的练习，这一篇可进行长交传的笔记训练，特别是要尝试一口气译完总理回答问题的内容，注意讲话人条分缕析的讲话方式。

5. Passage 3 节选自 2008 年 9 月外交部发言人姜瑜的例行记者会，选取了他对两个外国记者所提问题进行的回答。在练习之前要对国家各部委的专有译名尽可能多地掌握，还要了解中美商贸联委会的有关背景知识。其中第二个问题属于一般性外交问题，难度不大，但最好先了解中国与巴基斯坦及委内瑞拉之间的传统友谊，以及彼此合作的主要内容。

V Highlight for Interpreting

Directions: Interpret the following sentences from Chinese into English or vice versa.

1. 首先，我前一段时间已经说到，中央银行有若干个手段来压延市场上过多的流动性，包括公开市场业务操作、存款准备金率、再贷款利率以及其他一些手段，我们还会继续使用。
2. 另外，全球信息化的发展，使得信息非常灵敏，出口厂商很容易捕捉到全球的机会。现在流行一本书叫《世界是平的》，就是描述这种现象。包括服务业，现在外包也越来越多。
3. 作为辅助性政策，汇率政策作为价格杠杆也能起到一定作用，能够调节进出口之间的平衡。另外就是外汇管理可以配合上面提到的结构性政策和汇率政策来进行转变，比如给对外投资提供方便，(给)经常项目用汇提供方便。
4. 央行的金融服务有广义和狭义之分。您刚才谈到的诚信服务就是中央银行服务的一个内容。中央银行提供服务的有支付清算系统。
5. 还有就是反洗钱服务，这不是一个正面服务，但是为了保证金融稳定，主要是防止社会上出现不良现象，防止走私、贩毒、贪污受贿、金融诈骗、逃税漏税等。
6. 提到为"三农"服务，中央银行在本届政府和银行及其他金融机构一起做了几件事，也还有几件事没有做完，正在推进。
7. 这次股市波动在全球都有一定的相互关联影响，这说明全球化在逐步进展。过去中国认为自己的市场是一个相对比较小型的市场，也是一个正在建设中的、比较幼年的市场，或者说是在转轨经济中逐步发展的新兴市场。
8. 关于流动性过剩问题。流动性偏多是全球的现象，中国也存在流动性偏多的问题。美国财政赤字那么大，它那儿的流动性也很丰富。因此，资金面上的宽松是全球一体化之下相互影响的现象。
9. 从分析角度也要分析得更透一些，不见得流动性过剩会直接对某一个或者某一天的资产市场，包括股票市场和房地产市场，产生直接冲击和影响。

商务口译

10. 我们是要组建一个外汇投资机构，这个机构是超脱任何部门的，依照国家的法律来经营外汇，有偿使用，接受监管，保值增值。
11. 关于你提到的军品贸易，我没有这方面的具体信息。但是我们的政策是明确的。中国对军品出口一直采取非常慎重和负责的态度，实行严格的管理。
12. International investors are now very interested in China's stock market. Do you think the rise of the stock market over the past two years went too far, too fast?
13. The government has announced plans for a new agency to manage the diversification of China's foreign exchange reserves. Can you tell us what kind of assets this agency will invest in?
14. The 19th China-US JCCT meeting will be held next week in the US. Which Chinese departments will attend? What is your expectation? And how would you comment on the current China-US trade relations?
15. It is understood that the newly elected Pakistani President Zardari will visit China next week, and Venezuelan President Chavez shall follow. Is it fair to assume that they want to talk about civilian nuclear cooperation or military trade?

第7单元

企业社会责任

Corporate Social Responsibility

I Background Knowledge

Directions: Read the following English passages and then compare them with their Chinese equivalents.

Passage 1

So, what is CSR[1]? It can mean many different things to different people—both in terms of the different business and social issues which can be covered by the description "CSR" and in terms of the way in which businesses deal with them. CSR has become something of a sound-bite in business communities around the world, and in the media.

But fundamentally, CSR is about recognizing that business impacts upon society—in many different ways—and that social development can in turn affect business profits.

As the former British Chancellor of the Exchequer Gordon Brown has said, CSR should be seen as "enlightened self interest" at its best. CSR is not just charitable philanthropy—perhaps not even that. It is really about the corporate strategy of business—this is not about external giving, but about internal business processes. It is about making money—affecting your bottom line—not about giving it away.

Or, as China's Hong Kong Secretary for Financial Services and the Treasury Bureau said at a conference organized by our colleagues in the British Consulate-General in Hong Kong in February:

---

1 Corporate Social Resonsibility

"I do not accept and cannot subscribe to the view that a company is responsible to its shareholders but not to society. It is not right to say that corporate governance which seeks to protect shareholders and investors is legitimately a priority of a company, while CSR—which is about doing society good—is only a secondary, if relevant, consideration."

Indeed not! CSR must be about balancing these different issues.

Let us take another definition, a global definition, this time by the World Business Council for Sustainable Development. Their definition is as follows:

"Corporate Social Responsibility is the continuing commitment by business to behave ethically and contribute to economic development while improving the quality of life of the workforce and their families as well as of the local community and society at large."

什么是企业社会责任？就其可能涵盖的各种商业和社会问题而言，以及就企业的不同处理方式而言，它对于不同的人可以有不同的含义。在全球商界和媒体界，企业社会责任已经成为了一句响亮的口号。

但从根本上来说，企业社会责任就是要承认企业以各种不同的方式对社会产生影响，而同时社会发展反过来又影响企业利润。

前英国财政大臣戈登·布朗曾经说过，企业社会责任充其量可以被看成是"开明的自身利益"。企业社会责任不仅仅是慈善，甚至根本连慈善都谈不上。它实际上是企业的商业策略，不是对外施舍，而是内部商业流程。企业社会责任实际上就是要赚钱，作用于企业的基本利益，而不是要让钱白白流走。

或者，正如香港财经事务及库物局司长今年2月在一个由我们的英国驻香港总领事馆的同事组织的会议上所说的那样：

"我不接受也不赞成公司只对其股东负责而不对社会负责的观点。那种认为致力于保护股东和投资者利益的公司治理理应是企业的首要考虑因素，而对社会有利的企业社会责任只是企业的次要（如果是相关的话）考虑的说法是不对的。"

的确不对！企业社会责任必须平衡这些不同方面的问题。

让我们再来看看另一个定义，一个全球性的定义。这是世界商业可持续发展委员会给出的定义。他们的定义是这样的：

"企业社会责任是企业持续的承诺，以道德来规范自己的行为并为经济发展作出贡献，同时改善员工及其家庭的生活质量，改善整个地方社区乃至全社会的生活质量。"

Passage 2

How can CSR be achieved through better business practices? And in what sectors? As we will explore later, CSR can cover a range of issues which companies need to consider in their business planning and in their relations with their business partners, employees and customers. CSR includes issues such as:

• Labor laws, both domestically and in relation to international conventions agreed through organizations such as the International Labor Organization;

• Occupational health and safety;

• Environmental performance;

• Sustainable resources, and

• Supplies and buyers.

Within those broad headings, it is possible to break them down into many more categories as they affect the key stakeholders—employees, a company's contractors, the local community and wider society. Issues such as labor rights, ethics, working conditions, discrimination—for example against the disabled or against women—pay and working hours, both in a company and in those contractors which supply it. And CSR also extends out into issues such as directors' pay, ethical issues such as corruption, animal testing and so on.

Back in the 1980s in the UK, it was easier to argue that making money was all that mattered. But times have changed, and people are increasingly asking not just how much, but how money is made. The quantitative has become a qualitative.

Skeptics have been quick to dismiss this, what they might call "fluffy" approach to business—arguing that these kinds of questions occupy a minority of woolly headed do-gooders in developed countries. After all, companies already contribute to society and have no business in looking to address the welfare needs of communities. This should be the responsibility of governments. What else is taxation for?

This argument is a superficial one. For the qualitative we are talking about is actually a means by which to maximize profit by ensuring that it is sustainable. Increasingly, when an investor reads the annual reports of the companies in which he or she invests, this is an issue which they will look at more closely. And consumers are also asking pertinent questions about the ways in which companies behave, for example, whether or not they have meaningful CSR programs.

CSR is not about philanthropy, but about recognizing that business impacts upon society. And that social developments impact upon business profits. As I have said, it extends to considerations of human rights and labor standards, to the environment, to anti-corruption efforts, to supply chains and global sourcing, and even to issues such as conflict prevention.

怎样能够通过更好的商业实践来履行企业社会责任呢？由什么部门来履行这些责任呢？随着我们接下来的探讨，会发现企业社会责任涉及一系列的问题，企业需要在商业规划中、在管理与他们的商业伙伴、雇员以及客户的关系中考虑这些问题。企业社会责任包括问题如下：
- 劳动法，既指国内的劳动法，也指由国际劳工组织等制订的国际公约；
- 职业健康和安全；
- 环境绩效；
- 可持续的资源，以及
- 供应商和采购商。

在各个大标题下，可以根据受其影响的主要利益相关者——员工、承包商、当地社区乃至全社会——细分为多个类别，例如劳工权利、道德、工作条件、歧视——例如对残疾人或妇女的歧视——工资和工时等问题，既指公司本身的这些问题，也指承包商的这些方面的问题。此外，企业社会责任的内容还包括董事薪酬问题以及反腐败和动物试验之类的道德问题。

在20世纪80年代的英国，人们很容易就认为赚钱就是一切。但现在时代已经不同了，人们越来越多关注的不仅是赚了多少钱，还会问是怎样赚的钱。定量的问题已经变成了定性的问题。

怀疑论者很容易就拒绝这种经营方式——这种他们可能称为"愚蠢的"方式，他们认为这种问题占据了发达国家少数不实际的社会改良家的头脑。毕竟公司已经为社会作出了贡献，没有必要再努力满足公众的福利需要。这应当是政府的责任。税收不正是为了解决这类问题的吗？//

这种论点是很肤浅的。我们所讨论的定性问题，实际上是通过保证可持续发展来实现利润最大化的一种手段。投资者在阅读他/她所投资的公司的年报时，企业社会责任是其越来越为密切关心的问题。而消费者也会问及与公司的经营方式相关的问题，例如他们是否有实质性的企业社会责任计划。

企业社会责任不是慈善，而是意识到商业运作对社会产生影响，而社会发展反过来影响商业利润。正如我前面讲过的那样，企业社会责任涵盖对人权和劳工标准的考虑，涵盖环境、反腐败斗争、供应链和全球采购、甚至包括预防冲突之类的问题。

第7单元 企业社会责任

Ⅱ Warm-up

1 Directions: Give the English equivalents of the following Chinese expressions.

企业社会责任	重要法宝
非政府组织	赠人玫瑰，手有余香。
认证	《劳动合同法》
技术标准	增长方式
消费者群体	贯穿"一条主线"
利益相关人	突出"三个结合"
《关于企业社会责任合作的谅解备忘录》	实现"四个和谐"
	以点带面，循序渐进
投资者	

2 Directions: Give the Chinese equivalents of the following English expressions.

sound-bite	conflict prevention
corporate strategy	International Standard Organization
World Business Council for Sustainable Development	labor right
International Labor Organisation	compliance
occupational health and safety	Fair Labor Association (FLA)
buyer	external audit
contractor	transparency
local community	Universal Declaration of Human Rights
labor right	industrial relation
ethical issue	capacity building
animal testing	worker representative
annual report	secret ballot
labor standard	worker retention
anti-corruption effort	worker turnover
supply chain	
global sourcing	

87

III Passages for Interpreting

Passage 1

Directions: Listen to the passage and interpret from Chinese into English at the end of each segment.

对于社会责任问题，我们首先要做一些基本的理论分析。// 这里面存在这样几个问题，也希望提请我们与会的女士们、先生们的注意，第一个（问题是）社会责任和企业社会责任不一样。最开始我们谈企业社会责任，现在由于我们参加了一些ISO，就是国际标准化组织的一些社会活动，也在研究，已经召开了三次国际研讨会，今年将要研究的就是社会责任的具体指导意见。// 那么在这个问题上，到底是企业社会责任还是社会责任，在ISO的角度来看，也就是国际标准化组织已经提升到社会责任的角度来研究，而不仅仅是一个企业社会责任的问题，那么这个里面就存在在社会责任这个角度上，企业应当承担什么责任，政府应当承担什么责任，非政府组织应当承担什么，当然包括工会应该做什么。这是（第）一个问题。//

第二个问题，社会责任和社会责任标准不是一个概念。最开始的时候很多人把社会责任标准作为一种认证的技术标准，这是大大值得置疑和研究的。那么怎么来认证？刚才领导也谈到了这个问题，社会责任的标准到底按谁的标准来制定？按美国的标准来制定，对发展中国家是不是公平、公正和合理？按最不发达的国家的标准来制定，这种标准又究竟有没有意义呢？所以这是一个非常棘手的问题，我们也在考虑和研究。//

另外一个问题就是社会责任作为一个界定来讲，到底是广义的还是狭义的。我们现在讨论的社会责任问题，常常会谈论劳工标准这些问题。这些问题，有些是狭义的，有些是广义的。// 我们是怎么来看待这个问题的呢？关于广义的社会责任的问题，我们说它包括了一些劳工标准的问题，包括了环境保护问题，甚至包括反腐败问题——企业不能行贿，包括了我们所说的消费者群体，包括利益相关人。那么这样一个广大的社会责任问题恐怕不是某一个企业能够把它解决好的。//

Passage 2

Directions: Listen to the passage and interpret from Chinese into English at the end of each segment.

尊敬的赖因费尔特首相，各位来宾，女士们、先生们：

下午好！// 四月的北京，春意盎然，鲜花盛开。值此美好时刻，我们迎来了"中国－瑞典企业社会责任高层论坛"的召开。// 去年6月胡锦涛主席访问瑞典期间，商务部与瑞典外交部代表两国政府签署了《关于企业社会责任合作的谅解备忘录》，标志着两国在这一领域的合作正式启动，对促进两国经济的持续稳定健康发展具有十分重要的意义。今天，两国朋友们齐聚一堂，就企业社会责任开展深入交流，必将对两国企业社会责任建设产生积极的影响。//

企业社会责任运动自上世纪80年代兴起后，已经成为世界潮流。强调企业社会责任，就是要求企业对投资者负责的同时，对员工负责，对消费者负责，对商业伙伴负责，对环境和社会负责。// 国内外企业的成功经验表明，社会责任也是企业的品牌，是企业核心竞争力的组成部分，是企业长盛不衰的重要法宝。// 企业要生存和发展，就必须增强社会责任意识，积极履行社会义务。我们有理由相信，未来的企业竞争，将不再仅仅是产品的竞争、技术的竞争和人才的竞争，更是履行社会责任的竞争。"赠人玫瑰，手有余香"。企业在履行社会责任、促进社会和谐的同时，自身也会得到更大的发展。//

随着社会主义市场经济的逐步完善，中国大多数企业的社会责任意识也在不断增强。它们恪守诚信，合法经营，努力为国内外消费者提供高质量的商品，注重节约，保护环境，努力履行社会义务。// 一些企业还主动发布社会责任报告，公开履行社会责任状况，自觉接受社会监督。当然，受经济发展水平和发展阶段的制约，中国经济增长方式还比较粗放，能源资源消耗多，环境保护压力大，少数企业还存在一些片面追求经济效益、忽视社会责任的行为。//

中国政府历来重视企业社会责任建设，尤其是近年来的工作力度明显加大。// 2007年，商务部联合环保部门下发了《关于加强出口企业环境监管的通知》，限制不履行社会环境责任的企业从事对外贸易；出台了《国家级经济技术开发区加强社会责任的若干意见》，要求开发区企业加强履行社会责任；还调整了加工贸易政策，禁止不履行社会责任的企业开展加工贸易。// 国资委出台了《中央企业履行社会责任的指导意见》，要求央企带头履行社会责任。今年1月1日中国开始实施的新《劳动合同法》，为建设和谐的劳资关系奠定了法律基础。相信在企业和政府部门的共同努力下，中国的企业社会责任建设将不断取得新的成就。//

我个人认为，今后中国企业的社会责任建设要贯穿"一条主线"，突出"三个结合"，实现"四个和谐"。//

贯穿"一条主线"，就是要始终贯彻落实科学发展观。要在科学发展观的指导下，把加强企业社会责任作为转变经济发展方式的重要"抓手"，把企业的经济效益和社会效益结合起来，眼前利益和长远发展结合起来，局部利益和整体利益结合起来，企业发展和员工成长结合起来，走出一条经济效益好、社会效益高、资源消耗低、环境污染少、消费者权益得到充分保障、员工利益得到充分维护的有中国特色的企业社会责任建设道路，推动社会主义和谐社会建设，实现经济社会可持续发展。//

突出"三个结合"，一是政府倡导和企业实践相结合。政府要创造环境、营造氛围、积极引导、加强监管，规范企业承担法定社会责任，倡导企业承担道义性社会责任，惩戒企业严重违反社会责任的行为。企业要发挥主体地位，树立现代经营观念，对社会负责，自觉接受社会监督。//二是国外经验和中国国情相结合。要加强国际交流与合作，充分借鉴包括瑞典在内的其他国家的先进经验，推动中国企业社会责任建设健康发展。同时，要立足中国国情，充分考虑经济社会发展水平和企业承受能力，防止盲目追求不切实际的高标准，避免对企业和社会造成冲击。//三是重点突破和全面推进相结合。要抓薄弱环节，抓关键环节，抓影响全局的环节，尤其是高耗能、高污染、劳动力密集型以及容易出现安全事故的行业和领域。同时，要以点带面，循序渐进，不断总结经验，促进企业社会责任整体水平的提高。//

实现"四个和谐"，一是企业与员工之间的和谐。要促进劳资关系的协调，充分发挥人力资源潜能，保障员工分享企业经营成果，实现员工职业生涯与企业发展壮大的有机统一。//二是企业与企业之间的和谐。要构建健康的商业伙伴关系，既要立足竞争，又要重视合作，形成诚实守信、公平竞争、共同发展的良好市场环境。//三是企业与社会之间的和谐。企业要切实增强社会责任意识，充分履行作为社会"公民"的应尽义务，既努力为社会和谐服务，也为企业自身发展营造良好的社会环境。//四是人与自然的和谐。要把企业发展模式切实转变到依靠技术进步、产品创新和资源节约上来，通过节约发展、清洁发展和安全发展，建设资源节约型和环境友好型社会，实现人与自然的和谐共处。//

女士们、先生们。中瑞两国政府高度重视企业社会责任领域的合作。瑞典作为发达的市场经济国家，在企业社会责任建设方面拥有丰富经验；中国作为快速发展的新兴经济体，正在积极开展企业社会责任建设。//今天上午，双方共同启动了社会责任合作网站，举办了培训班开班仪式。我衷心地希望，中瑞政府相关部门和企业界按照两国高层领导人达成的共识，不断加强交流与合

作，相互学习和借鉴，把企业社会责任建设不断推向前进。//

预祝论坛圆满成功！谢谢大家！//

Passage 3

Directions: Listen to the passage and interpret from English into Chineses at the end of each segment.

Zao Shang Hao, Wo De Peng You! //

We just want to give a very short story about our experience on one project. So we just describe very briefly. But I wanted to at least give some history about the Reebok program that we have now. // Our program for the compliance area began in 1992. So we have a very long history of working in this area. Our current obligation, we are (a) participant in the Fair Labor Association (FLA). The reason I mention this is that some of our suppliers now receive independent external audits, not from our staff but from outside. // And those audits are posted on the websites of the FLA. And the factory name is not shown, but our name is shown. So we are trying to have transparency, so the consumer who buys our products can understand what we are doing for managing our practices. //

Our program, our requirements that we work with are based first on China law, secondly the Universal Declaration of Human Rights and lastly we also look at the covenants of the International Labor Organization. These are the primary sources of our material. // And right now, we have almost two hundred and fifty business partners in China, and I predict every year we will have more partners. So, we have some partners with us here today. Thank you for coming. //

I want to, before I describe the project, explain why... why we are presenting this project to you. // In our experience since 1992, we have been doing auditing of our independent business partners. And our conclusion is that this is helpful but it does not solve any problems in the long term. So what we want to do is (to) promote a more local solution. We find that poor communication is often the heart of any problem at a particular factory site. // It is not unusual that the general manager at the factory does not even know that there may be a problem with a line leader and a worker. The information flow is not occurring. We also find that our own staff, our monitors, don't know as much about the work place as the workers who are there every day. Maybe we can only go there two days or three days in a year. But the workers are there every day and have the best understanding of the local condition. // So consequently when we are thinking about this issue, we want to, we ask ourselves the question: how can the workers be involved in the solution to improving the work place standard, because really it is the workers and the managers together who must have the dialog in order to create a harmonious work place. // So we are, after our long experience, we are not completely satisfied with the monitoring or the audit process. So we began to try to seek other creative ways that we could address long-term, good industrial relations. //

We have many approaches to the issue. So I just give a brief... a list. I just want to say we try many different things in order to increase the dialog in the work place. So we have things like our own staff may be involved, but we also encourage workers, if they can, to talk to our staff. // And most importantly, I want to draw your attention to the last two bullets on this slide, which is that we started a worker communication system in different countries around Asia and we used this system to collect workers' feedback, and then we went to the managers at the factories and sort of mentored them in how to respond to the workers' suggestions. // So we use worker communication system which is our program as a training tool for local managers. And we also believe in offering trainee capacity building wherever possible, whether it's a venue like the one that we share today, or whether it's some internal training that we do. // One example is that last year we offered our own internal program whose theme was "problem-solving methods". And we offered this in different regions in China. And the goal, again, is (to) help people negotiate a local solution at the site where they work. //

But the one innovation I want to talk with you today, we have so many tools, I just gave a list on this slide, we have many approaches to try to find a better work place, and to try to have problems that are not recurring year on year. We want to see, you know, continuous improvement in our work and in our suppliers' business also. // One idea that we had was really to use the China law as the basis for promoting a better industrial relation. So we decided to look at the possibility of promoting election of worker representatives in the factory. The thing that is innovative about this particular program is that each worker at the factory can vote using a secret ballot. This is a different process from how they may have done things before that. We also offer the opportunity that any worker who had an interest could try to be a candidate for this election. // So the candidates are not chosen. The candidates can decide if they would like to run for the office of worker representative. They may need to have a certain level of seniority at the business, such as three months or six months' experience. But if they pass that level, then they can decide to participate in the election process. This is the innovation, but we see our role in this process as just trying to provide the facilitation. // This is not our decision, and we do not want to tell any worker what to think about this or what they should do. But we can help the factory management if they decide to pursue this. We have some tool(s) we can offer to help them pursue this type of innovation. //

I want to describe the benefits in a general sense before I discuss some of the challenges or difficulties that we encounter. We have been attempting this process for approximately four years. And we feel that the results of this innovation is somewhat mixed. We don't see a huge change in the work place. But we do see some small type of benefits that we think may be worthwhile. // One is that the senior management who are involved in this kind of process have the opportunity to learn more information about their own company. And this is very linked to the fact that when worker representatives are elected, we find that workers across the factory will go to their union representative more often with their problems, because they elected this person. Now they are interested to talk to this person in order to receive help. // We do think this is the opportunity for both managers and workers to gain some more skills in problem solving. We find that this process of having an election with a secret ballot has been very well received by workers in general. They do find excitement in the process, because Vincent, my colleague, has been able to observe an election. I will have him give you some more examples and show you some photographs of what this looks like. //

But I don't want to come here and say that we have found an answer, because the truth is we don't have an answer to what is the best sustainable approach to industrial relations. We have many challenges in fact and we want to be very honest with you about what they are so that if you were to ever consider this, you can [could] really have a realistic view. // On the one hand, what is happening in these types of situations is that workers are coming into a new role especially if they are elected as a worker representative. They may not be familiar with their responsibility as a representative. It's a new concept really. And if the worker representative would look around for some role models, it can be difficult for them to find a good example. // So it is very demanding to ask workers to take on such a new experience. We find it difficult to get a training resource to help these workers. In one example actually in three factories, we went ahead and offered a short course on communication skills. And the only reason that we decided to do this was in these three locations we could not find any local resource to help them. And the workers need maybe some understanding of taking the first step how to communicate. // So in that case we did try to give some small training. But we find that the worker retention and the worker turnover, which is such a challenge to us for our business, is also a challenge for the worker representatives, because after—one year after the election or two years after the election, not all the representatives may still be at that factory. // So you always have the challenge of training, just like you have the same challenge with the normal turnover for the normal worker. This is also our challenges too, that, getting a representative who can understand their job. //

So what we consider this case, we don't consider a huge dramatic change to have the election. We find we consider this trial and error. We try something new and we see maybe in some cases it does provide us strong benefit, and in some cases maybe we don't see as clear benefit. // The positive thing, the impression that we have, but we really don't have data which I am sure some people would be interested in, but we do have the impression that workers who become representatives and those who elect representatives have a stronger sense of participation in that company. So we do believe that having the sense of participation in their company can promote their willingness to stay longer at that work place. //

However, we really have still a long way to go to study whether worker representation can assist worker retention rates. So this is still an area of consideration. We had the first election that we helped to facilitate and then we observed the election in 2002. // So since that time approximately four years ago, we have now been able to facilitate or to observe eight elections in eight different work places. Over 15,000 workers have voted in these elections. As you can imagine, some footwear suppliers can be quite large, so we can have a lot of people involved. // We find at these eight different facilities that the worker committees are functioning at every different level. In some—a couple of cases we have committees that meet every month and they are very active. In others we have cases where the committee doesn't really have any idea what they want to do. And maybe they don't even have the idea how to talk to the people in their section of the factory. So we have every range of worker representative. //

第 7 单元　企业社会责任

IV Guide to Interpreting

1. 近年来企业社会责任已成为许多企业必须关注的热门话题。背景知识介绍节选目前英国驻广州总领事胡克定先生在 2004 年英国道德贸易组织（Ethical Trading Initiative）大会上的发言。Passage 1 是和背景知识相配套的姊妹篇，取自企业社会责任研讨会上某位学者的讲话。讲话人先总说，后分说，讨论了 CSR 的三个理论问题，语言较为通俗易懂。译员在进行交传时应注意笔记内容的相应排列，即围绕 CSR 与一般社会责任的区别、CSR 的概念标准界定以及 CSR 的广义、狭义内涵等展开。笔记要体现"纲举目张"的原则，核心信息点抓住了，其他支撑性的信息也就八九不离十了。

2. Passage 2 取自中国商务部于广州副部长的正式演讲稿，语篇风格正式，用语规范，具有礼仪祝词常见的套语以及富有中国特色的习语，例如"春意盎然，鲜花盛开"、"赠人玫瑰，手有余香"，以及"一条主线"、"三个结合"和"四个和谐"，译员在译前应做好应对此类中国特色表达的充分准备。此外，于副部长还列举了政府出台的各项规章制度，对这些专有名词的翻译也必须在口译之前就要准备好。

3. Passage 3 转写自国际知名运动品牌公司锐步（中国）有限公司内部员工培训的现场录音。讲话人来自美国总部，用流畅的英语详细介绍了 1992 开始启动的合规项目，内容牵涉到一些国际劳工组织公约方面的法律知识，例如"外部审计"、"透明管理"等概念，以及锐步公司在公平劳工方面的具体措施，还有其在良好的劳资关系方面的创新尝试。译员在练习之前应该上网查阅有关这些专业知识的背景和该公司的举措。企业的可持续发展与企业的伦理建设分不开，与建立公平、合法的劳工组织密切相连，弄清这些措施和 CSR 之间的关系对顺利完成这一专题的口译任务至关重要。此外，译员应有针对性地做好有关工会选举和人力资源方面的词汇准备。

V Highlight for Interpreting

Directions: Interpret the following sentences from Chinese into English or vice versa.

1. 国际标准化组织已经提升到社会责任的角度来研究，而不仅仅是一个企业社会责任的问题，那么这个里面就存在在社会责任这个角度上，企业应当承担什么责任，政府应当承担什么责任，非政府组织应当承担什么，当然包括工会应该做什么。

2. 社会责任的标准到底按谁的标准来制定？按美国的标准来制定，对发展中国家是不是公平、公正和合理？按最不发达的国家的标准来制定，这种标准又究竟有没有意义呢？

3. 关于广义的社会责任的问题，我们说它包括了一些劳工标准的问题，包括了环境保护问题，甚至包括反腐败问题——企业不能行贿，包括了我们所说的消费者群体；包括利益相关人。那么这样一个广大的社会责任问题恐怕不是某一个企业能够把它解决好的。

4. 它们恪守诚信，合法经营，努力为国内外消费者提供高质量的商品，注重节约，保护环境，努力履行社会义务。一些企业还主动发布社会责任报告，公开履行社会责任状况，自觉接受社会监督。

5. 要在科学发展观的指导下，把加强企业社会责任作为转变经济发展方式的重要"抓手"，把企业的经济效益和社会效益结合起来，眼前利益和长远发展结合起来，局部利益和整体利益结合起来，企业发展和员工成长结合起来，走出一条经济效益好、社会效益高、资源消耗低、环境污染少、消费者权益得到充分保障、员工利益得到充分维护的有中国特色的企业社会责任建设道路，推动社会主义和谐社会建设，实现经济社会可持续发展。

6. 三是重点突破和全面推进相结合。要抓薄弱环节，抓关键环节，抓影响全局的环节，尤其是高耗能、高污染、劳动力密集型以及容易出现安全事故的行业和领域。同时，要以点带面，循序渐进，不断总结经验，促进企业社会责任整体水平的提高。

7. Our requirements that we work with are based first on China law, secondly the Universal Declaration of Human Rights and lastly we also look at the covenants of the International Labor Organization. These are the primary sources of our material.

8. We find that poor communication is often the heart of any problem at a particular factory site. It is not unusual that the general manager at the factory does not even know that there may be a problem with a line leader and a worker.

9. So consequently when we are thinking about this issue, we want to, we ask ourselves the question: how can the workers be involved in the solution to improving the work place standard, because really it is the workers and the managers together who must have the dialog in order to create a harmonious work place.

10. We started a worker communication system in different countries around Asia

and we used this system to collect workers' feedback, and then we went to the managers at the factories and sort of mentored them in how to respond to the workers' suggestions.

11. We want to see, you know, continuous improvement in our work and in our suppliers' business also. One idea that we had was really to use the China law as the basis for promoting a better industrial relation.

12. We do see some small type of benefits that we think may be worthwhile. One is that the senior management who are involved in this kind of process have the opportunity to learn more information about their own company. And this is very linked to the fact that when worker representatives are elected, we find that workers across the factory will go to their union representative more often with their problems, because they elected this person.

13. We have many challenges in fact and we want to be very honest with you about what they are so that if you were to ever consider this, you could really have a realistic view.

14. But we find that the worker retention and the worker turnover, which is such a challenge to us for our business, is also a challenge for the worker representatives, because one year after the election or two years after the election, not all the representatives may still be at that factory.

15. The positive thing, the impression that we have, but we really don't have data which I am sure some people would be interested in, but we do have the impression that workers who become representatives and those who elect representatives have a stronger sense of participation in that company.

第8单元

企业文化

Corporate Culture

I Background Knowledge

Directions: Read the following English passages and then compare them with their Chinese equivalents.

Passage 1

Corporate culture refers to notions, cultural forms, value systems and behavioral norms gradually established, accepted and observed by the company and its employees during production and management under certain circumstance. Every organization has its own unique culture. Most organizations don't try to create a certain culture consciously. The corporate culture is typically created unconsciously.

Corporate culture drives the development of an organization. It guides how employees think, act and feel. It is dynamic and fluid, and it is never static. With development of corporate culture, the overall strength and core competitiveness of an organization can be improved and corporate development can be sustained; meanwhile, corporate culture is also the ideological basis of realization of modern corporate system as well as mechanism innovation.

企业文化是指在特定的条件下，企业及企业员工在生产和管理中逐步形成的、为全体员工普遍接受和共同奉行的思想观念、文化形式、价值体系和行为准则。每一个企业都有它自己独特的企业文化。大多数企业都不是有意识地试图建立某一种文化。企业文化一般是自然而然形成的。

企业文化促进企业的发展。它指导员工的思想、行为和感受。它是动态的、流动的，不是一成不变的。开展企业文化建设可以提高企业的综合实力，提升企业的核心竞争力,保持企业的可持续发展。同时,企业文化又是实行现代企业制度,进行企业机制创新的思想基础。

Passage 2

Globalization and technological advancement—while bringing forth tremendous prosperity throughout the world—has generated heightened competition between nations, regions and enterprises. Gaining a competitive edge on the global stage, therefore, no longer depends on the exploitation of natural comparative advantages in factors of production (i.e. land and population), but on the ability to develop and, most crucially, capitalize on new knowledge and technologies.

There are many definitions of innovation, and they differ depending on whether we view innovation in the context of economics, business or government policy. We usually assume that innovation is about creating something new, whether a product or technology. But just as often, innovation is about creating new uses for older things or adapting technologies already in use. The different definitions have a big effect on the benefits innovation can bring. The goal of innovation is to improve and allow progress, at an individual and collective level (in the private and public sectors). Innovation can be either incremental or breakthrough, and can focus on products or services. For example, breakthrough innovation was the first airplane powered with a propeller, and incremental innovation was a jet-propelled airplane. The first CD player was a breakthrough, and the DVD was an incremental innovation.

Innovation is a major driver of the economy, and an economy's and company's long-term international competitiveness and sustainable growth are increasingly dependent upon innovation.

全球化和科技进步极大地促进了全球的繁荣,但与此同时,也在国家、地区及企业之间引发了日益激烈的竞争。因此,要想在国际舞台上获得竞争优势,就不能仅仅依赖于开发生产所需的自然资源优势(如土地资源和劳动力等),更要增强自我发展的能力,尤其是科技创新及科技成果转化的能力。

创新有多种定义,它们在不同的经济、商业和政策环境中有所区别。我们经常认为创新是创造全新的产品或者技术,但是很多时候,创新是对旧有事物开辟新用途或者对现有技术进行改进。不同的定义能够在很大程度上影响创新带来的收益。创新的目标是改进,并允许在个人和集体的层面上(在私人和公共部门)取得进步。创新可以是渐进式的,也可以是突破性的;可以是产品上的，也可以是服务上的。例如：第一架使用螺旋桨的飞机是突破性的创新，而喷气式飞机是渐进式的创新。第一台CD播放器是突破，而DVD是渐进式的创新。

创新是经济的一个主要推动力，任何经济体、企业要获得长效的国际竞争力、实现可持续发展，都必须依靠创新。

Warm-up

1 **Directions:** Give the English equivalents of the following Chinese expressions.

企业竞争力	市场规则
精神支柱	讲究信用
企业管理	假冒伪劣（产品）
市场竞争力	经济效益
社会主义先进文化	文明经营
企业价值观	可持续性
企业精神	伦理规范
以人为本	公益事业
公平竞争、诚信共赢的精神	义无反顾
诚信互利	中国特色

2 **Directions:** Give the Chinese equivalents of the following English expressions.

corporate culture	affordable product
managing director	in situ
core value	institution set-up
cost-consciousness	manufacturing company
real bond	public sector
store concept	innovative culture
Walking the Talk	boundary-breaking
retail skill	CLSA
career development	novel technology
management introduction	economic tie

closed innovation	core business
open innovation	ever-accelerating
internal capability	strategic agility
do it alone	go-to-market agility
start-up	strategic partner
open-source community	ever-widening
spin-off	mobile communications
business model	significant break from established thinking
market presence	
innovation move	

III Passages for Interpreting

Passage 1

Directions: Listen to the passage and interpret from Chinese into English at the end of each segment.

同志们，朋友们：

中国企业文化国际论坛，是新世纪中外企业家、企业文化研究专家的盛大聚会，我对论坛的举办表示热烈的祝贺，并向出席论坛的中外企业家、专家、学者，致以亲切的问候和崇高的敬意！//

文化是一个国家的身份证，是一个国家根之所系，脉之所维，是精神和智慧的长期积累和凝聚。文化是人创造的，是为人服务的。而文化反过来又熏陶人，塑造人，发展人。//

当今时代，文化在经济社会发展中的作用日益突出，文化与经济的一体化正在成为令人激动的一道风景线。文化作为综合国力的重要因素，逐步成为一种生产力。文化是明天的经济。//

企业是现代社会经济的基本细胞。现代企业间的竞争不仅是管理的竞争、市场的竞争，而且是文化的竞争。管理也是一种文化。文化就是资源，就是品牌。文化是一个社会进步的标志，同样也是企业竞争力的标志。// 企业文化是社会文化的重要组成部分，是一个企业的灵魂，是企业不断发展壮大的精神支柱。加强企业文化建设不仅是提高我国企业管理水平，提升企业市场竞争力的

第8单元 企业文化

重大战略,而且是发展社会主义先进文化的重要环节。//

企业文化的核心是企业价值观,是企业精神。现代企业应该具有什么样的价值观,应该具有什么样的企业精神?这是众多企业家和专家关注的课题。借此机会,我谈几点看法,同大家讨论。//

现代企业应该具有不断创造的精神。在处理企业与员工、企业内部人与物的关系时,现代企业强调"以人为本",而在企业管理中,坚持"以人为本",从根本上说,就是要不断激发员工的创造精神,有创造,才会有贡献。//

现代企业应该具有公平竞争、诚信共赢的精神。在处理企业与市场的关系时,现代企业强调公平竞争,诚信互利。有竞争,企业才能壮大,经济才能发展。// 现代市场经济是法制经济,企业必须遵守市场规则,讲究信用。制售"假冒伪劣",不仅贻害社会,而且是企业的自杀行为。//

现代企业应该具有责任意识。在处理企业与社会的关系时,现代企业既追求经济效益,又注重社会效益,坚持文明经营。// 企业的可持续性必须以社会的可接受性为前提,企业的产品要满足社会需要,企业行为要符合社会的伦理规范,同时,企业要积极投身社会公益事业,形象地说,企业与社会的关系就像鱼和水的关系一样。//

现代企业应该具有学习的精神。在处理企业与企业之间的关系时,现代企业强调互相学习,共同进步。学习是一种态度,更是一种文化;是一种方法,更是一种哲学。// 一个善于学习的人才能不断进步,一个善于学习的民族才有光明的未来,一个善于学习的企业才能做大、做强、做久。// 当代中国的企业不但要学习我国管理文化的优良传统,而且要学习国外先进的管理经验、企业文化,学习人类文明的一切成果,滋养我们的企业精神。//

现代企业应该具有高尚的英雄精神。一个时代,一个国家和民族,应该有自己的英雄。优秀企业家就是我们这个时代的英雄。// 优秀企业家应当是社会的楷模,受到社会的喜爱,他们不仅创造了产品,也同时创造了文化。// 我们的社会需要一大批创造财富的英雄,需要一大批在世界上有影响的著名企业,需要成千上万的优秀企业家。//

中国已经加入WTO,这意味着我国企业走进世界经济的汪洋大海,在大风大浪中搏击,这是又一次更加深入、广泛的改革。// 竞争的对手是有几百年历史的国际知名企业,必然会有新的观念、理念上的深刻变革。// 这次转变是历史性的,义无反顾。转变的好坏、成败,将直接决定中国企业走向世界、走向国际的步伐。//

相对发达国家的企业而言,我国企业的科技和管理水平还比较落后,市场竞争力不高;现代企业文化建设刚刚起步,缺乏特色和优势,远远不能适应参

商务口译

与国际市场激烈竞争的需要；// 加强企业文化建设，已经成为我国企业走向世界，参与国际市场竞争的迫切任务。//

中国企业界要努力创建中国特色、中国风格、中国气派的企业文化，创造一大批中国的世界名牌企业，为中国经济持续、健康、快速发展做出更大的贡献。//

中国企业文化国际论坛为我国企业向世界著名企业学习提供了难得的舞台。我相信，它一定会受到中外企业家的欢迎。//

最后，祝中国企业文化国际论坛圆满成功！//

Passage 2

Directions: Listen to the following interview and interpret from English into Chinese at the end of each segment.

I = Interviewer   G=Göran Nilsson

I: And now to IKEA. The Swedish furniture retailer has just reported turnover of 56 billion euros from its 150 stores worldwide. Now, IKEA puts its success down to corporate culture. // So with me today to explain the secret of IKEA's culture is Managing Director of IKEA UK, Göran Nilsson. Good morning, Mr. Nilsson.//

G: Good morning.//

I: Now is every IKEA store really exactly the same? //

G: Well, in terms of culture they're pretty well uniform. Although our culture will bond with the local culture to some extent, our core values such as simplicity and cost-consciousness are valid in all cultures. So we don't need to adapt the way we operate to run our stores. // And as for products, although we make some minor adaptations to suit local tastes, we produce exactly the same catalog in all 26 countries. //

I: And where do these values originate? //

G: It all goes back to Sweden in the 1950's and 1960's. IKEA's founder, Ingvar Kamprad, started the company. //

I: Are IKEA's values those of its founder, then? //

G: Well, they have evolved over the last 65 years, of course, but I think our mission statement "a better life for the majority of people" still very much reflects the spirit of those early years. // Having said that though, I think

Ingvar's ability to relate to a co-worker in China would be pretty limited, though. //

I: You mentioned China. How does IKEA cope with such diversity among its employees? //

G: Well, funnily enough, I've been working for IKEA for 15 years in Sweden, Italy, Canada, the USA and what's struck me most is how much we have in common. // People may interpret certain concepts such as responsibility and freedom differently but core values such as humbleness exist in every country. //

I: So, what are the advantages of such a strong corporate culture? //

G: They're tremendous. For one, there's a real bond between our operations around the world. It's easy to transfer across borders because you know the values will be exactly the same. And from a marketing and positioning point of view it's very advantageous as well. // But the real pay-off is that it makes IKEA unique. You can clone our products and our store concept but not our culture. It takes years to build and has to be maintained daily. //

I: But how do you educate 40,000 workers? //

G: We begin by making sure people understand the values. That's why the IKEA Way seminars are so vital. All managers attend them and then it's their responsibility to pass the message on. Corporate culture also figures in the meetings...//

I: Do you use educational videos and brochures as well? //

G: Videos and brochures are helpful tools but only if used in conjunction with *Walking the Talk* and discussing values with management. // We have various initiatives which regularly provide co-workers with the opportunity to participate and contribute to these discussions.//

I: So, does culture affect IKEA's recruitment process? //

G: It has a major impact. Although it's important for us to get highly-skilled people into the company, we're not interested if there's a conflict of value systems. Anyone expecting a flash car or status symbols has not [no] future with us. // Recruitment at IKEA is an extensive process, based on judgments about the candidate's value systems and attributes. We can add retail skills, no problem, but it's tough to change one's mindset. //

I: Does that go for career development too? //

G: Yes, it does. //

I: So Swedish managers will always have more chance of promotion then? //

G: We find that many Scandinavians identify more easily with our culture but there is no written or unwritten rule concerning the nationality of senior managers. It would be impossible, however, for anyone to advance within IKEA without wholly understanding and buying into the company's philosophy and culture. // So managers are encouraged to visit Sweden and learn the language, etc., and management introductions include at least one week in Almhult, where the company began. //

I: And finally, Ingvar Kamprad stepped down as President in the mid-1980's, replaced by Anders Moberg. What effect did this have on the development of IKEA's culture? //

G: Both Moberg and our current CEO, Anders Dahlvig, worked closely with Kamprad for many years and have a deep knowledge and understanding of Kamprad's original vision and philosophy. // Naturally, IKEA is different today than it was 10 years ago, primarily because it is three times bigger and has entered many more diverse and challenging markets. // But our values and mission—to provide quality, affordable products for the majority of people—remain very much in situ. //

Passage 3

Directions: Listen to the passage and interpret from English into Chinese at the end of each segment.

Innovation will not happen automatically. Broadly speaking, there are two kinds of mechanisms to encourage innovation: one is our corporate culture, the other is institution set-up. // I would like to focus on these specific topics to illustrate Nokia's incentive mechanism for innovation and Nokia initiatives how to create a policy environment to encourage innovation at Nokia, and relate them with Guangdong. //

This is the most direct innovation inducing measure. // In the past five years, Nokia's annual R&D expenditure has been consistently nearly four billion euros, and this was significantly more than 10% of Nokia's net sales except for 2006; and more than 20% of all our employees are in the R&D functions. //

China has been active in investing in innovation in the past few years, and has overtaken Japan to become the world's second largest investor in R&D behind the US. // However two things generally separate China's R&D investment from that of the developed economies. // The first is the size of the investment at the corporate level. We know that the best companies in China, and some of them are based in Guangdong, can match Nokia's R&D investment in percentage's terms, but they are exceptions rather than norms. // The second is the private sector involvement: 75% of US' industry R&D funding is made by the manufacturing companies, while the major part of R&D investment in China is made by the public sector. //

Innovation is an attitude. It does not stop at building a strong R&D, but extends through the whole organization. // Therefore we have elevated innovation as one of the key Nokia values: Engaging You, Achieving Together, Very Human, and Passion for Innovation. This was created, debated, and summarized by a broad participation of Nokia employees of all levels across the organization. // For us, "Passion for Innovation" is based on the desire we have to live our dreams, to find our courage, and make the leap into the future through innovation in technology, ways of working, and the passion for understanding the world around us. //

This may not be intuitive to the Chinese companies and employees at first sight. // China has a long and rich history in inventions, but it's very important for China and Chinese companies to continue to encourage and create an innovative culture and environment, especially boundary-breaking and risk taking, etc. // To quote the CLSA analyst Andy Rothman, China has not produced many major breakthroughs "that resulted in commercialization of products or services based on the novel technology". // For innovations to become successful, a large number of people need to change their behaviors. This happens when people realize that an innovation gives them distinct advantages and improves their quality of life. //

As mentioned above, you need to build an innovation culture that is business and value driven, but not solely internally focused. // There is no better way to secure the future prosperity and competitiveness of all regions than to build on our strengths and look for our role in building strongly integrated and open economic ties. //

Here lies a fundamental transition from conventional "closed innovation" to "open innovation". // Closed innovation is one of discovering things yourself, then transferring them into development, production, distribution, service, and support within the four walls of your company. // The logic is: If you want something done right, you've got to do it yourself. // On the other hand, even the best companies with the most extensive internal capabilities have to take external knowledge and ideas into account when they think about innovation. // It is no longer possible for one company to "do it alone". The speed and complexity of today's markets and technologies require new ways to look at business relationships, ideas, projects, and innovation. // There are too many good ideas held by people who don't work for you to ignore them all. // Some key benefits of open innovation include a greater effectiveness of R&D, a wider source of innovations for new products, and decreased risk of missing market opportunities. //

A good first step toward taking an open-innovation approach is to open up to what is going on in your industry—listen to what consumers are saying. // Then, find a way to work with other companies, and tap into the many sources around you: academia, start-ups, developers, and inventors; innovation labs, the open-source community, suppliers, competitors, and spin-offs. // The main thing is to think in terms of collaborative relationships that balance the core strengths and capabilities of both sides. //

Discovery, or invention, is really about creating fundamental new knowledge—but without a business model, this is usually worth little. // Business models are not just ways of turning technology into money. They're also filtering devices to help you decide what you need to react to and what information you need to process. // There are a lot of benefits to be gained from modeling your business around partnerships and collaboration. //

The benefits can work both ways in terms of greater efficiency at lower costs, building upon established processes, market presence, and local insights. // On another level, both sides can gain from added insights, real world input, and research opportunities. // One of the greatest benefits of collaborative business models is the opportunity for sharing new ideas that can open your eyes to new possibilities. //

Here lie some key challenges companies are facing when they are going through big innovation moves. // The first challenge concerns the danger of trying to create too many big innovations simultaneously, and stretching organizational capabilities too thin. // However, it would be difficult to select innovation in just one area and drive toward that success. You have to place several bets and push for several to succeed. // The resources are there for each, and we are making sure that the business cases and business models are clear. //

This is closely tied to the second challenge—how to maintain the core business through innovation. // In Nokia's case, our core business is mobile devices. Increased competition and the ever-accelerating speed of innovation mean that we need to be able to shift course and scale up and down quickly, i.e. maintaining our strategic agility. // The balance of technology innovation and go-to-market agility continues to be very important. //

Nokia will continue to drive innovation in the direction of open innovation with strategic partners. // The best way to do this is to support research and business efforts within an ever-widening network of colleagues, institutions and external partners, and accept a responsibility for encouraging more dialog between different fields of expertise. This is the best way to foster a culture of openness and fairness that allows the best opportunities for exploration, discovery and invention. // As a world leader in mobile communications, Nokia is continuing to open up and further expand many different channels for innovation. //

Our external partnerships continue to develop in quality and capability. External suppliers can increasingly offer solutions of equal or even higher quality to what can be done in-house. // In these close working relationships, we expect all partners to share the same philosophy—that none of us can innovate alone, and that we can all build upon each other's insights and core strengths. // As we seek to push research toward new horizons, we need to understand that effective innovation requires a courageous focus on quickly growing and changing your business. // We also need to ensure that researchers have the opportunity to put their results into practice and create new solutions to the challenges we all face. // Only by embracing a truly global sense of cooperation can we ensure that possibilities to engage in research and to share the benefits of innovations are open and available to all. //

Here, again, the culture is playing a big role. // If people prefer to work, communicate, and share information with people of their "group", people they know and trust, then this tradition not only hinders efficient operation of a company, but also discourages and excludes different ways of thinking, behaviors, and participation of people from outside. // However, we are happy to see that the new generation of Chinese is showing a significant break from the previous generations in challenging established thinking, taking what is given, and doing what is told. This will bode well in innovating when they join the workforce. //

IV Guide to Interpreting

1. Passage 1节选自李铁映在一个企业文化论坛上的讲话，语言较为正式。在

商务口译

翻译具有中国文化特色的讲话时，要认真处理一些汉语习语。例如"一个国家根之所系，脉之所维"，尽管是两个短句，但因表达的意思是一样的，故可以将其只翻译为"root of a nation"，表达出基本意思即可。汉语重意合，英语重形合，因此在汉译英时需要把隐含在句与句之间的关系翻译出来。例如，"文化作为综合国力的重要因素，逐步成为一种生产力。文化是明天的经济。"在这句话中，后一句应该是前一句的进一步说明，因此，翻译时需在中间添加"that is"以表明两者的关系。"借此机会，我谈几点看法，同大家讨论。"在这句话的翻译中，译员可采用增词的策略，增加"would be pleased to"，听起来更口语化，更符合演讲的表达习惯。对于"以人为本"的翻译，除了"people-orientated"外，还可以译为"people-foremost"或"put people first"、"take people in the first place"等，在此只要译出其含义即可。对于"有创造，才会有贡献"的翻译，译员不妨巧妙地套用谚语"有志者，事竟成"的英文翻译，即"where there is a will, there is a way"。套用已有的、约定俗成的句子也是在口译中经常使用的一种技巧。汉语喜欢重复，而英语则相反，因此在"一个善于学习的人才能不断进步，一个善于学习的民族才有光明的未来，一个善于学习的企业才能做大、做强、做久"这句话的翻译中，"一个善于学习的"连续出现了三次，为避免累赘，不妨在后两个的处理上用"of this kind"来代替，使语言简洁明了。在口译中，对长句要学会拆分，同样，对短句要学会合并。在"优秀企业家应当是社会的楷模，受到社会的喜爱，他们不仅创造了产品，也同时创造了文化"中出现了四个短句，译员可以通过一个定语从句结构"those ... who"将它们合并在一起，使整个句子听起来更加紧凑；在"走进世界经济的汪洋大海，在大风大浪中搏击"这句话中，"汪洋大海"和"大风大浪"是形象的说法，没有实质性含义，因此在口译中可以省去不译。

2. Passage 2选自某位记者对宜家公司负责人的采访，介绍这一国际知名家居企业的文化内涵。在对话口译中，像"well"、"so"这类语气词可以省去不译。汉语表达中习惯用动词，而英语则习惯用名词，在口译时要注意语言使用上的这种转换。例如，在"there's a real bond between our operations around the world"一句中就可以把"bond"一词译成动词词组"形成了纽带"。此外，在对话口译中，因为口语性比较强，所以要尽可能地翻译其意义。例如，在"we're not interested if there's a conflict of value systems"这句话中，根据上文的含义，应把"not interested"译为"不会考虑雇佣此人"，意思更加直接；在"a flash car or status symbols"的翻译中也是只把它要传达的真实含义——"金钱和地位"表达出来就可以了。"quality, affordable products"指的是"质量高、消费者买得起的产品",所以可以将其译为"优质、实惠的产品"或"物美价廉的产品"。

3. Passage 3节选自诺基亚公司首席执行官康培凯在广东经济发展国际咨询会上的发言稿,介绍该公司的文化创新,语言较为正式规范。下面是针对一些句子口译处理技巧的点评。例如,"Therefore we have elevated innovation as one of the key Nokia values: Engaging You, Achieving Together, Very Human, and Passion for Innovation."在这句话中,演讲者不会将冒号读出,因此为了使上下意思连贯,译员有必要将冒号的解释作用译出,即译为"那就是"或重复前面的内容——"我们的核心价值观是"。再来看下面这个句子,"For us, 'Passion for Innovation' is based on the desire we have to live our dreams, to find our courage, and make the leap into the future through innovation in technology, ways of working, and the passion for understanding the world around us."这句话虽比较长,但译员通过使用四个由"渴望"引导的短语来译,不但加强了语气,又符合汉语重复的表达习惯,读起来朗朗上口。在翻译"a greater effectiveness of R&D, a wider source of innovations for new products, and decreased risk of missing market opportunities"这句话时,同样要遵循汉语喜欢用动词的习惯,将三个名词短语分别译为动词短语"研发的效率大大提高了"、"新产品的创意来源更广了"和"错过市场机会的风险降低了"。"spin-offs"是"剥离企业"或"抽资分离"的意思,指母公司收回其在子公司的全部股本,将股份分发给股东,使之脱离。"spin-offs"的含义还包括"让产易股",即原企业以部分资产换取另一企业的新股份,并以其股票分配给原企业股东。另外,对于定语从句的翻译,能直接翻译成定语固然好,但如果定语比较长通常要将其单独译出,例如,"This is the best way to foster a culture of openness and fairness that allows the best opportunities for exploration, discovery and invention."在这个句子的口译中,译员就应把句子进行拆分,把"that"引导的定语从句单独译出。

V Highlight for Interpreting

Directions: Interpret the following sentences from Chinese into English or vice versa.

1. 文化是一个国家的身份证,是一个国家根之所系,脉之所维,是精神和智慧的长期积累和凝聚。文化是人创造的，是为人服务的。而文化反过来又熏陶人，塑造人，发展人。

2. 企业文化是社会文化的重要组成部分，是一个企业的灵魂，是企业不断发展壮大的精神支柱。加强企业文化建设不仅是提高我国企业管理水平，提升企业市场竞争力的重大战略，而且是发展社会主义先进文化的重要环节。

3. 现代企业应该具有不断创造的精神。在处理企业与员工、企业内部人与物的关系时，现代企业强调"以人为本"，而在企业管理中，坚持"以人为本"，从根本上说，就是要不断激发员工的创造精神，有创造，才会有贡献。

4. 现代市场经济是法制经济，企业必须遵守市场规则，讲究信用。制售"假冒伪劣"，不仅贻害社会，而且是企业的自杀行为。

5. 企业的可持续性必须以社会的可接受性为前提，企业的产品要满足社会需要，企业行为要符合社会的伦理规范，同时，企业要积极投身社会公益事业，形象地说，企业与社会的关系就像鱼和水的关系一样。

6. 相对发达国家的企业而言，我国企业的科技和管理水平还比较落后，市场竞争力不高；现代企业文化建设刚刚起步，缺乏特色和优势，远远不能适应参与国际市场激烈竞争的需要。

7. Well, in terms of culture they're pretty well uniform. Although our culture will bond with the local culture to some extent, our core values such as simplicity and cost-consciousness are valid in all cultures.

8. For one, there's a real bond between our operations around the world. It's easy to transfer across borders because you know the values will be exactly the same. And from a marketing and positioning point of view it's very advantageous as well.

9. Although it's important for us to get highly-skilled people into the company, we're not interested if there's a conflict of value systems. Anyone expecting a flash car or status symbols has not future with us.

10. Recruitment at IKEA is an extensive process, based on judgments about the candidate's value systems and attributes. We can add retail skills, no problem, but it's tough to change one's mindset.

11. Innovation will not happen automatically. Broadly speaking, there are two kinds of mechanisms to encourage innovation: one is our corporate culture, the other is institution set-up.

12. In the past five years, Nokia's annual R&D expenditure has been consistently

nearly four billion euros, and this was significantly more than 10% of Nokia's net sales except for 2006; and more than 20% of all our employees are in the R&D functions.

13. There is no better way to secure the future prosperity and competitiveness of all regions than to build on our strengths and look for our role in building strongly integrated and open economic ties.
14. Discovery, or invention, is really about creating fundamental new knowledge—but without a business model, this is usually worth little. Business models are not just ways of turning technology into money. They're also filtering devices to help you decide what you need to react to and what information you need to process.
15. If people prefer to work, communicate, and share information with people of their "group", people they know and trust, then this tradition not only hinders efficient operation of a company, but also discourages and excludes different ways of thinking, behaviors, and participation of people from outside.

第9单元

国际会展

International Exhibitions

I Background Knowledge

Directions: Read the following English passages and then compare them with their Chinese equivalents.

Passage 1

After China's accession to the WTO, its convention and exhibition market will be gradually opened up. This is an active step to keep its entry promise. Due to this policy, foreign institutions will have access to China's exhibition industry as nationals.

For convention and exhibition industry overseas, they could adopt two means to enter China's market. They can set up joint ventures with domestic convention and exhibition companies or cooperate with the hosting cities by making investment in building exhibition facilities to expand operation scale and then to tap China's convention and exhibition market. They can also establish representative agencies or offices in China to investigate and further exploit China's convention and exhibition market.

No matter which one they use, it would be very hard for them to get success without the cooperation of China's convention and exhibition industry, including its service industry. Only upon this cooperation, could exhibitors from home and abroad share complementary advantages, increase the standard of China's convention and exhibition industry and further promote the development of China's market.

Nowadays, convention and exhibition industry in China is still at the stage of development. Ministry of Commerce of the People's Republic of China, as the governing body of this industry, is responsible for the construction of domestic market system and the adjustment of market operation. Furthermore, it has direct connection with quite a few domestic companies.

For those overseas exhibition companies, which enter China's market for the first time, it is of great importance for them to establish company's recognition. It is necessary to create a platform for self-promotion whether they intent to seek Chinese partners for the exploitation of Chinese market or to organize Chinese companies to participate in conventions and exhibitions abroad for targeting prospects.

中国加入世贸组织以后，中国的会展市场也将逐步开放以积极实现其入世的承诺。这一开放政策的实施意味着外国的组织机构将以国民待遇进入中国会展行业。

外国会展商可以通过两种形式进入中国市场。其一，他们可以和国内的会展单位组建合资企业；或者和会展举办城市合作，投资兴建会展设施，拓展运营规模，开发中国会展市场。其二，他们可以先在中国设代表处或者办公室，做好调研后，再开拓中国会展市场。

无论外国会展商采取什么方式进入中国市场，要取得成功的关键始终是要和本土会展企业和服务业合作。只有通过合作，中外会展单位才能实现优势互补，提高本土会展行业的从业标准，从而促进中国会展市场的发展。

目前，中国的会展行业仍处于发展阶段。作为会展业的主管部门，中华人民共和国商务部对该行业的国内市场体系建设和市场运营调控负责。并且，国内目前就有好几家商务部直属的会展公司。

对于首次进入中国市场的外国会展商而言，重中之重是建立市场认可。我们需要搭建一个平台，供外国会展行业进行自我推销，他们既可以"走进来"和中国国内单位合作共同开发市场，又可以组织国内企业"走出去"，实现目标愿景。

Passage 2

Exhibition industry, MICE, is a comprehensive tourism service offering combining meeting, incentive, conference and exhibition. The differentiations of MICE from normal tourism are fourfold: the marginal pull effect to various related industries; the promotion of the recognition and goodwill of the city; the improvement of infrastructure; and the increase of regional exchanges. The pull ratio between MICE and related industries is estimated to be between 1:6 and 1:10.

MICE is referred to, in China, as sunrise industry. Through major conferences and exhibitions, numerous economic opportunities are brought forward to neighboring industries like logistics, hotel, catering, and tourism.

At present, China's exhibition industry has become a new economic growth point with an annual 20% increase on average. MICE is one of the nation's top 10 potential industries. The significance of the success of Beijing Olympic Games and the Shanghai World Expo bid success is far reaching. They have not only introduced China to the world, but more importantly, have attracted abundant foreign capital, technology and talents right into the exhibition industry in China. China's exhibition industry has enormous potential which is yet to be tapped.

However, we must also be well aware of the constraining drawbacks of China's exhibition industry. MICE was not seen or developed as an independent industry until very recently. Both the emergence and the development of the industry are spontaneous and random. Thus the overall quality of Chinese exhibitors is not satisfying enough. And the development of exhibition industries varies drastically across the country. In terms of market-orientation, exhibition facility, professionalization of practitioners and legitimacy of the industry, there are still a lot to be done.

会展业，也称MICE，是一种综合的旅游服务形式，包括集体会议、奖励旅游、大型会议和展览。与常规旅游相比，会展旅游具有四重特点：能带动各种相关产业；可以提升一个城市的知名度和整体形象；促进城市基础设施的完善；有助于增进地区间的交流。据估算，会展业对其他相关产业的带动比例在1∶6至1∶10之间。

会展行业在中国被誉为朝阳产业。大型会议和展览的举办给诸如物流、酒店、餐饮和旅游业这些相邻产业带来无限商机。

目前，中国的会展业以年均20%的增长速度成为新的经济增长点。它已成为中国最具潜力的10大产业之一。北京奥运会的成功举办和上海世博会的竞标成功对中国的会展业发展意义深远。这两件国际盛事不仅让世界认识了中国，更为重要的是为中国会展产业引入了大量的外国资金、技术和人才。中国会展业的前途无可限量。

但是，我们也必须清楚地认识制约中国会展业发展的因素。中国的会展业起步较晚，直到最近才发展成为一个独立产业，行业的出现和发展都带有自发性和随意性。因此，国内会展商的总体素质还难以令人满意。再者，全国的行

商务口译

业内发展程度也极不平衡。在市场化、会展设施、从业人员的专业化和行业的合法性等问题上，我国的会展业均还有很大的改进空间。

II Warm-up

1 **Directions:** Give the English equivalents of the following Chinese expressions.

会展城市	中国—东盟商务与投资峰会
相关产业拉动效应	市场准入
集聚效应	大湄公河（次区域）
政府主导、政府主体	东盟东部增长区
展场面积	次区域经济合作
中国会展经济国际合作论坛	山水相连
中国国际贸易促进委员会	文化相通
国际展览业协会	经济互补
国际展览与项目协会	北部湾经济区
独立组展商协会	增长极
"汇聚成长的力量"	抗震救灾
中国国际展览会议展示会	坚定不移
（展中展）	始终不渝
中国—东盟博览会	

2 **Directions:** Give the Chinese equivalents of the following English expressions.

entry promise	China International Exhibition
convention and exhibition industry	Corporation (CIEC)
MICE	Deutsche Messe Hanover
sunrise industry	Messe Düsseldorf
Shanghai World Expo	Shanghai New International
Munich International Trade	Expo Centre (SNIEC)
Fairs (MMI)	

第9单元　国际会展

III Passages for Interpreting

Passage 1

Directions: Listen to the passage and interpret from Chinese into English at the end of each segment.

女士们、先生们，朋友们：

上午好！首先，请允许我代表成都市人民政府向莅临本次盛会的各位领导、各位嘉宾、各位朋友表示热烈的欢迎。刚才大家观看了成都会展业的宣传片，对成都的会展环境有了初步的了解。下面，我从成都经济社会的基本情况、成都展会经济发展的体会和成都未来三年会展产业发展的构想，给大家介绍一下成都这座理想的会展城市的情况。//

成都把会展业作为现代服务业的重要组成部分，在"十一五"期间列为重点产业加以扶持发展。成立专门的会展发展机构——成都会展业发展办公室，建成一批功能、设施完善的会展场馆，培养锻炼出一支有经验的专业队伍。// 近年来，我市承接展会数量大幅增加，自办展会品质不断提升，会展经济规模不断扩大，呈现出又好又快的发展态势，对我市相关产业拉动效应明显。//

一是会展活动是举办城市营销的重要载体。会展活动能产生较大的集聚效应，高层次、大规模的展会更是吸引媒体的广泛关注，有利于提高举办城市的知名度。// 目前，成都每年举办各类展会、节庆活动260多个，不仅在媒介上宣传、推广城市，还带来了200多万参展、参会的客商直接来到成都。//

二是会展业是城市经济发展的重要推手。特色产业和优势产业的崛起可以为专业展会提供坚实的产业基础。专业展会的举办又是对当地产业整体的营销，并为产业的配套发展和提档升级开拓了空间。// 举办植根于产业基础的专业展会，将会形成产业与会展互动双赢的良性发展格局。//

三是会展业的发展需要坚持"政府主导、政府主体"的运行模式。会展经济涉及面广，相关性强。成都市在培育会展经济的过程中，形成了"政府主导、部门协调、企业运作"的办展办会模式，市政府成立了专门部门即成都会展办，建立了涵盖交通、公安、工商、城管、旅游、税务、卫生、商检、海关等部门的会展政务服务工作体系，为承接展会的办展机构最大限度地提供便利，保证了30多个国内外大型知名展会来蓉成功举办。// 同时，成都市政府十分重视市场主体的培育，支持形成了一批会展企业。全市已有展场面积20万平米、酒店配套的4个场馆设施，使承接展会的能力不断提升。//

商务口译

四是会展业的发展需要坚持承接外来展和自办本地展并重。这是成都发展会展业的长期战略。高水平的外来展会带来了新的创意和办会经验，可以开阔本地业界思路，促进自办展水平提升。// 我市在总结外来展会经验的基础上，依托产业特点、市场特性、文化特色和资源优势，采取招标、重组、新建公司和引进办展机构等多种方式，分类打造自主品牌展会。现已培育出展览面积超过5万平米的展会3个。//

谢谢大家！//

Passage 2

Directions: Listen to the passage and interpret from English into Chinese at the end of each segment.

In the year 2008 we commemorate the 30th anniversary of (the) economic and social reforms in China, which started with the Third Plenary Session of the Eleventh Central Committee of the Chinese Communist Party. //

Thirty years is only a short period in China's history. But never before has China in such a short period of time generated such an increase in public welfare. //

The main reason for this success story is twofold: openness with regard to the economy on the one hand and pursuit of trustworthiness on the other. This is especially true concerning China as a place for investment in exhibitions and conventions. //

The upkeep of free trade, especially since China became a member of the World Trade Organization in 2001, is inevitably linked to a free exchange of business information on what is necessary to trade. Thus, the exhibition industry is crucial for China's continuous growth and economic expansion. //

Munich International Trade Fairs (MMI) is a good example on reviewing the history of the trade fair sector during the last 30 years. //

• As early as 1975, IMAG—Internationaler Messe- und Ausstellungsdienst—a subsidiary of Munich International Trade Fairs organized the first German industrial exhibition in Beijing. During the 1980s other international exhibition companies joined us in testing the opportunities of investing into the Chinese exhibition market. //

• In 1995, IMAG and joint venture partner China International Exhibition Corporation (CIEC) in Beijing founded Jing Mu, the first joint venture company in Chinese exhibition industry. Today, our subsidiary MMI Singapore is the joint venture partner of CIEC. //

• In 1999, experiences made during this period guided the decision of three leading German exhibition companies, Munich International Trade Fairs, Deutsche Messe Hanover and Messe Düsseldorf, to band together and enter a joint venture with a Chinese partner, Lujiazui Development Group, to build and operate a trade fair center in Shanghai. //

Looking back on the Shanghai New International Expo Centre (SNIEC), which was inaugurated in 2001, the Chinese and German partners can be proud to have created a strategic beacon of success at the beginning of the new century. //

This century is characterized by globalization, a development also driven by China and driving China. At the heart of this progress is the explosive growth of trade, and again, at the core of this continuous advance we find trade fairs as marketing hubs for China and its international business. //

Thank you. //

Passage 3

Directions: Listen to the passage and interpret from Chinese into English at the end of each segment.

经国务院批准，第四届中国会展经济国际合作论坛将于2008年1月14日至16日在成都世纪城国际会议中心举行。这是继2005年、2006年和2007年成功举办三届中国会展经济国际合作论坛之后，中国国际贸易促进委员会、国际展览业协会、国际展览与项目协会、独立组展商协会合作，共同主办的又一次会展业国际盛会。//

根据往届论坛的参会规模，预计将有400多名全球会展业界精英和商界人士齐聚成都，并有来自十几个国家和地区的中外嘉宾在论坛上发表演讲，共同研讨当代中国会展业发展现状、外资在华拓展展览业务的经验和战略、中型会展城市发展的新机遇、会展营销与主题策划对会展品牌的影响等方面的问题。//

本届中国会展经济国际合作论坛主题为"汇聚成长的力量"，旨在为中外会展业构建交流与合作的平台，将通过五场全体会议和六个分组论坛等系列主题活动，在国际会展巨头、会展城市官员、经济研究与会展相关领域的专家学者和会展业界代表之间开展交流与对话，共同分享行业发展经验与合作成果。同期还将继续举办中国国际展览会议展示会（展中展）。//

商务口译

Passage 4

Directions: Listen to the passage and interpret from Chinese into English at the end of each segment.

尊敬的各位嘉宾，女士们、先生们，朋友们：//
　　我代表中国政府，对莅临会议的东盟国家领导人和各位嘉宾表示热烈的欢迎！//
　　中国与东盟各国政府高度重视发展友好关系和互利合作。自2004年首次举办中国—东盟博览会和商务与投资峰会以来，双方积极推进中国—东盟自由贸易区建设，先后签署并实施货物贸易协议、服务贸易协议，不断降低关税水平和扩大市场准入，深化大湄公河、东盟东部增长区等次区域经济合作，推动贸易和投资更加便利化。// 中国与东盟贸易额由2004年的1,059亿美元增加到2007年的2,025亿美元，提前三年实现双方领导人提出的2,000亿美元的贸易目标。今年1至9月，双方贸易额达1,804亿美元，比去年同期增长23%，已互为第四大贸易伙伴。// 相互投资不断扩大，东盟对华投资已形成相当规模，中国企业对东盟投资快速增长。东盟10国都已成为中国公民的旅游目的国，人员往来更加频繁。双方各领域合作呈现出平等互信、互利共赢的良好发展态势。//
　　中国和东盟各国同处于经济快速发展的阶段，山水相连，文化相通，经济互补，加强合作不仅具有牢固的基础，而且具有巨大的潜力。// 当前，国际经济不确定、不稳定因素明显增多，美国金融危机继续蔓延，国际金融市场动荡加剧，世界经济增长明显减缓，对亚洲地区已产生重大影响。面对这样前所未有的挑战，加快推进中国与东盟合作具有特别重要的意义。为此，我愿就加强中国—东盟经贸合作提出以下建议：//
　　（一）深化贸易和投资合作。进一步深化双方货物贸易、服务贸易合作。继续就《中国—东盟自贸区投资协议》加强沟通协商，力争早日结束谈判并签署协议，确保如期建成中国—东盟自贸区。中国政府将鼓励和支持企业进一步加大对东盟国家的投资，推动在东盟国家建立经济贸易合作区。//
　　（二）加强次区域合作。中方积极支持东盟经济一体化建设，与有关国家共同推动大湄公河次区域由交通走廊向经济走廊转型，探讨开展泛北部湾经济合作。中国政府将支持加快北部湾经济区开放开发，使之成为中国—东盟合作新的增长极。//
　　（三）完善合作机制。进一步发挥现有沟通与合作机制的作用，继续办好中国—东盟博览会和商务与投资峰会，推动多层次、多领域交流对话。鼓励中

介机构为企业合作提供服务，特别是支持中小企业开展更有效的合作。//

（四）共同应对挑战。顺应经济全球化的潮流，加强区域经济合作，有利于抓住发展机遇，应对重大挑战。中方将继续以负责任的态度，与东盟各国加强在金融、能源、环保、粮食安全等领域的协调与合作，共同促进本地区经济金融稳定健康发展。//

女士们、先生们、朋友们！对中国来说，今年是极不平凡的一年。在国际形势发生复杂变化和国内出现突发性困难的情况下，我们继续保持经济较快增长和金融安全稳定，夺取了汶川特大地震抗震救灾重大胜利，成功举办北京奥运会、残奥会，圆满完成神舟七号载人航天飞行任务。这充分显示出中国改革开放30年奠定的坚实国力基础。// 总的看来，中国经济发展的基本面没有改变，正朝着宏观调控的预期方向发展。今年前三季度，国内生产总值同比增长9.9%，近几个月物价涨幅逐步回落。当前，最重要的是把自己的事情办好。// 中国政府已经并将继续采取措施应对外部冲击，努力保持经济稳定、金融稳定、资本市场稳定。我们有信心、有条件、有能力战胜各种困难和挑战。//

中国的发展将为世界各国特别是周边国家带来更多机遇。我们将坚定不移地走中国特色社会主义道路，深入贯彻落实科学发展观，加快转变经济发展方式，灵活审慎地调整宏观经济政策，着力扩大国内需求特别是消费需求，努力实现发展的速度与结构、质量、效益相统一，促进国民经济持续平稳较快发展。// 中国将继续推进改革开放，实施互利共赢的开放战略，推动贸易和投资自由化、便利化，反对任何形式的保护主义。// 我们将始终不渝走和平发展道路，坚持与邻为善、以邻为伴，加强同周边国家的睦邻友好和务实合作，努力以自身的发展促进本地区的共同发展。//

广西作为中国—东盟博览会和商务与投资峰会的举办地，在推动中国和东盟合作中具有独特的优势和重要的作用。希望中国和东盟国家各界朋友充分运用这个平台，加强交流，增进了解，努力达成更多的合作成果，为不断扩大中国与东盟经贸合作，巩固和发展战略伙伴关系作出新贡献。//

祝本届中国—东盟博览会和商务与投资峰会圆满成功！//

谢谢大家。//

IV Guide to Interpreting

1. Passage 1节选自2008年成都市人民政府副秘书长在第四届中国会展经济国际合作论坛上的主题发言。此篇口译练习的重点是要对原文中的逻辑关系进行深度加工，按照英文受众的思维习惯进行条理梳理工作。下面以第

商务口译

二段发言为例进行分析，将它划分为四块内容：①成都把会展业作为现代服务业的重要组成部分，②在"十一五"期间列为重点产业加以扶持发展。③成立专门的会展发展机构——成都会展业发展办公室，建成一批功能、设施完善的会展场馆，培养锻炼出一支有经验的专业队伍。④近年来，我市承接展会数量大幅增加，自办展会品质不断提升，会展经济规模不断扩大，呈现出又好又快的发展态势，对我市相关产业拉动效应明显。

上述这四块内容其实可概述为四大意群：①描述了会展业在成都的定位；②进一步描述定位；③一个综合信息，共同之处是它们都是例子，是为了解释和支持前面两点的论断，目的是说明会展业很重要；④努力后的结果。这样的层次划分和理解才符合英语的思维，而不能生硬地按照原文的句法，统统处理成并列的关系。

2. Passage 2是德国慕尼黑国际博览集团首席执行官曼弗雷德·乌茨霍夫（Manfred Wutzlhofer）在2008年第四届中国会展经济国际合作论坛上的英语演讲，句型较为简单，也是书面语特征非常明显的一篇演讲稿。译员要重点准备好演讲里涉及到的德国公司的中译名和合资公司的中译名，否则将严重影响听众的理解。

3. Passage 3是对中国会展经济国际合作论坛的新闻发布，口译时，需引起译员注意的同样是诸多专有名词的准备。在翻译之前，浏览主办方的专门网站，了解主办方和参展方的相关背景，掌握专有名词的缩略语使用等准备都至关重要。

4. Passage 4是王岐山在第五届中国—东盟商务与投资峰会开幕式上的发言稿，具有鲜明的时代气息和中国官方独有的礼仪特征。中国官员讲话擅长逻辑条理的使用，译员在做口译笔记时应注意信息的相应分层，礼仪祝词中的套语在此讲稿中也体现得淋漓尽致。此外，了解中国—东盟博览会的背景知识和涉及中国方面内容常用的英语表达形式对顺利完成口译任务也十分必要。

V Highlight for Interpreting

Directions: Interpret the following sentences from Chinese into English or vice versa.

1. 成立专门的会展发展机构——成都会展业发展办公室，建成一批功能、设施完善的会展场馆，培养锻炼出一支有经验的专业队伍。

2. 近年来，我市承接展会数量大幅增加，自办展会品质不断提升，会展经济规模不断扩大，呈现出又好又快的发展态势，对我市相关产业拉动效应明显。

3. 会展活动是举办城市营销的重要载体。会展活动能产生较大的集聚效应，高层次、大规模的展会更是吸引媒体的广泛关注，有利于提高举办城市的知名度。
4. 举办植根于产业基础的专业展会，将会形成产业与会展互动双赢的良性发展格局。
5. 会展业的发展需要坚持"政府主导、政府主体"的运行模式。
6. 会展业的发展需要坚持承接外来展和自办本地展并重。
7. 自2004年首次举办中国—东盟博览会和商务与投资峰会以来，双方积极推进中国—东盟自由贸易区建设，先后签署并实施货物贸易协议、服务贸易协议，不断降低关税水平和扩大市场准入，深化大湄公河、东盟东部增长区等次区域经济合作，推动贸易和投资更加便利化。
8. 当前，国际经济不确定、不稳定因素明显增多，美国金融危机继续蔓延，国际金融市场动荡加剧，世界经济增长明显减缓，对亚洲地区已产生重大影响。面对这样前所未有的挑战，加快推进中国与东盟合作具有特别重要的意义。
9. 广西作为中国—东盟博览会和商务与投资峰会的举办地，在推动中国和东盟合作中具有独特的优势和重要的作用。希望中国和东盟国家各界朋友充分运用这个平台，加强交流，增进了解，努力达成更多的合作成果，为不断扩大中国与东盟经贸合作，巩固和发展战略伙伴关系作出新贡献。
10. Thirty years is only a short period in China's history. But never before has China in such a short period of time generated such an increase in public welfare.
11. Munich International Trade Fairs (MMI) is a good example on reviewing the history of the trade fair sector during the last 30 years.
12. In 1999, experiences made during this period guided the decision of three leading German exhibition companies, Munich International Trade Fairs, Deutsche Messe Hanover and Messe Düsseldorf, to band together and enter a joint venture with a Chinese partner, Lujiazui Development Group, to build and operate a trade fair center in Shanghai.
13. This century is characterized by globalization, a development also driven by China and driving China.

第10单元

政治与经济

Political & Economic Issues

I Background Knowledge

Directions: Read the following English passages and then compare them with their Chinese equivalents.

Passage 1

Wall Street is a street in lower Manhattan, New York City, New York, United States. It runs east from Broadway to South Street, through the center of the Financial District. Wall Street was the first permanent home of the New York Stock Exchange which was built in 1903. Over time Wall Street became the name of the surrounding geographic neighborhood. Wall Street is also shorthand for the "influential financial interests" of the American financial industry, which is centered in the New York City area. Several major US stock and other exchanges remain headquartered on Wall Street, including the NYSE, NASDAQ, AMEX, NYMEX, and NYBOT.

华尔街位于美国纽约州纽约市下曼哈顿区,自百老汇大街向东绵延至南街,贯通整个金融中心区域。纽约股票交易所建于1903年,并以华尔街为第一个永久家园。经年累月,华尔街逐渐成为整个周边地区的统称。与此同时,华尔街还是以纽约为中心的美国金融业具有影响力的金融利益的简称。另外,许多主要的美国证券和其他交易公司都将总部设在华尔街,如纽约证券交易所、纳斯达克、美国证券交易所、纽约商业交易所以及纽约期货交易所等。

商务口译

Passage 2

The subprime mortgage crisis is a financial crisis characterized by contracted liquidity in global credit markets and banking systems triggered by the failure of mortgage companies, investment firms and government-sponsored enterprises which had invested heavily in subprime mortgages. The crisis, which has roots in the closing years of the 20th century but has become more apparent throughout 2007 and 2008, has passed through various stages exposing pervasive weaknesses in the global financial system and regulatory framework.

The crisis began with the bursting of the United States housing bubble and high default rates, beginning in approximately 2005-2006. For a number of years prior to that, declining lending standards, an increase in loan incentives such as easy initial terms, and a long-term trend of rising housing prices had encouraged borrowers to assume difficult mortgages in the belief they would be able to quickly refinance at more favorable terms. However, once interest rates began to rise and housing prices started to drop moderately in 2006-2007 in many parts of the US, refinancing became more difficult. Defaults and foreclosure activity increased dramatically as easy initial terms expired, home prices failed to go up as anticipated, and ARM[1] interest rates reset higher. Foreclosures accelerated in the United States in late 2006 and triggered a global financial crisis through 2007 and 2008.

次贷危机指的是一种金融危机，其特点是由抵押公司、投资公司和政府注资公司在次贷市场过度投资失败所引发的全球信贷市场和银行系统的流动性紧缩。此次危机源自20世纪末期，在2007至2008年间变得日益明显，已在不同的阶段暴露出全球金融系统和监管机构普遍存在的弱点。

此次危机始于美国房产市场泡沫的破灭以及高按揭款违约率，在2005年至2006年间已初现端倪。在此前的数年间，美国调低借贷信用分值，降低首付款以刺激贷款，加之民众预期房价长期向好，这些都鼓励了借贷者承担沉重的借贷，使他们相信，在更为优惠的条件中他们可以迅速再融资。然而，在2006至2007年间，美国许多城市由于利率不断升高，房价下跌，再融资变得更加困难。越来越多的次级房贷借款人不能按时还款，违约和房产被没收的现象激增，房价向好并没有预期的那么乐观，可调整抵押贷款利率调高。2006年末美国国内抵押赎回权取消的加速，引发了贯穿2007年至2008年的全球金融危机。

---

1 adjustable rate mortgage.

第10单元 政治与经济

Ⅱ Warm-up

1 **Directions:** Give the English equivalents of the following Chinese expressions.

高层互访	美国商会
双边贸易额	美国中国总商会
同比增长	百人会
组团旅游	美中政策基金会
通胀压力	美国中国论坛
趋利避害	商业圆桌会议
部长级会议	华美协进社
零关税待遇	共叙情谊
投资兴业	合则两利，斗则俱伤
商业融资	战略对话机制
美中关系全国委员会	执教
美中贸易全国委员会	花样游泳队
美国对外关系委员会	金融动荡
亚洲协会	能源紧张、粮食短缺

2 **Directions:** Give the Chinese equivalents of the following English expressions.

NYSE	financial recovery plan
NASDAQ	defining moment
AMEX	Great Depression
NYMEX	rescue effort
NYBOT	get oversight over
subprime mortgage crisis	final verdict
contracted liquidity	shred regulation
regulatory framework	trickle down
high default rates	fair shake
refinance	work out a solution
initial terms	Wall Street
defaults and foreclosure	Main Street

129

商务口译

come up with a package	Secretary of the Treasury
subprime lending mess	stakeholder
lax regulation	economic philosophy

III Passages for Interpreting

Passage 1

Directions: Listen to the following dialog and interpret from English into Chinese at the end of each segment.

I = Interviewer   O = Obama   M = McCain

I: Gentlemen, at this very moment tonight, where do you stand on the financial recovery? First, response to you Senator Obama. You have two minutes. //

O: Well, thank you very much, Jim, and thanks to the commission and the University of Mississippi, "Ole Miss", for hosting us tonight. I can't think of a more important time for us to talk about the future of the country. // You know, we are at a defining moment in our history. Our nation is involved in two wars, and we are going through the worst financial crisis since the Great Depression. //

And you're wondering, how's it gonna affect me? How's it gonna affect my job? How's it gonna affect my house? // How's it gonna affect my retirement savings or my ability to send my children to the college? So we have to move swiftly, and we have to move wisely. // And I've put forward a series of proposals that make sure that we protect taxpayers as we engage in this important rescue effort. //

No. 1, we've got to make sure that we've got oversight over this whole process; $700 billion, potentially, is a lot of money. //

No. 2, we've got to make sure that taxpayers, when they are putting their money at risk, have the possibility of getting that money back and gains, if the market, and when the market returns. //

No. 3, we've got to make sure that none of that money is going to pad CEO bank accounts or to promote golden parachutes. //

And, No. 4, we've got to make sure that we're helping homeowners, because the root problem here has to do with the foreclosures that are taking place all across the country. //

Now, we also have to recognize that this is a final verdict on eight years of failed economic policies promoted by George Bush, supported by Senator McCain, a theory that basically says that we can shred regulations and consumer protections and give more and more to the most, and somehow prosperity will trickle down. //

It hasn't worked. And I think that the fundamentals of the economy have to be measured by whether or not the middle class is getting a fair shake. That's why I'm running for president, that's what I hope we're gonna be talking about tonight. //

I: Senator McCain, two minutes. //

M: Well, thank you, Jim. And thanks to everybody. I also want to thank the University of Mississippi for hosting us tonight. // And, Jim, I—I've been not feeling too great about a lot of things lately. So have a lot of Americans who are facing challenges. But I'm feeling a little better tonight, and I'll tell you why. //

Because as we're here tonight in this debate, we are seeing, for the first time in a long time, Republicans and Democrats together, sitting down, trying to work out a solution to this fiscal crisis that we're in. //

And I have no doubt about the magnitude of this crisis. // And we're not talking about failure of institutions on Wall Street. We're talking about failures on Main Street, and people who will lose their jobs, and their credits, and their homes, if we don't fix the greatest fiscal crisis. //

But the point is—the point is, we have finally seen Republicans and Democrats sitting down and negotiating together and coming up with a package. //

This package has transparency in it. It has to have accountability and oversight. It has to have options for loans to failing businesses, rather than the government taking over those loans. // We have to—it has to have a package with a number of other essential elements to it. //

But I want to emphasize one point to all Americans tonight. This isn't the beginning of the end of this crisis. This is the end of the beginning, if we come out with a package that will keep these institutions stable. // And we've got a lot of work to do. And we've got to create jobs. And one of the areas, of course, is to eliminate our dependence on foreign oil. //

商务口译

I: All right, let's go back to my question—how (do) you stand on the recovery plan? And talk to each other about it. We can wait (for) five minutes, we can negotiate a deal right here. I mean, you favor this plan, Senator Obama? And you, Senator McCain? Are you in favor of this plan? //

O: Er... and I do think that there's constructive work being done out there. So, for the viewers who are watching, I am optimistic about the capacity of us to come together with a plan. // The question, I think, that we have to ask ourselves is, how did we get into this situation in the first place? //

Two years ago, I warned that, because of the subprime lending mess, because of the lax regulation, that we were potentially gonna have a problem and tried to stop some of the abuses in mortgages that were taking place at the time. // Last year, I wrote to the Secretary of the Treasury to make sure that he understood the magnitude of this problem and to call on him to bring all the stakeholders together to try to deal with it. //

So—so the question, I think, that we've got to ask ourselves is, yes, we've got to solve this problem short term. And we are going to have to intervene; there's no doubt about that. //

But we're also going to have to look at, how is it that we shredded so many regulations? We did not set up a 21st-century regulatory framework to deal with these problems. // And that in part has to do with an economic philosophy that says that regulation is always bad. //

Passage 2

Directions: Listen to the passage and interpret from Chinese into English at the end of each segment.

女士们、先生们，朋友们：//

很高兴参加中国—太平洋岛国经济发展合作论坛投资、贸易、旅游部长级会议。我谨代表中国商务部，对部长级会议的召开表示热烈祝贺，对来自岛国的各位朋友表示热烈欢迎，对岛国政府和人民在中国汶川地震后所给予的同情和无私帮助表示衷心感谢。//

近年来，中国与太平洋岛国的友好关系进一步加强，高层互访更加频繁，合作领域不断扩大。汤加、瓦努阿图和密克罗尼西亚相继在北京设立了大使馆，为中国和太平洋岛国关系的进一步发展创造了良好条件。// 在贸易领域，2007

年双边贸易额超过15亿美元。今年上半年，双边贸易超过9亿美元，同比增长8%，全年有望达到或者突破20亿美元。// 在投资领域，2006年以来，中方企业累计在岛国地区的直接投资超过3亿美元，先后实施了巴新[1]拉姆镍钴矿和马绍尔水产品加工厂等重大项目。经过共同努力，根据《中国—太平洋岛国经济发展合作行动纲领》确定的原则，双方在人力资源开发、投资、旅游、农业、教育、交通运输、基础设施建设以及经济援助等各个领域的合作日益深化。// 同时，中国已与巴新、斐济、瓦努阿图、汤加、密克罗尼西亚签署了中国团队赴各国旅游实施方案的谅解备忘录，启动了赴斐济、瓦努阿图、汤加等国的组团旅游业务。//

女士们、先生们！当今世界正处于大变革、大调整之中，经济全球化深入发展，国与国相互依存日益紧密，求和平、谋发展、促合作成为不可阻挡的时代潮流。// 同时，世界经济增长中的不稳定因素增多，金融市场持续动荡，能源价格快速上涨，粮食安全日益突出，通胀压力不断增大，建设和谐世界仍面临诸多严峻考验。// 在此大背景下，如何趋利避害、实现可持续发展，是摆在包括中国和太平洋岛国在内的广大发展中国家面前的一项重大课题。//

为适应新形势下加强合作、共谋发展的需要，2006年4月，中国—太平洋岛国经济发展合作论坛首届部长级会议在斐济楠迪成功举办。温家宝总理代表中方宣布了支持岛国经济发展的六项重大举措，受到普遍欢迎。// 两年来，中方在各岛国的大力支持和配合下，积极推进各项工作的落实，取得了较好成效。//

到2009年4月，我们将迎来中国—太平洋岛国经济发展合作论坛斐济会议三周年。中方有信心在未来的八个月内，本着"互惠互利、共同发展"的原则，和岛国政府通力合作，把六项措施逐一落到实处，为岛国人民的福祉做出实实在在的贡献。//

为把中国—太平洋岛国经贸合作提高到新水平，今后一个时期，双方可以重点在以下方面作出努力：

第一，扩大双边贸易规模，力争到2010年双边贸易在2007年的基础上翻一番，达到30亿美元。// 中方将通过多种形式鼓励企业扩大进口岛国具有比较优势的产品，逐步扩大从最不发达岛国进口享受零关税待遇的税目范围。//

第二，鼓励投资合作。中方将一如继往地鼓励有实力、守信誉的中方企业赴岛国投资兴业，积极探讨利用政府贷款和商业融资等多种方式在岛国进行基础设施、通信以及农、林、渔业开发等领域的合作。//

---

[1] 巴布亚新几内亚。

商务口译

　　第三，鼓励双向合作开发旅游市场。中方积极鼓励旅游企业开展中国旅游团队赴岛国的旅游业务；将继续邀请岛国旅游官员来华出席每年一届的中国国际旅游交易会，增进双方旅游部门相互交流。//

　　第四，将能源合作列为双边合作的重要领域。中方已为多个岛国援建了小水电、太阳能、风能等清洁能源项目，在此基础上，中方将继续与岛国分享节能及利用再生和替代能源的成功技术，帮助岛国更好应对能源安全问题。//

　　第五，在良种培育、农业科技、病虫害防治、粮食储备等方面开展技术交流和务实合作，帮助岛国提高农业综合生产能力。// 中方将继续在双边渠道和南南合作框架内向岛国派遣农业专家，传授水稻、蔬菜种植技术，并在华组织各类农业技术培训班，帮助岛国培养农技人员。//

　　女士们、先生们！中国政府高度重视同太平洋岛国的友好合作关系。发展与太平洋岛国的友好合作关系不是中国的权宜之计，而是一项长期的战略决策。//

　　政治上，我们主张国家不分大小、强弱、贫富，都是国际社会的平等一员。我们尊重各岛国根据各自国情选择发展道路，尊重各国为维护主权和地区稳定所做的努力。//

　　经济上，中国致力于落实联合国千年发展目标，努力帮助各岛国增强自主发展能力，支持岛国提出的旨在推进区域合作进程的"太平洋计划"。// 作为发展中国家的一员，我们将继续向岛国提供力所能及的援助，并且不附带任何条件。//

　　在国际事务中，中国作为联合国安理会常任理事国，将一如既往地维护包括太平洋岛国在内的广大发展中国家利益，支持各岛国在可持续发展问题上的合理诉求，通过提供资金、分享技术和经验等手段帮助岛国更好应对在气候变化、能源和粮食安全、海洋资源保护等问题上面临的挑战。//

　　历史已经并将继续证明，中国永远是太平洋岛国真诚、可信、可靠的朋友和合作伙伴。//

　　女士们、先生们！中国与太平洋岛国经济互补性强，合作潜力巨大，具有广阔的发展前景。// 只要双方共同努力，就一定能把中国和太平洋岛国的合作推向新的高度。这不仅有利于本地区的稳定与繁荣，也是对世界和平与发展做出的重要贡献。//

　　最后，预祝本届部长级会议取得圆满成功！//

　　祝各位朋友在华访问愉快！//

Passage 3

Directions: Listen to the passage and interpret from Chinese into English at the end of each segment.

女士们、先生们：

　　首先，我要感谢美中关系全国委员会、美中贸易全国委员会、美国对外关系委员会、亚洲协会、美国商会、美国中国总商会、百人会、美中政策基金会、美国中国论坛、商业圆桌会议和华美协进社共同举办这场活动，使我们有机会同各位老友新朋再次相聚，共叙情谊。//

　　记得2003年我对美国进行正式访问期间，你们在华盛顿也举办了这样盛大的宴会。那次我发表了题为《共同谱写中美关系新篇章》的演讲，对中美关系作出三条结论：一是中美两国合则两利，斗则俱伤；二是中美两国有合作的基础和共同的利益；三是中美合作有利于亚太地区的稳定，也有利于世界的和平与发展。//

　　转眼五年过去了，我高兴地看到，这三条结论经受住了时间的检验，中美关系取得了重要的发展。//

　　首先，中美高层接触比以往任何时期都要频繁。中美之间各种对话和磋商机制已超过60个，特别是中美战略经济对话和战略对话机制，为增进双方战略互信发挥了重要作用。//

　　第二，双边贸易额从2003年的1,260亿美元增加到去年的3,020亿美元，五年中增长了近一倍半，中美互为第二大贸易伙伴。// 不久前，两国签署的《中美能源环境十年合作框架》文件就是一个突出例子。//

　　第三，中美在反恐、防扩散等全球安全领域和朝鲜半岛核问题等地区和国际热点问题上保持了沟通与协调，共同致力于维护世界和平与稳定。//

　　女士们、先生们。// "国之交在于民相亲"。中美关系的发展还体现在两国人民之间的友好感情不断加深。在上个月结束的北京奥运会上，我们同样见到许多中美友好的感人场景。// 例如，布什总统全家三代人来到北京，与中国观众一起为两国运动员加油；由中国教练执教的美国女排和体操队与中国队同场竞技；在美国NBA打球的中国运动员很受人们喜爱；美国花样游泳队在赛场上高举"谢谢你，中国"的标语，中国观众对此报以热烈的掌声，等等。这些例子再次证明，中美两国人民心灵是相通的，情感是相连的。// 借此机会，我要向长期致力于促进中美友好事业的美国各界人士表示崇高的敬意，对美国政府和人民对中国抗震救灾和举办奥运会的大力支持表示衷心感谢！//

商务口译

女士们、先生们。// 再过一个多月美国将举行总统选举。有不少人问我如何看待美国大选后的中美关系？我告诉他们，不管谁出任美国下届总统，中国都希望与美国保持和发展建设性合作关系。// 同时，我们坚信，无论谁入主白宫，中美关系都要向前发展，历史的潮流不会逆转。这是因为：//

第一，中美两国从未像今天这样拥有广泛的共同利益。从维护世界和平与稳定，到应对日益增多的全球性经济和金融挑战，中美合作的领域和意义已远远超出双边范畴，正在全球产生越来越重要的影响。中美关系稳定发展符合两国人民的根本利益，也顺应时代潮流。//

第二，中美社会制度、发展水平和历史文化不同，两国在一些问题上存在分歧，这并不是什么可怕的事情。只要双方坚持在相互尊重的基础上开展平等对话协商，就能够逐步消除疑虑，加深互信。//

第三，中美两个民族都具有海纳百川、好学求新的品质。美国在短短200多年时间里，成为世界上最强大的国家，在经济、科技领域取得了辉煌成就。// 中国悠久的文明绵延5,000年不中断，在新的时代日益焕发出勃勃生机。不同的历史，同样精彩，靠什么？靠开放包容、博采众长。两个相互欣赏、相互学习的民族，也应该是友好相处、共同进步的民族。//

第四，中国的发展不会损害任何人，也不会威胁任何人。中国是国际体系的积极参与者和建设者，不是破坏者。// 中国是一个负责任的大国。中国经济对世界经济增长的贡献率已超过10%。中国积极参与解决朝鲜半岛核问题、伊朗核问题等重大国际和地区问题。中国愿与国际社会一道，共同应对金融动荡、能源紧张、粮食短缺、气候变化等全球性挑战。//

中美不是竞争对手，而是合作伙伴，也可以成为朋友。布什总统在出席北京奥运会期间对我说，美中关系不是一种你输我赢或你赢我输的关系，中国所得并不意味着美国所失，反之亦然。// 美国可以从中国的繁荣发展中获益，美中两国可以共同发展。我也高兴地看到，美国共和、民主两党阵营都重视中美关系。我认为，这体现了布什总统和美国两党阵营的战略眼光和政治智慧，也代表了全体美国人民的愿望。//

我要强调的是，中国政府历来重视发展中美关系。我们真诚希望，中美友好合作能够走出一条不同文化背景的大国和谐相处、共同发展的光明大道。//

女士们、先生们。我们即将迎来中国改革开放30周年和中美建交30周年。30年来，中国大地发生了翻天覆地的变化，中美关系也实现了巨大发展。// 这一切与其说是历史的巧合，不如说是历史的必然。富兰克林·罗斯福总统曾经说过，"时代要求我们大胆地相信，人类经过努力可以改变世界，可以达到新的、更美好的境界"。// 今天，我们有充分的理由期待和相信，一个世界上

最大的发展中国家和最强的发达国家,有足够的勇气和智慧跨越任何艰险和阻碍,继往开来,共创更加光明、美好的未来！//

谢谢大家！//

IV Guide to Interpreting

1. Passage 1 节选自 2008 年美国总统候选人奥巴马和麦凯恩关于美国金融复兴计划与政治决策思考的电视辩论录音。7,000 亿美元的金融援助尽管最终获得国会通过,但是面对席卷全球的金融海啸,如何应对给美国经济乃至全球经济所带来的前所未有的挑战是摆在政府决策人面前最为棘手的问题。在就这一问题进行的唇枪舌剑的激烈辩论中,奥巴马展现出他的非凡辩论天赋,有效地攻击了前任政府在经济政策上的败笔。众所周知,这次肆虐全球的金融海啸的罪魁祸首就是"次贷危机",这次危机也成为奥巴马当选的催化剂之一。译员应对这一点有充分的认识,然后才能正确理解和翻译两位总统候选人的观点和逻辑推理。

2. Passage 2 节选自 2008 年 9 月 7 日中国商务部部长陈德铭在中国—太平洋岛国经济发展合作论坛部长级会议上的讲话。听众是来自太平洋岛国的部长级官员,讲话人代表中国商务部陈述中国的商务政策,用语正式,内容丰富,涉及外交、双边贸易、投资合作、旅游开发、能源合作以及农业技术合作等方面的政策。口译训练之前,译员要准备好相关的语汇,尤其是与太平洋岛国相关的国家名、地名和地理方面的知识。同时也要了解中国对太平洋岛国的外经贸政策以及已出台的相关政策文件,做到"no surprises in interpreting"。

3. Passage 3 节选自国务院总理温家宝 2008 年 9 月 23 日在美国友好团体欢迎午宴上题为《继往开来,共创中美关系更加美好的明天》的演讲,具有鲜明的外交礼仪祝词的特征,体现出温总理一贯的讲话风格,即善于引经据典,用一些寓意深刻的汉语习语,逻辑性极强,但又不乏轻松愉快的表述。这无疑给译员的现场口译带来极大的挑战。因此平时多收集温总理的讲话录音,研究讲话人的言语风格,多积累一些典故的翻译知识,就显得十分必要了。在此篇口译训练之前,词汇热身必不可少,不仅要熟悉诸多专有名词的翻译,比如"美中关系全国委员会"、"美中贸易全国委员会"、"美国对外关系委员会"、"亚洲协会"、"美国商会"、"美国中国总商会"、"百人会"、"美中政策基金会"、"美国中国论坛"、"商业圆桌会议"和"华美协进社"等。还要熟悉一些富有中国文化特色的表达,例如"合则两利,斗则俱伤"、"国之交在于民相亲"等。另外，还要注意温总理讲话时喜欢用的"条分缕析"的手段，在做口译笔记训练时不妨就中美关系将向前发展的四条原因做一个针对性的练习。

V Highlight for Interpreting

Directions: Interpret the following sentences from English into Chinese or vice versa.

1. You know, we are at a defining moment in our history. Our nation is involved in two wars, and we are going through the worst financial crisis since the Great Depression.
2. So we have to move swiftly, and we have to move wisely. And I've put forward a series of proposals that make sure that we protect taxpayers as we engage in this important rescue effort.
3. No. 3, we've got to make sure that none of that money is going to pad CEO bank accounts or to promote golden parachutes. And, No. 4, we've got to make sure that we're helping homeowners, because the root problem here has to do with the foreclosures that are taking place all across the country.
4. But the point is, we have finally seen Republicans and Democrats sitting down and negotiating together and coming up with a package.
5. We did not set up a 21st-century regulatory framework to deal with these problems. And that in part has to do with an economic philosophy that says that regulation is always bad.
6. 我谨代表中国商务部，对部长级会议的召开表示热烈祝贺，对来自岛国的各位朋友表示热烈欢迎，对岛国政府和人民在中国汶川地震后所给予的同情和无私帮助表示衷心感谢。
7. 近年来，中国与太平洋岛国的友好关系进一步加强，高层互访更加频繁，合作领域不断扩大。
8. 当今世界正处于大变革、大调整之中，经济全球化深入发展，国与国相互依存日益紧密，求和平、谋发展、促合作成为不可阻挡的时代潮流。
9. 中国政府高度重视同太平洋岛国的友好合作关系。发展与太平洋岛国的友好合作关系不是中国的权宜之计，而是一项长期的战略决策。
10. 中国与太平洋岛国经济互补性强，合作潜力巨大，具有广阔的发展前景。只要双方共同努力，就一定能把中国和太平洋岛国的合作推向新的高度。

11. 一是中美两国合则两利，斗则俱伤；二是中美两国有合作的基础和共同的利益；三是中美合作有利于亚太地区的稳定，也有利于世界的和平与发展。
12. 双边贸易额从2003年的1,260亿美元增加到去年的3,020亿美元，五年中增长了近一倍半，中美互为第二大贸易伙伴。
13. "国之交在于民相亲"。中美关系的发展还体现在两国人民之间的友好感情不断加深。
14. 中美关系稳定发展符合两国人民的根本利益，也顺应时代潮流。
15. 中国悠久的文明绵延5,000年不中断，在新的时代日益焕发出勃勃生机。不同的历史，同样精彩，靠什么？靠开放包容、博采众长。两个相互欣赏、相互学习的民族，也应该是友好相处、共同进步的民族。
16. 中国愿与国际社会一道，共同应对金融动荡、能源紧张、粮食短缺、气候变化等全球性挑战。
17. 富兰克林·罗斯福总统曾经说过，"时代要求我们大胆地相信，人类经过努力可以改变世界，可以达到新的、更美好的境界"。
18. 今天，我们有充分的理由期待和相信，一个世界上最大的发展中国家和最强的发达国家，有足够的勇气和智慧跨越任何艰险和阻碍，继往开来，共创更加光明、美好的未来！

第11单元

营销与全球采购

Marketing & Global Sourcing

I Background Knowledge

Directions: Read the following English passages and then compare them with their Chinese equivalents.

Passage 1

Marketing, simply put, means the process of finding a need and then filling it. It sounds rather simple, but it is greatly affected by its environment. Marketing is an ongoing process of planning and executing the marketing mix (Product, Price, Place, Promotion, often referred to as the 4Ps) for products, services or ideas to create exchange between individuals and organizations.

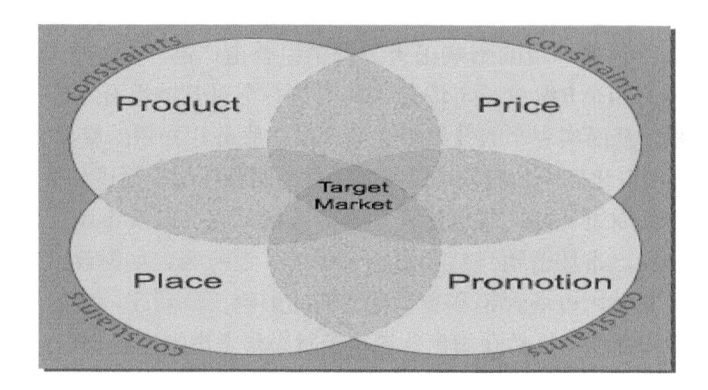

The marketing environment is so varied that we can think of it as four different environments, described briefly below:

The first is the proximate environment, which includes the other departments in the firm and the other firms with which the marketing operation has direct contact. Marketing naturally affects the other activities of the firm, such as finance, accounting, production, and personnel, and is also affected by them. The firm competes and cooperates with other firms in the environment, and obviously these other firms must be considered when marketing decisions are made.

The second is called the socio-cultural environment. Market, by definition, reflects what people want, and that in return is a reflection of our society and culture. Marketing and society have always been related, and social trends as the human rights movement, environmentalism, and consumerism have a heavy impact on how marketing is practiced and how it performs.

The third is the economic environment. Marketing is an economic phenomenon. It benefits from the country's economic well-being and also contributes to it. The two are so closely bound together that marketers must always keep a sharp eye on the economy.

The last is the public environment. More and more, every day, marketing is regulated. It faces thousands of regulations issued by dozens of local and central regulatory agencies. Marketing managers must not only make their decisions within this intricate framework, but also consider the possible impact of their decisions on future regulatory activity. Yet it is a mistake to regard regulation only as a burden. The wise marketer sees it as simply another alteration of the marketplace, giving rise to as many opportunities as problems.

市场营销，简而言之，指的是找到客户的需要然后满足它。这听起来很简单，但市场营销受环境的影响很大。营销组合由产品、价格、渠道和促销，即人们常说的四个P组成，市场营销其实是一个对营销组合不断进行计划和实施的过程，从而实现个人及组织之间产品、服务和知识的交换。

营销环境变化万千，我们可以将其考虑为四种环境，简述如下：

第一个是周边环境，它包括公司内的其他部门，以及市场营销操作中直接接触的公司。市场营销自然会影响公司的其他行为，如财政、会计、生产和人事等，同时，市场营销本身也受它们的影响。公司在一定的环境中与其他公司竞争和合作，显然在作出营销决策时必须考虑到这些公司。

第二个是社会文化环境。从定义看，市场反映人们的需要，也就反映出我们的社会和文化。市场营销始终与社会相联。人权运动、环境保护主义、用户至上主义等社会倾向都对营销的实践和操作有很大的影响。

第三是经济环境。市场营销是一个经济现象。它受惠于国家的经济福利，也为其做出贡献。市场营销和经济联系紧密，营销人员必须密切关注经济。

最后是公共环境。市场营销每天都要受到越来越多的管制。它面对的是从地方到中央数十个部门所确立的数千个规章。营销经理不仅必须在这个复杂的框架内进行决策，还要考虑到这些决策可能对未来管制行为的影响。不过，只将规章视为负担是错误的。明智的营销者将规章看作是市场的一种变更，在带来麻烦的同时，也带来同样多的机会。

Passage 2

Marketing management is the process of analyzing, planning, implementing, coordinating, and controlling programs for the conception, pricing, promotion, and distribution of products, services, and ideas designed to create and maintain beneficial exchanges with target markets. Thus, the marketing management process involves the following steps:

Monitor and evaluate potential threats and opportunities in the external environment, including those shaped by market, competitive, social, economic and political/legal forces;

Assist in the development of corporate and business unit strategies;

Develop marketing objectives and a strategic marketing program—including specification of the controllable components of products, price, promotion, and place (distribution)—for a given product-market entry. These must fit the constraints of corporate and business-level strategies;

Implement, monitor, and control the strategic marketing program over time, making adjustments when performance falls short of objectives.

营销管理指的是通过对产品、服务和概念的酝酿、定价、推广和经销等程序进行分析、策划、实施、协调和控制以创造和保持与目标市场有益沟通的过程。因此，营销管理包括以下几个步骤：

监督和评估外部环境中潜在的风险和机遇，包括那些由市场、竞争、社会、经济以及政治或法律因素所形成的风险和机遇；

协助公司和企业单位的战略发展；

为既定的产品市场进入开发出营销目标和战略营销计划，包括产品、价格、推广和分销等可控因素明细。这些都应与公司和企业层面的战略配合。

即时实施、监督和控制战略营销计划，在绩效未达标时做出调整。

商务口译

II Warm-up

1 **Directions:** Give the English equivalents of the following Chinese expressions.

销售代表	销售老手	无人能及	行之有效
年度会议	纷扰不断	思维敏捷	重演
开场白	变幻莫测	经年累月	

2 **Directions:** Give the Chinese equivalents of the following English expressions.

marketing mix	prospective partner
human rights movement	extract maximum value
consumerism	complete ownership
threat and opportunity	strategic alliance
potential threat	buy the market
product-market entry	prequalified vendor
corporate and business-level strategy	bidding process
look further afield	vulnerable to fluctuation
catalyst	availability
key criteria	primary ingredient
island hop	short-term saving
negative publicity	venture capital
weigh up	

III Passages for Interpreting

Passage 1

Directions: Listen to the passage and interpret from Chinese into English at the end of each segment.

朋友们：

欢迎出席"可柔丝纺织公司"销售代表的年度会议。// 身为本公司总裁，

第11单元　营销与全球采购

我想在此针对各位在本公司的角色问题以及有关做推销员的一些想法说几句话，作为这一周末会议的开场白；这次周末会议的议程是由我们最佳的研究小组所策划，其目的是让各位完全熟悉我们的新系列产品及新制造技术，同时还有一些销售老手提供有用的建议及经过证明有效的行销策略，以提升业绩。//

营销部门是本公司和其他企业及买主间最重要的联系部门之一。我们过去两年的销售纪录是各位努力工作及奉献的直接结果，我知道这个趋势还会持续许多年，而且我们若将纷扰不断的地方性商业景况及变幻莫测的国际贸易局势一并予以考虑的话，各位的纪录尤其难能可贵。//

在准备今晚的演说时，我想起了一位在我所认识的人中表现最杰出、同时也是这里最成功的销售员，我们之中只有从事这一行很久的人才会记得约翰逊·史密斯先生。// 我认为此人之所以会成功，要归因于一些重要观念：首先，史密斯先生的毅力相当惊人，他会全方位地开展工作，他会努力地全面了解买主的需求并提供他们最合意的货品。他对客户个别的关怀和照顾使客户们了解到，他所关切的是客户的福利与满意，而非仅是做买卖而已。//

他对公司产品及其制造程序方面的知识，在这个行业中无人能及。// 他思维敏捷，不过多半都会潜心地用在研究市场上，他会阅读所有能弄到手的有关他目前正在从事的特殊领域的资料。// 经年累月下来，这样的求知使得他对许多其他行业制造程序的各个方面都有所了解。// 但是，事情还不只如此，他还具有对人类心灵的理解力。所有的时事他全知道，还能针对新闻上的重大议题发表权威性的看法。他不是那种强记许多事实以备随时应用的人，而是一个热爱生命的人。//

我认为要做一个成功推销员的最重要部分，就是把你客户的需要放在第一位，对你所从事的行业有透彻的了解，而且先要待客户如朋友，再发展成生意上的伙伴。//

当各位想到自己的生意往来时，如果你也能把这些建议并入你的计划内，或许它们能行之有效。我希望大家都能成功，也希望我们已创的销售纪录能在明年重演。//

Passage 2

Directions: Listen to the following dialog and interpret from Chinese into English at the end of each segment.

I = Interviewer　C = Craig

I:　We keep hearing all about the globalization of markets and supply chains and

so on, but why has global sourcing suddenly become so widespread? //
C: Well, I think there are several factors, really. I mean, as companies expand internationally their outlook becomes increasingly global. What's more, hyper-competitive domestic markets have driven companies to look further afield in their search for competitive advantage. // Although I think the process has really been accelerated by rapid advances in IT and telecoms. That's been the real catalyst for change. //
I: And what's the great attraction? Why are companies so keen to source abroad? //
C: It depends on the circumstances of the company in question. It could be anything from better access to overseas markets, lower taxes, lower labor costs, quicker delivery or a combination of any of these. //
I: But it would be fair to say the financial benefits are the main incentive, wouldn't it? //
C: Yes, in most of the circumstances. Otherwise, I think few of the companies will be interested in it. Anyway, you know there is risk in it. //
I: For example? //
C: Well, the most common mistakes companies make is they only see the savings and don't bother to think about the effect on other key criterias [criteria] like quality and delivery. // A clothing company that only buys from Asian suppliers at low cost, for instance, will find that as labor rates increase over time, it'll have to island hop to find new low cost sites. // And this, of course, introduces uncertainty about quality—and that's critical for a clothing company. There are other possible risks as well. //
I: Such as? //
C: Well, such as negative publicity as a result of poor working conditions in the supplier's country. And, of course, there's always currency exchange risk. //
I: So how do you go about weighing up all these factors and choosing a supplier? //
C: It's crucial that companies know precisely what they're after from a supplier and that they fully understand their key selection criteria. // They need to be careful to define them and make sure they're measurable and then rank them. It's dangerous to select a particular supplier just because they happen to deliver outstanding performance in one objective such as cost or flexibility. //
I: So, having selected a prospective partner, what then? //
C: Well, then you have to negotiate how closely the two parties need to work to-

gether. // If it's going to be a long-term relationship, you need to discuss how much sharing of information and resources will be necessary to extract maximum value from the collaboration. The prospective partners need to sit down and decide on the best form for the relationship to take. //

I: And what's the most common form of this relationship? //

C: Well, once again it depends on individual circumstances. The relationship can be anything, I suppose, from complete ownership through strategic alliance to buying the market. //

I: Buying the market? //

C: That's when companies just publish their specifications and ask prequalified vendors to bid for the contract. // General Electric is currently doing $1 billion of business this way over the Internet. It's a short-term deal with almost no interaction with the supplier and the links of the bidding process is cut by half. But most importantly for companies like GE, order processing is $5—an order as opposed to $50 when it's done on paper. //

I: You mentioned strategic alliance. When do they make sense? //

C: Well, for an aircraft manufacturer like Boeing, for example, an alliance with its engine manufacturers is logical because of the complex interaction between the body of the aircraft and its engines. // And this complexity means everything has to be developed together. The arrangement also has the added bonus of reducing the financial risk of long-term development programs. //

I: And how about actually owning the supplier, then? When is that preferable? //

C: Well, companies take over suppliers when they're vulnerable to fluctuations in the availability of key supplies. // Take DuPont for example, the chemicals giant. Since oil is a primary ingredient of many of its products, DuPont is very much affected by the availability, and therefore cost, of oil. DuPont reduced these uncertainties by purchasing Conoco, its main oil supplier. //

I: Thus keeping its costs down. //

C: Possibly. Owning the supplier definitely increases financial control of the supply chain. But when you take the cost of acquisition into account, there are no short-term savings. //

I: So, all in all, does global sourcing make sense? //

C: Well, there are lots of very powerful benefits but managers have to consider all the main operational factors very carefully first. //

商务口译

Passage 3

Directions: Listen to the following interview and interpret alternatively from Chinese into English or vice versa at the end of each segment.

I= Interviewer S = Schultz

I: 其实在采访您之前,我看到很多有关于您和星巴克的报道。但是我们想知道,在1981年之前,您对咖啡了解多少? //

S: I did not know very much about coffee, and it was an experience that I had. Walking into Starbucks store for the first time in Seattle Washington, when I tasted it for the first time, I was really intrigued with a taste that I had never experienced before. I wanted to learn more about it. And that brought me to being able to meet the people behind Starbucks initially and ultimately going to work for Starbucks in 1982. //

I: 他答应您了吗? //

S: They turned me down. They turned me down because they didn't think they needed someone to come in and help them build Starbucks to another level. And I was very fortunate and very lucky that they had a change of mind and they did offer me a position and I moved from New York city to Seattle Washington. in September, (19)82, and joined Starbucks. //

I: 可是仅仅进入到星巴克两年的时间,您又要走了,什么原因? //

S: One year after I joined Starbucks, I went on a trip to Italy, a business trip, for Starbucks and while visiting Italy, I became enamoured, and curious, and intrigued with the phenomenon of the Italian coffee bar. Er, for example, there's [were] 1,500 coffee bars alone in the city of Milan and what I saw in the coffee bar was not just great coffee but the sense of community and human connection. Starbucks only sold pounds of coffee for home consumption. They never sold one cup of coffee. // It was a different business. It was a business created for home use. So I rushed back from Italy with tremendous enthusiasm and excitement and sat down with the founders of the company and said, "I've seen the future. The future is the Italian coffee bar and what we can create—the sense of community". // And as enthusiastic and excited as I was—that's how disappointed and non-interested they were. With the idea and they... once again, they turned me down. It was a disagreement about strategy. // He was the owner; I was the employee. He was the boss, and he was in charge and I had to follow that, but the way that I thought about this over a period of almost two years is that I couldn't allow this incredible opportunity that I saw in Italy and what I thought was an opportunity to create a different kind of business in America to go by. And so I guess you can say for almost two years, I just continued to be so frustrated and disappointed, and disappointed in myself that I wasn't taking action and that I found myself really unhappy and I had to kind of look myself in the mirror and say, "Ok, it's up to you. You are responsible (for) what you want to do." And that's why I decided to leave. //

I: 希望能自己开店来实现自己的理想。可是开门七件事：柴、米、油、盐、酱、醋、茶。当然最重要的应该是要有钱才能解决这一切。//

S: First of all, I had zero money. //

I: 没有钱的一个人敢去创业，这真是让人不可思议。//

S: So... but I knew that the way to start the business was to raise what in America is called "venture capital". And so, I wanted to go to private individual investors who could perhaps see the future with me and invest with me and I was a terrible salesman. In the first year, when we were trying to raise the money, I literally talked to 242 individual investors and about 98 percent of them turned me down. I meet many of those people today. I remind them. //

I: 他们拒绝你的理由是什么呢？//

S: At the time when I was trying to raise money for this new company, coffee consumption in America was down. We're gonna charge 2, 3, 4 dollars for a cup of coffee. We were gonna serve in a paper cup and also we were gonna call each drink by an Italian name that no American could pronounce. Would you have it invested? //

While think you are trying to raise money from a sophisticated investor, you have to create for them a very very bright picture, a vision of what the company is going to look like and ultimately what it is you are trying to accomplish. But you also obviously have to create an economic return. I should tell you this: the first business plan was—over a five-year period, I believe that we could open 100 stores. And things were going so badly that I actually rewrote the business plan and crossed out 100 and wrote 75 stores and even then, people said that there was no way that you were gonna open 75 stores in five years. It's impossible. And well, there's [are] 11,000 today. //

I think I mentioned to you earlier that when I walked into the Starbucks store for the first time, I had an emotional experience and that emotional experience was that I could feel and see that this rough diamond was not yet polished, but it had so many assets and so many unique characteristics that if positioned properly, could be something of extraordinary quality and so that gave me the idea and perhaps gave me the confidence. // But also I recognized that the Starbucks' name, the name itself I believed, was a magic and the people who were working for the company were so passionate about the coffee and the customer. And I believe that, if given the opportunity to grow the business and expand it reliterally and I wasn't just kidding—I really believed that we could make history. //

I: 但是我想后面还会有很多的风险在等待着您。//

S: Any time you are growing a company, I think, at this pace, there's risk attached to it. As we examine what has taken place over the years, in terms of number of new stores, number of new markets, the foundation of our success has been the cultural values of the company, so that the risk that we constantly address is... and sounds kind of trivial way is how do you get big and stay small, how do you maintain the local relevancy of the stores, how do you maintain the intimacy with the customer, how do you maintain trust with your people, and so what we've tried to do in every place that we've gone is to make sure that the fundamental foundation of what has built the company around the cultural values is in place first. //

I believe strongly, that people, irregardless of the differences, want to be part of something larger than themselves. They want to be part of something that they can go home at night, and share with their family and friends that they are proud to be part of. So we've created an environment both for our customers and our people. That is aspirational. // And I think also, when you are managing a company and managing people, it's really important, no matter where you are, if you are the CEO, or if you are the lowest person in the company, that everyone is treated respectfully, and there is no arrogance. And I think in the end of the day, as managers, and I would say this to future entrepreneurs and business people as well, you wanna demonstrate to your people not how much you know, but how much you care, and if you can do that in a genuine(ly) authentic way, that is gonna cross over all of the culture differences, because you want to build an emotional connection with people. // And I've learnt that even though there are differences, that emotional connection—there is a common language. Even though I am the chairman of the company, my main job is to ensure the fact that they are heard, that they are valued, and that they are supported. // What we've created as a company, I think, is a fantastic environment for our customers to both enjoy coffee itself and to experience the opportunity to share coffee with friends and family in a sense of community that exists in Starbucks. // We call that "The Third Place", this place between home and work. And as a result of what we've created and its universal appeal, we keep repeating it, because this is what customers all over the world want. // Now, having said that, we also are in the business of retail, which means we have to consistently provide new ideas, new innovation. But for me, I believe the foundation and the framework—what Starbucks does everyday, couple with innovation in our stores, is exactly the way to go. //

IV Guide to Interpreting

1. 市场营销组合（Marketing Mix）这一概念是由美国哈佛大学教授尼尔·博登（N. H. Borden）于1964年最早采用的，它确定了营销组合的12个要素。随后，理查德·克鲁维（Richard Clewett）教授把营销组合要素归纳为产品（Product）、定价（Price）、分销（Distribution）和促销（Promotion）。之后又有人提出6Ps的市场营销组合：产品（Product）、地点（Place）、价格（Price）、促销（Promotion）、权力（Power）和公共关系（Public Relations）。营销学大师菲利普·科特勒（Philip Kotler）新提出的4Ps：探查（Probing）、分割（Partitioning）即细分（Segmentation）、优先（Prioritizing）即目标选定（Targeting）、定位（Positioning），称为战略营销。他认为，战略营销计划过程必须先于战术性营销组合的制订，两者相加成了10Ps: 产品（Product）、地点（Place）、价格（Price）、促销（Promotion）、权力（Power）、公共关系（Public Relations）、探查（Probing）、分割（Partitioning）、优先（Prioritizing）、定位（Positioning）。到了20世纪90年代，又有人认为，6Ps组合是战术性组合，企业要有效地开展营销活动，首先要有为人们服务的正确的指导思想，又要有正确的战略性营销组合，即4Ps的指导。

2. Passage 1节选自台湾某公司总经理在年度销售代表会议上的致词。讲话人以一个典型案例来简要阐述市场部以及市场推销人员的角色和素质，语言简洁流畅，用词务实到位，没有太多花哨的用语。就内容而言，译员如果已经熟悉这个专题的有关知识，译起来应该没有多大的难度。

商务口译

3. Passage 2节选自BBC访谈节目，由Craig回答有关"全球采购"这一市场现象的问题。全球采购（global sourcing），又被称为跨国采购。其英文解释如下：Global sourcing is a term used to describe strategic sourcing in today's global setting. Most companies now include global sourcing as part of their procurement strategy. Global sourcing often aims to exploit global efficiencies in the delivery of a product or service. Common examples of globally-sourced products or services include: labor-intensive manufactured products produced using low-cost Chinese labor, call centers staffed with low-cost English-speaking workers in India, and IT work performed by low-cost programers in India and Eastern Europe. While these examples are examples of low-cost country sourcing, global sourcing is not limited to low-cost countries. 全球采购从广义上讲，指的是在全球范围内建立生产与运营链，采购质价比最高的原料、人力、技术、设备等，保证产品的总成本最低。在这篇专业性较强的练习中，对专业词汇的熟悉是译前准备必不可少的环节。此外，还要了解全球采购与全球化的关系、全球采购的具体步骤、全球采购的诸多益处，当然，还有全球采购的具体操作和潜在的风险。

4. Passage 3节选自中央电视台《对话》节目录音，是一段对星巴克董事长霍华德·舒尔茨（Howard Schultz）的访谈。英文由现场录音转写而来，里面有许多典型的口语表达，口语性很强，有的句子结构松散并且相当长。节目现场配有同声传译，而在做这篇材料的交替传译训练时应注意断句技巧。在节选内容里，舒尔茨先生幽默诙谐地讲述了他是如何将创新的市场理念运用于星巴克这个全球知名公司的经营和管理中的。了解该公司的一些背景知识非常重要。对于爱喝咖啡的人来说，星巴克是一个耳熟能详的名字，它最早来源于19世纪美国文坛杰出大师赫尔曼·梅尔维尔（Herman Melville）的经典著作《白鲸——莫比·迪克》中的主人公。1971年，杰拉德·鲍德温和戈登·波克在美国西雅图开设第一家咖啡豆和香料的专卖店——星巴克公司。

1987年，霍华德·舒尔茨斥资400万美元重组星巴克，推动了星巴克向意式咖啡馆的转型，并完全以自己的理念来经营星巴克，为公司注入了长足发展的动力。1992年6月26日，作为一家传统的咖啡连锁店，星巴克在美国号称"高科技公司摇篮"的纳斯达克（NASDAQ）成功上市。1996年8月，为了寻求更广阔的海外发展，舒尔茨飞到日本东京，亲自为第一家海外店督阵。之后，星巴克大力开拓亚洲市场，并进入中国大陆和台湾地区。经过10多年的发展，星巴克已从昔日西雅图一条小小的"美人鱼"

进化到今天遍布全球40多个国家和地区、连锁店达一万多家的"绿巨人"。星巴克的股价攀升了22倍，收益之高超过了通用电气、百事可乐、可口可乐、微软以及IBM等大型公司。今天，星巴克公司已成为北美地区一流的精制咖啡的零售商、烘烤商及一流品牌的拥有者，它的扩张速度让《财富》、《福布斯》等世界顶级商业杂志津津乐道。

V Highlight for Interpreting

Directions: Interpret the following sentences from Chinese into English or vice versa.

1. 这次周末会议的议程是由我们最佳的研究小组所策划，其目的是让各位完全熟悉我们的新系列产品及新制造技术，同时还有一些销售老手提供有用的建议及经过证明有效的行销策略，以提升业绩。
2. 史密斯先生的毅力相当惊人，他会全方位地开展工作，他会努力地全面了解买主的需求并提供他们最合意的货品。他对客户个别的关怀和照顾使客户们了解到，他所关切的是客户的福利与满意，而非仅是做买卖而已。
3. 我认为要做一个成功推销员的最重要部分，就是把你客户的需要放在第一位，对你所从事的行业有透彻的了解，而且先要待客户如朋友，再发展成生意上的伙伴。
4. I mean, as companies expand internationally their outlook becomes increasingly global. What's more, hypercompetitive domestic markets have driven companies to look further afield in their search for competitive advantage.
5. A clothing company that only buys from Asian suppliers at low cost, for instance, will find that as labor rates increase over time, it'll have to island hop to find new low cost sites.
6. They need to be careful to define them and make sure they're measurable and

then rank them. It's dangerous to select a particular supplier just because they happen to deliver outstanding performance in one objective such as cost or flexibility.
7. If it's going to be a long-term relationship, you need to discuss how much sharing of information and resources will be necessary to extract maximum value from the collaboration. The prospective partners need to sit down and decide on the best form for the relationship to take.
8. General Electric is currently doing $1 billion of business this way over the Internet. It's a short-term deal with almost no interaction with the supplier and the links of the bidding process is cut by half. But most importantly for companies like GE, order processing is $5—an order as opposed to $50 when it's done on paper.
9. Take DuPont for example, the chemicals giant. Since oil is a primary ingredient of many of its products, DuPont is very much affected by the availability, and therefore cost, of oil.
10. DuPont reduced these uncertainties by purchasing Conoco, its main oil supplier.

第12单元

人力资源管理

Human Resources Management

I Background Knowledge

Directions: Read the following English passages and then compare them with their Chinese equivalents.

Passage 1

Human resource is a kind of economic resource which exists in human's body in form of carriers such as physical condition, knowledge, skill, competence, personality and tendency. Similar to other resources, human resource also has qualities of materiality, possibility and finiteness.

Human resource has the following four characteristics: first, human resource is the "live" resource which is mobile, periodical and wearable; second, human resource is the major resource to make profit; third, human resource is a kind of strategic resource; fourth, human resource is limitless.

人力资源是存在于人的体能、知识、技能、能力、个性特征与倾向等载体中的经济资源。人力资源与其他资源一样也具有物质性、可能性和有限性。

人力资源具有以下四个特征：第一，人力资源是"活"的资源，它具有移动性、周期性和耐用性；第二，人力资源是创造利润的主要源泉；第三，人力资源是一种战略性资源；第四，人力资源是可以无限开发的资源。

Passage 2

Human resource management (HRM) is the strategic approach to the management of an organization's most valued assets—the people working there who individually and collectively contribute to the achievement of the objectives of the business. The terms "human resource management" and "human resources (HR)" have largely replaced the term "personnel management" as a description of the processes involved in managing people in organizations. Human resource management is evolving rapidly. Human resource management is both an academic theory and a business practice that addresses the theoretical and practical techniques of managing a workforce. The goal of human resource management is to help an organization meet strategic goals by attracting and maintaining employees, and also to manage them effectively.

人力资源管理（HRM）是对一个组织内最有价值的资产，即人进行管理的一种策略方法，从个人和集体的角度讲这些人都对公司目标的实现做出了贡献。"人力资源管理"和"人力资源（HR）"在很大程度上已经取代了"人员管理"这个词，用于描述机构内部对人员管理的过程。人力资源管理发展迅速，它既是一个学术理论又是一种商业做法，它探讨的是管理劳动力的理论和实践技巧。人力资源管理的目标是通过吸引、留住员工并对员工进行有效管理来帮助一个机构实现其战略目标。

II Warm-up

1 **Directions:** Give the English equivalents of the following Chinese expressions.

就业市场	附加福利
人力资源	员工留用
工作和生活平衡	收益递减规律
有效措施	双赢局面
人才竞争	咨询服务
人员更替	开明就业
职位空缺率	大力推广
薪酬制度	共同携手

2 **Directions:** Give the Chinese equivalents of the following English expressions.

legislative proposal	Auditor General
SHRM	rules-driven
snapshot	staffing system
rippling effect	externally and internally
strong resiliency	deputy head
unemployment rate	PSC
payroll employment	Public Service Employment
purchasing power	Act (PSEA)
wage earner	exclusive authority
knowledge-based economy	oversight capacity
post-secondary education	values-based
healthcare provider	assessment process
technical specialist	oversight function
thoughtful comment	accountability instrument
routine process	Staffing Mangement Account-
one-size-fits-all	ability Framework
beacon of opportunity	Commission for Public Com-
recruitment and staffing	plaints Against the RCMP
Public Service Modernization	audit plan
Act (PSMA)	external staffing
tight labor market	political partisanship
multiple objectives	Public Service Staffing Tribunal
fast-paced environment	at arm's length

III Passages for Interpreting

Passage 1

Directions: Listen to the passage and interpret from Chinese into English at the end of each segment.

邱教授，各位嘉宾，女士们、先生们： //

应邀在本次论坛上讲话我感到十分荣幸。首先，我必须感谢由香港浸会大学和香港董事学会组织的这次重要而有意义的活动，对他们在促进建立雇佣幸福员工的幸福公司中所表现出的激情我表示衷心的感谢。//

首先请允许我向大家介绍一下目前就业市场的大体状况，这会为我们的人力资源管理提供一个背景，然后我会重点讲一下工作和生活平衡的重要性，以及怎样把这个概念转变成有效措施来吸引和留住人才。//

我们的就业市场依然很活跃，但这种乐观的就业市场必然会导致激烈的人才竞争和人员更替的增加。// 人员更替及职位空缺率的增加已经给雇主和负责员工招聘及留用的人力资源专家提出了巨大的挑战。我相信你们中许多人已经在积极地审查薪酬制度，制定主动战略来吸引和留住人才。更高的工资和更好的附加福利会吸引更多的求职者，但这可能还不足以来留住人才。//

事实上，随着社会的进步，我们的雇员不仅仅关心自身的物质福利，他们也期望过一种平衡的生活，以便能有足够的时间关注其他各种需要。帮助雇员实现工作与生活之间的平衡已经成为一个越来越重要的员工留用策略。//

很显然，工作与生活的平衡是一个易于理解的概念。它可以被定义为能够使人有效地同时处理工作、家庭和社会多重责任的一种完美状态。// 实现这种平衡的人会感到很幸福，对工作和生活也会更加满意，因为他们能够根据自己不同的角色有效地履行其责任。另一方面，生活不平衡的人可能会感到倦怠，不能有效地处理各种生活任务。//

香港雇员一贯以勤奋而著称，我们的传统文化高度重视勤奋和毅力。许多人要长时间工作以处理繁重的工作，满足雇主高的期望。但是，长时间工作不一定会带来生产力的提高。// 一些研究已经证实，工作（时间）太长对雇员的身心有害。马萨诸塞大学做的一项研究发现，经常加班的工人受伤害或得病的几率要高 61%。一天工作超过 12 个小时会把这种风险提高三分之一以上。//

此外，有许多证据证明，工作时间的延长与健康问题有关，例如，高血压、心脏病、胃肠功能紊乱以及心理问题。工作时间越长，损坏或患病的风险就越大，雇员的积极性和生产力就越低。这就是收益递减规律。//

另外，如果雇主帮助其雇员实现工作和生活平衡的话，双方都会得到巨大的利益，创造一个双赢的局面。//

政府作为香港最大的雇主，自 1999 年以来就已经为雇员设立了一项类似的服务。政府委托第三方机构为政府雇员提供免费的咨询服务。服务范围包括电话和面对面的咨询服务以及推荐给合适的专业机构。这收到了雇员的积极的反馈。//

另一个帮助雇员实现工作生活平衡的有效策略是实行每周五天工作制，这

第 12 单元　人力资源管理

种制度有助于鼓舞员工士气，提高家庭生活质量，同时，能够节省雇主的运行成本。// 你们知道，自 2006 年 6 月份以来，政府已经率先分两个阶段实施了这一举措。我必须说，自从实施这一举措以来，不但生产力没有损失，而且没有增加额外支出。// 另一方面，员工的士气和积极性有了明显的提高。我有理由相信，女公务员的生育率也已经上升！我很高兴地注意到越来越多私营机构的雇主也正在仿效这一举措。//

政府现正致力于帮助公众来理解工作与生活平衡的概念。劳工署对雇主和人力资源经理提倡开明就业的做法，并鼓励在工作场所使用这种做法。另外，该署十分重视所有雇员的职业健康，并通过多方面的宣传和推广活动努力提高他们的安全和健康意识。// 我们正在大力推广在工作中进行锻炼和有效管理工作压力。在锻炼方面，该署已经出版了一套名为《更多锻炼，潇洒工作》的视频光盘和宣传册，介绍一些在办公室中就能做的简单锻炼来放松身体的不同部位。在工作压力方面，该署印制了一份名为《工作与压力》的小册子，介绍工作压力的常见来源和影响以及有效的预防措施。// 所有这些出版材料和视频光盘都能从该署免费获得，也可以从其网站主页上下载。在 2003 年到 2007 年间，共发放了九万多份这样的材料。//

鉴于政府和各个机构的共同努力，我完全相信更多的雇主会很快意识到帮助员工实现工作与生活平衡的重要性。我必须重申，实现工作与生活的平衡会给雇主和雇员带来双赢。这也是确保可观分红的一种投资。// 当雇员有一个平衡的生活时，他们就会愉快而又高效地工作，这样雇主就能招聘并留住最好的员工。因此，我想利用这次机会邀请在座的雇主、董事或人力资源专家与我们共同携手推动工作与生活平衡，创造一个既愉快又有活力的香港劳动力。//

谢谢大家！//

Passage 2

Directions: Listen to the passage and interpret from English into Chinese at the end of each segment.

Ladies and Gentlemen, //

This afternoon, I'd like to share some thoughts on the state of our nation's economy, the competitiveness of America's workforce, and a few legislative proposals SHRM members may be concerned about. But first, let me give you a snapshot of our nation's economy. //

Today, America's economy is healthy and resilient. It is one of the fastest growing among the industrialized nations, with a 3.1 percent GDP growth rate in 2006. Recently, we saw the rippling effects of the growing integration of the worldwide economy and the strong resiliency of United States financial markets and economy. //

Our country's unemployment rate remains low at 4.5 percent. That's more than one full percentage point lower than the average 5.7 percent unemployment rate of the 1990s. You can contrast this with Europe, where two countries in particular—France and Germany have unemployment rates near 9 percent. And their long-term unemployment is three times higher than the United States. //

Our economy has created 7.6 million new jobs since August 2003. That's more jobs than the European Union and Japan combined have created. Furthermore, the latest revisions to the payroll employment survey show that our country actually created one million more jobs over the past two years than had previously been estimated. //

America's workers are among the most productive of any major industrialized economy. And strong productivity growth in recent years is translating into higher wages and a higher standard of living. // Real hourly earnings for workers increased 2.2 percent over the past 12 months. That's an extra $1,279 of new purchasing power for the typical family of four with two wage earners. And overall compensation, including both wages and benefits, has increased 3 percent over the past 12 months. //

America's workforce is also characterized by its flexibility and mobility. That's important because our country is transitioning to a knowledge-based economy. But our country does face a skills gap. Two thirds of all the new jobs being created require higher skills and more education. // By definition, these jobs pay above average wages. But workers will require post-secondary education to access these opportunities. This means that workers with higher skills and educational levels are more in demand. Therefore the wages of these higher-skilled workers have risen much more quickly than those of lower-skilled and less-educated workers. //

Over the decade, end in 2014, for example, the US will need over three million healthcare providers and technical specialists, including physicians, therapists, and over 1.2 million registered nurses. // There will also be over three and a half million job openings in the education, training, and library occupations fields. // Other high growth fields include geospatial technology, biotechnology, nanotechnology, and advanced manufacturing. So, more than ever before, education, training, and retraining are the keys to future earnings. //

Today, our country has a workforce of over 150 million. And every year approximately 50 million workers change jobs, usually for better opportunities. Each year, the federal government spends nearly $15 billion on worker training and employment services. The Labor Department administers nearly $10 billion of this amount. The Department of Education spends the rest. And the private sector spends much more. //

Overall, the best way to build a brighter future and ensure America's competitiveness is not through bigger, more expensive government programs, but by empowering the individual. //

Now let me turn to another workforce issue that many workers and employers are concerned with. As many of you know, the Labor Department published a request for information regarding the Family and Medical Leave Act in December 2006. We received over 15,000 comments, many of which were from SHRM and SHRM members. // We appreciate all the data that was provided, your thoughtful comments and the time that it took to put this information together. // We will be weighing them carefully and listening to what you have to say in response to this routine request for information. This is part of the routine process that the Department goes through when a regulation has been on the books for a long period of time, in this case more than 10 years. //

Today, our country benefits because we give workers and employers the freedom to work out solutions to family and work balance issues, rather than imposing a one-size-fits-all approach. //

Whether it's through reforms to improve the workplace as a whole or protecting the rights of workers, this Administration will continue to promote strategies that emphasize the empowerment of the individual. By working together, we can continue to ensure that our nation's economy remains strong, competitive and the beacon of opportunity in the world. //

Thank you! //

Passage 3

Directions: Listen to the passage and interpret from English into Chinese at the end of each segment.

Ladies and Gentlemen, //

I am pleased to be here today to talk about modernizing human resources management and in particular, the recruitment and staffing component of public service modernization. As a former academic myself, I welcome the opportunity to exchange views with leading specialists in public administration, management and political science. //

The changes to recruitment and staffing undertaken in the Public Service Modernization Act (PSMA) are in response to a number of important challenges facing the public service: the public service workforce is aging, meaning more and more employees will be retiring. To replenish the workforce, the Public Service Human Resources Management Agency has estimated that the government will need to attract and hire up to 7,000 new employees each year. //

Competition for talents with the private sector and with other governments is already intense and will become even more so in an increasingly tight labor market. // Public service work has changed and is continuing to do so in response to the rapidly changing environment. The result is an increasing demand for knowledgabe workers, capable of dealing with complex issues and reconciling multiple objectives in an increasingly fast-paced environment. //

The previous system was unable to respond to these challenges. A number of studies and reports over the years have recommended changes to the framework. // In particular, the Auditor General pointed out in 2001 that the complex and rules-driven nature of the staffing system had become an obstacle to recruiting qualified applicants, given the challenges facing the public service. That needed to change. //

The government hopes to accomplish a number of objectives with the PSMA which Mr. Burton has outlined for you. In terms of recruitment and staffing, the Act is designed to improve the government's ability to attract and hire the people it needs—both externally and internally. //

For employees, it should lead to more transparent and faster staffing; for managers, greater flexibility to hire the right people. // In conjunction with this greater flexibility, the Act strengthens accountabilities and clarifies roles for deputy heads and their managers. //

One of the most important changes in the new regime is increased delegation. The PSC administers the Public Service Employment Act (PSEA) which applies to over 80 departments and agencies and grants us exclusive authority to make appointments to the core federal public service. //

In the past, we have delegated authorities for internal staffing to departments

第 12 单元　人力资源管理

and agencies but we have not delegated authorities for higher risk activities such as executive resourcing and external recruitment. //

With the full implementation of the new PSEA about seven months from now—in December 2005—we will also delegate most executive staffing and most authorities for external recruitment. // But the risk associated with these activities will remain. That is one reason we will need to increase our oversight capacity which I will discuss shortly. The Act provides that these various authorities be delegated to deputy heads, and through them, to the lowest level possible within the organization. //

Another important feature of the new regime is that it provides deputies with the flexibility to establish appointment processes and programs tailored to their own organizational needs—a direction that we've been moving towards for some time now. While the regime will continue to be values-based, it will no longer be rules-driven. The new legislation is less prescriptive and eliminates most of the procedural aspects of the current legislation. // This means that deputies have much more flexibility to develop the types of processes that best meet their organization's human resources plans and business plans. When establishing these processes and programs, deputies are expected to establish policies that respect the values of transparency, fairness and equity of access. //

A third important change is the new definition of merit set out in the Act. In the previous system, merit has generally been taken to mean the most qualified person based on a ranking derived from the assessment process. Under the new legislation, merit will have two components. // The first will be that the person meets the essential qualifications of the work. The second component allows managers to bring other factors into consideration for the appointment decision, such as asset qualifications, operational requirements and current and future organizational needs. The goal of this new definition of merit is to ensure that the person who is appointed is the right fit for the job. //

The passage of the Public Service Modernization Act has set the PSC on a new course—with the same mission but a clearer direction on changing how it is to be carried out. We will no longer be running parts of the staffing system. Instead, we will be overseeing it. //

As I have explained, the new legislation gives departments and agencies a greater role in hiring. But with this increased role comes accountability to the PSC.

And that means a shift in the PSC towards our oversight function. We will hold deputy heads accountable for respecting the values that underlie staffing in the public service. In turn, the PSC remains accountable to Parliament for maintaining the integrity of appointments in the public service. //

Over the last year, we have been working with departments and agencies to develop an appointment framework. This framework, which was recently approved by the Commission, will guide deputy heads in building their own staffing systems adapted to their needs. // It provides the essential policies that must be followed in their systems to respect legislative requirements and the core values. The framework encompasses high-level policies on key issues that arise during an appointment process. It also includes an appointment delegation and accountability instrument which identifies the authorities being delegated, the conditions of delegation and accountability. It also consists of other accountability tools and guides such as the Staffing Management Accountability Framework which sets out the expectations for a well managed appointment system that respects the new legislation. //

The PSC will hold deputies accountable through these instruments, as well as through audits and investigations. To do so, we have been increasing our audit capacity. We have already seen results with two reports released last year. // We are currently conducting a number of other audits including: an audit of the Industrial Security of Public Works and Government Services Canada; an audit of the Commission for Public Complaints Against the RCMP and an audit of the Canadian Space Agency. We are also undertaking a number of government-wide audits such as of staffing files. You can find our audit plan on our web-site. //

We are transforming our investigative function from one that is related to staffing appeals to one that will undertake investigations in the areas of external staffing, political partisanship and fraud. // As of the end of this year, the PSC will no longer accept staffing appeals. Much more of recourse will become the responsibility of deputy heads and the new Public Service Staffing Tribunal. //

To further separate the service delivery function from our strengthened oversight role, we have put in place a separate recruitment and service agency which will operate at arm's length from the Commission and report directly to me, the president and chief executive officer. // Under the new legislation, departments and agencies will have the flexibility to choose various options for recruitment; however, the new service agency is seeking to be the provider of choice for departments and agencies wishing to obtain such services. //

Thank you for your attention. I look forward to hearing your views on public service modernization. //

IV Guide to Interpreting

1. Passage 1 节选自 2008 年香港劳工及福利局负责人在一个人力资源专题论坛上的讲话稿。这是一篇专业性较强的讲话，在人力资源中有许多惯用的专业术语，例如，人员更替 (staff turnover)、薪酬制度 (remuneration package)、附加福利 (fringe benefit)、员工留用 (staff retention) 等，翻译时要尽量做到准确无误。其中"package"一词指的是一整套的计划、建议、制度等，如 package deal（一揽子交易）、package tour（包办旅游）、salary package（工资待遇）。在翻译"风险提高三分之一以上"这句话时要注意"提高到"与"提高（了）"在翻译时的区别。表示提高的结果时用介词"to"，表示提高的幅度时用介词 by，所以在 Passage 1 中把"提高三分之一以上"这句话译成"raised the risk by more than one third"。另外，在处理汉译英的长句时，要理清句子之间的关系，遵循汉语句子短小精干，英语句子逻辑严密的特点。在"另一个帮助雇员实现工作生活平衡的有效策略是实行每周五天工作制，这种制度有助于鼓舞员工士气……"的翻译中，译员可用"which"引导一个定语从句来译出句子的后半段，从而避免在英语中出现"制度"一词重复的现象。

2. Passage 2 节选自美国劳工部部长赵小兰在 2007 年人力资源管理学会会议上的讲话。有一些专业性较强的词汇需要译员在翻译之前予以注意，例如，"snapshot"本意是"快照"，在此引申为"简单描述，简单介绍"；在"their long-term unemployment is three times higher than the United States"中，根据上下文，"unemployment"应翻译为"失业人数"或"失业率"，而不是"失业"；"payroll"指的是薪金名册，即领工资或薪金的雇员名单，"payroll employment"在此译为"非农业就业人口"既符合上下文的意思又符合汉语的表达；又如句子"Two thirds of all the new jobs being created require higher skills and more education.""new"和"being created"有重复之意，因此在翻译时可以将后者省去不译；"So, more than ever before, education, training, and retraining are the keys to future earnings."这句话中的"more than ever before"放于英语句首起强调作用，但若放于汉语句首则显得有些突兀，因此应将其语序颠倒进行翻译，以便理解；文中"our

country"一词的在翻译时应注意变通，因为演讲者是美国本国人，可以说"我们国家"，但听众不一定都与演讲者来自同一个国家，因此译员在翻译时应将其具体的国别翻译出来；像"SHRM"这样的缩略语，并不是所有听众都知道其含义，所以在翻译时应将其全称翻译出来，便于听众理解；"Today, our country benefits because we..."这句话比较长，在翻译时应遵循汉语中原因在前、结果在后的表达习惯，先译原因，再译结果。

3. Passage 3 节选自加拿大公共服务委员会主席玛丽亚·芭拉朵思（Maria Barrados）2005 年在加拿大公共服务学院第 19 届年度大学研讨会上的讲话，因为听众对象均是这方面的专家和学者，因此讲话内容难度较大，有的句子结构复杂，书面语特色浓厚，专业性极强。译前上网查阅该委员会的有关背景和业务知识非常必要，而掌握一些核心缩略语则显得尤为重要。此外，在翻译时，不能局限于原文的句式结构，应根据需要做出适当调整。例如，在"As a former academic myself..."和"With the full implementation of the new PSEA about seven months from now..."的翻译中，为了使句子更加通顺，译员可将两个介词短语分别译成两句话。在翻译中为了使句子更加通顺，更加符合汉语的表达习惯，可以对词性进行适当的调整。例如，在"it provides deputies with the flexibility to establish appointment processes and programs tailored to their own organizational needs"的翻译中，为了表达的需要，可以将原本的名词"flexibility"翻译为副词"灵活地"来修饰后面的动词"establish"，意思没变，但表达变得更加流畅；在译第 11 段中的"under the new legislation"时，根据上下文的含义，前后两句应是对比关系，因此译员可以采用加词的策略，在前面添加"然而"或"但是"。不管是英译汉还是汉译英，译员要善于将句子与句子之间的关系恰当地翻译出来，以便听众理解。

V Highlight for Interpreting

Directions: Interpret the following sentences from Chinese into English or vice versa.

1. 人员更替及职位空缺率的增加已经给雇主和负责员工招聘及留用的人力资源专家提出了巨大的挑战。我相信你们中许多人已经在积极地审查薪酬制度，制定主动战略来吸引和留住人才。

2. 事实上，随着社会的进步，我们的雇员不仅仅关心自身的物质福利，他们也期望过一种平衡的生活，以便能有足够的时间关注其他各种需要。

第12单元 人力资源管理

3. 一些研究已经证实,工作时间太长对雇员的身心有害。马萨诸塞大学做的一项研究发现,经常加班的工人受伤害或得病的几率要高61%。一天工作超过12个小时会把这种风险提高三分之一以上。

4. 另一个帮助雇员实现工作生活平衡的有效策略是实行每周五天工作制,这种制度有助于鼓舞员工士气,提高家庭生活质量,同时,能够节省雇主的运行成本。

5. 我必须说,自从实施这一举措以来,不但生产力没有损失,而且没有增加额外支出。另一方面,员工的士气和积极性有了明显的提高。

6. 我必须重申,实现工作与生活的平衡会给雇主和雇员带来双赢。这也是确保可观分红的一种投资。当雇员有一个平衡的生活时,他们就会愉快而又高效地工作,这样雇主就能招聘并留住最好的员工。

7. Recently, we saw the rippling effects of the growing integration of the worldwide economy and the strong resiliency of United States financial markets and economy.

8. America's workers are among the most productive of any major industrialized economy. And strong productivity growth in recent years is translating into higher wages and a higher standard of living. Real hourly earnings for workers increased 2.2 percent over the past 12 months.

9. America's workforce is also characterized by its flexibility and mobility. That's important because our country is transitioning to a knowledge-based economy.

10. Overall, the best way to build a brighter future and ensure America's competitiveness is not through bigger, more expensive government programs, but by empowering the individual.

11. This is part of the routine process that the Department goes through when a regulation has been on the books for a long period of time, in this case more than 10 years.

12. As a former academic myself, I welcome the opportunity to exchange views with leading specialists in public administration, management and political science.

13. Competition for talents with the private sector and with other governments is already intense and will become even more so in an increasingly tight labor market.

14. In the past, we have delegated authorities for internal staffing to departments and agencies but we have not delegated authorities for higher risk activities such

as executive resourcing and external recruitment.
15. We are transforming our investigative function from one that is related to staffing appeals to one that will undertake investigations in the areas of external staffing, political partisanship and fraud.

第13单元

战略管理

Strategic Management

Background Knowledge

Directions: Read the following English passages and then compare them with their Chinese equivalents.

Passage 1

Strategic management is the art, science and craft of formulating, implementing and evaluating cross-functional decisions that will enable an organization to achieve its long-term objectives. It is the process of specifying the organization's mission, vision and objectives, developing policies and plans, often in terms of projects and programs, which are designed to achieve these objectives, and then allocating resources to implement the policies and plans, projects and programs. Strategic management seeks to coordinate and integrate the activities of the various functional areas of a business in order to achieve long-term organizational objectives. A balanced scorecard is often used to evaluate the overall performance of the business and its progress toward objectives.

Strategic management is the highest level of managerial activity. Strategies are typically planned, crafted or guided by the Chief Executive Officer, approved or authorized by the Board of Directors, and then implemented under the supervision of the organization's top management team or senior executives. Strategic management provides overall direction to the enterprise and is closely related to the field of Organization Studies. In the field of business administration it is useful to talk about "strategic alignment" between the organization and its environment or "strategic consistency". There is strategic consistency when the actions of an organization are consistent with the expectations of management, and these in turn are with the market and the context.

战略管理是企业为了实现其长期目标而制定、执行和评估跨部门决策的艺术、科学和工艺。它是厘清公司使命、远景和目标,以项目和行动计划等常用形式来发展为既定目标而设计的政策和计划,并分配资源以执行政策与计划,项目与行动计划的过程。战略管理的目的是有效协调和整合企业内各职能部门的活动,以实现企业的长期组织目标。平衡计分卡是常用的管理工具,用以衡量企业整体绩效以及明确进度。

战略管理是最高级别的管理活动。首席执行官经董事会的授权和同意对组织的战略进行规划、加工和指引。然后,该战略在组织的最高领导团队或者高管的监督下执行。战略管理能为组织的发展掌舵,它也是一门类似于组织学的学科。在商业管理领域,对组织和大环境之间的"战略协同",或者"战略一致性"的谈论是很有效的。所谓一致性,指的是组织的行为与管理层的期望一致,而管理层的期望与市场和大环境一致。

Passage 2

Specifying Strategic Goals of the Organization

First, the organization needs to identify its strategic goals and map a strategic planning with them. A process of evaluation, approval and amendment (if necessary) will be completed on the draft of the strategic planning to finalize the plan. Indeed, the very first step is to identify the strategic goals of the organization. The specification will start from a status quo analysis of the organization.

Very often organizations will use SWOT to carry out the analysis. SWOT means strength, weakness, opportunity and threat of the organization. Based on the analysis, organizations can make decision if this is the right time for change in the coming three or five years, depending on the cycle of your strategic planning. If the decision is negative, will the leaders or shareholders be happy? If the answer is positive, then the organization can maintain its existing strategy and not change. If the answer is negative, then the organization will have to dive deep into the analysis and generate a plan for change. The plan has to be detailed and comparative. If you side with change, what differences will it bring to the organization? Are they appealing to the management of the organization? When the decision is made and written into documents, a strategic goal is formed.

确定组织机构战略目标的步骤

首先一个组织机构需要确定战略目标,然后制定配套的战略规划,最后对战略规划文本进行评估、审批,如果有需要的话还要进行修改,然后再定稿。其中第一个步骤是要确定企业的战略目标。确定战略目标的第一步是对企业现状进行分析。

最常见的是进行 SWOT 分析,所谓 SWOT 分析就是分析企业的优势、劣势、机会和威胁,然后基于分析的结果给出一个判断,主要是考虑在这样一个分析结果下,在未来的三至五年(根据你制定战略规划的周期长短)是否是进行变革的好时机,如果企业不进行变革,那么企业的领导者或者股东们会不会满意?如果满意的话,就保持企业现有战略,不做变革;如果不满意,那么就得深入研究分析结果并制定变革计划,而这计划必须是具体和有比较性的。如果你拥护变革,那么就要确定变革能给组织机构带来什么不同,变革是否对机构管理有吸引力?一旦做出变革的决定并把它写成正式的文件,一个战略目标就形成了。

II Warm-up

1 Directions: Give the English equivalents of the following Chinese expressions.

百年老店	茁壮成长	居安思危
诚信	创业之本	东山再起
第一个吃螃蟹的人	诚信为基	狼来了
内控体系	危机感	
标准普尔	措手不及	

2 Directions: Give the Chinese equivalents of the following English expressions.

mission, vision and objective	Advisory Board
balanced scorecard	"more of the same"
strategic alignment	reach the limit of one's capacity
strategic consistency	oil and gas field
SWOT analysis	complex social and economic
BP (British Petroleum)	organism

商务口译

IPIC Annual Meeting	outreach
CIPO	average total pendency
Five-Year Strategic Plan	accessibility
dual mandate	turnaround time
fine-tuning performance measure	performance metric

III Passages for Interpreting

Passage 1

Directions: Listen to the passage and interpret from Chinese into English at the end of each segment.

　　平安的愿望是成为国际一流的金融保险集团，成为世界金融保险企业中的百年老店。历数一下世界上的百年企业，没有哪一家企业不是坚守诚信原则，在各种困境中走过来的，世界金融保险企业中的百年老店更是如此。平安要建成百年老店，就只有一条法则——诚信。//

　　平安是一个敢于创新的企业，平安是第一个吃螃蟹的人，遭螃蟹咬并不可怕，关键是我们被螃蟹咬了之后，能不能长记性，能不能从这件事情中吸取教训，总结经验。//

　　以前的市场，是风平浪静的小河，中国加入WTO，与我们竞争的是全球最著名的金融保险集团。今天的市场是一个大海，是一个以诚信为准则的市场经济的大海。//

　　今天的平安已经是大海里的一艘航空母舰，我们不仅是一艘守规则的航母，更是一艘抗风浪的航母，因为我们拥有优秀的销售队伍、杰出的职业经理、强大的技术平台、完善的内控体系、高效的管理系统、雄厚的资本实力、亚洲最好的资产质量和国内最好的保险服务品牌。// 去年，平安被评为中国唯一一家 AAA 级信誉的金融企业。在标准普尔刚刚发表的 "2002 全球大保险公司" 中，按照标准普尔的计算方式，平安是唯一入选的中国保险公司，而且，我们排在世界第 20 位。//

　　我有两个期望，一个是与同事们携起手来，在有生之年，将平安建设成为行业道德标准最高的保险企业，为建设平安百年老店奠定坚实的基础；另一个是让诚信在平安的每一个角落生根发芽，茁壮成长。诚信是我们的创业

之本，诚信是我们的立思之本，百年老店，诚信为基！//

Passage 2

Directions: Listen to the passage and interpret from English into Chinese at the end of each segment.

Good morning. Thank you for inviting BP[1] to contribute once again to the discussions of the Advisory Board.// It has been a fascinating experience for us to be a part of the extraordinary growth and development of Guangdong over the last few year(s). //

This is a province that has become a leader in many respects: //

a. leading China in a range of industries, from electronics to plastics, watches to footwear;

b. leading the program of reform and openness to world markets; and

c. leading in economic growth, with the Pearl River Delta being the fastest growing part of the fastest growing province in the fastest growing large economy in the world. //

So the question now is this: what next for Guangdong? How can we build on this success? Can we recreate the economic miracle of the last two decades in the years ahead? // Two overall messages come through clearly. The first is that some of this additional work needs to be radical in its nature. There comes a point in the growth of any organization or region when future development cannot be secured simply by "more of the same". New approaches, new solutions and new thinking are required. //

This is the case, for example, when a manufacturing company has reached the limits of its capacity. It has to invest in new plant if it is to continue growing strongly. // This was the case for BP a few years ago—our established oil and gas fields had become mature, and we needed to discover new ones in order to maintain strong growth. //

Similarly for Guangdong Province. The record has been a proud one, but now new engines of growth are needed for the future. //

The second general message is that future growth must be "sustainable"—

---

1 British Petroleum Co.Ltd.

商务口译

which means ensuring that Guangdong has the business environment, workforce and external relationships to sustain its prosperity long term. //

So keeping those two principles in mind, let me pick out some of the main priorities. //

First, the role of cities. Guangdong is a beneficiary of globalization, and as the globalization writer Saskia Sassen puts it: "The work of globalization goes on in cities." Nowhere is that more true than in Guangdong, where people have poured into the major cities over the past two decades. Guanzhou alone is now home to nearly 10 million people. With China's accession to the WTO and improvements in agricultural efficiency, many more people are bound to move from the country to the city in the next few years. //

But cities are not merely dormitories. They are complex social and economic organisms. And if cities are to be engines of growth, they require good planning and high quality services. // For a healthy and motivated workforce, strong public services are required, such as education, health care, housing and transportation. //And for competitive enterprises, good business services are required, such as financial, professional and communication services. //

In Guangdong, we need to ensure that the planning of cities anticipates population growth rather than falling behind it. //

In Guangzhou, in particular, such a change is being made, with the movement of factories to the edge of town, the development of residential communities and the redevelopment of the center. This is a massive undertaking and shows a vision for the cities of tomorrow and serves as a role model for other cities. //

BP is already engaged in this process, partnering with Petro China in a joint venture which is developing a network of dual branded petrol retail sites—we have approx. 350 such sites already—to support the growth of automobile transportation in Guangdong's major cities. //

Passage 3

Directions: Listen to the passage and interpret from Chinese into English at the end of each segment.

10年来我天天思考的都是失败，对成功视而不见，也没有什么荣誉感、自豪感，而是危机感。// 也许是这样才存活了10年。我们大家要一起来想，

第 13 单元　战略管理

怎样才能活下去，也许才能存活得久一些。失败这一天是一定会到来，大家要准备迎接，这是我从不动摇的看法，这是历史规律。//

目前情况下，我认为我们公司从上到下还没有真正认识到危机，那么当危机来临的时刻，我们可能是措手不及的。我们是不是已经麻木？是不是头脑里已经没有危机这根弦了？是不是已经没有自我批判能力或者已经很少了？// 那么，如果四面出现危机时，那我们可能是真没有办法了。那我们现在不能研究出出现危机时的应对方法和措施来，我们就不可能持续活下去。//

在当前情况下，我们一定要居安思危，一定要看到可能要出现的危机。大家知道，有个是世界上第一流的公司，确实了不起，但去年说下来就下来了，眨眼之间这个公司就几乎崩溃了。当然，他们有很好的基础研究，有良好的技术储备，他们还能东山再起。最多这两年衰退一下，过两年又会世界领先。// 而华为有什么呢？我们没有人家雄厚的基础，如果华为再没有良好的管理，那么真正的崩溃后，将来就会一无所有，再也不能复活。//

华为公司老喊狼来了。喊多了，大家有些不信了，但狼真的会来。// 今年我们要广泛展开对危机的讨论，讨论华为有什么危机，你的部门有什么危机，你的科室有什么危机，你的流程的那一点有什么危机，还能改进吗？还能提高人均效益吗？如果讨论清楚了，那我们可能就不死，就延续了我们的生命。// 怎样提高管理效率，我们每年都写了一些管理要点，这些要点能不能对你的工作有些改进？如果改进一点儿，我们就前进了。//

Passage 4

Directions: Listen to the passage and interpret from English into Chinese at the end of each segment.

Good afternoon. It is a pleasure for me to attend my 1st IPIC[1] Annual Meeting, and indeed a pleasure and honor to have been appointed CEO of CIPO. // Our Five-Year Strategic Plan for the period of 2007-2012 is a key step in outlining how CIPO will improve our administration of the Intellectual Property (IP) regime and better enable innovators and creators to more effectively use the IP regime to enhance their performance, as well as that of the Canadian economy. // This is the dual mandate for CIPO. // We are now in the process of fine-tuning performance measures for the Strategic Plan and will publish it on our website and share it with you no later than January 2008. //

1　Intellectual Property Institute of Canada

商务口译

In preparing this plan, we listened to your ideas and expectations as well as those of other key clients, staff, partners and stakeholders—we thought about our environment and opportunities—and we translated this into specific directions and outcomes. //

I would like to take this opportunity to thank you for your input, and also recognize the leadership of David Tobin as he led this effort this past year. //

In moving forward, we will focus on five strategic directions to achieve our vision of becoming a leading intellectual property office. These five directions are:

a. client services (managing the granting of IP rights);

b. outreach—these two together constitute the core of our business;

c. the IP administrative framework;

d. our efforts on the international front; and

e. our people. //

These last three are fundamental to achieving success in our core business. Further, to become a leading IPO we must continue to provide:

a. quality examination in all product lines;

b. access to well-trained and knowledgeable staff;

c. comprehensive online services; and

d. we must be proactive in our service offerings and in improving legislation. //

Our 2007-2008 Business Plan, now available on our website for the first time (and copies in the room) articulates in detail how we will go about increasing efficiencies in order to support increased productivity, and to make progress on our Strategic Plan. // These two plans are closely linked. The activities highlighted in our Business Plan in this bridge year represent our core-functions and Year 1 delivery of our Five-Year Strategic Plan. // In addition to tracking our progress on implementing the key activities in our Business Plan, we are currently fine-tuning performance measures that will help us assess our performance on achieving our Strategic Plan. // Some of these longer-term measures include:

a. average total pendency—in order to track improvements in the average time required to process an application.

b. client satisfaction with CIPO's service standards—in order to assess whether or not CIPO is performing up to our clients' expectations. //

We look forward to sharing these measures and to keeping you updated on our performance. // As evidence of our desire to build in this area, we intend to begin publishing, starting on a semi-annual basis, operational performance statistics so that you too can track our performance over time. //

CIPO will also continue the work it is doing to address clients' evolving needs and priorities by progressing on the three main service improvement areas identified in its 2005 National Client Survey—communications, accessibility, and turnaround times. //

Let me conclude by reminding you that: CIPO as an organization has sound fundamentals—we understand and are delivering well on our core business; we will continue to look for ways to improve CIPO's focus and to pursue our assigned mandate; we will strive for continuous improvement of services based on client feedback, offerings from other IP offices worldwide, and technological advances over time; we will use our strategic and management performance metrics to measure how well we are staying on track; and we will continue to build on already solid client relationships. //

I look forward to working with you. Thank you for your attention. //

IV Guide to Interpreting

1. Passage 1 的语言优美、生动，并且用词形象。口译时主要应考虑因文化差异而造成的对比喻的理解障碍。例如，译"百年老店"、"航空母舰"和"吃螃蟹的人"时，译员需要做解释和概念转换才能起到同样的效果。

2. Passage 2 相对比较简单。演讲的背景是广东省省长顾问咨询会，主题是广东省的发展战略。因此，对译员的挑战主要在于要译出有中国特色的用语，而不在于对专业词汇的理解。以下面的几句为例："more of the same"字面上的意思是"更多同样的东西"，但是这样直译将会是无效的翻译。译者如果对其进行更深层次的加工，就能得出"规模效应"这一更为贴切的翻译。又如"The work of globalization goes on in cities."如果直接译成"全球化的工作在城市里进行"，就没能真正解释全球化和城市的关系，而译成"全球化要从城市抓起"则更符合听众的理解水平。

3. 和 Passage 1 相比，Passage 3 的讲演者使用的语言更通俗，逻辑也不太强。这意味着译员要把握好话里话外的声音，进行逻辑的修复才能翻译。试举两例："我天天思考的都是失败"，实际上他思考的是"失败的可能性"；还有，"华为公司老喊狼来了"，讲演者自己并不认为华为是在喊"狼来了"，而是有人这样认为。这些信息需要译员进行补充，听众才能明白。

4. Passage 4 文章节选自加拿大知识产权局新任局长 2007 年的工作报告，语言较为专业和难懂，在口译过程中除了要熟悉知识产权方面的专业词汇

商务口译

外，还要重点准备战略管理方面的词汇。英译汉时，在许多情况下译员会被一些貌似简单的英文用法所迷惑，翻译时要注意运用补充的方法，多用汉语中的动词词组予以补充说明。

V Highlight for Interpreting

Directions: Interpret the following sentences from Chinese into English or vice versa.

1. 平安是第一个吃螃蟹的人，遭螃蟹咬并不可怕，关键是我们被螃蟹咬了之后，能不能长记性，能不能从这件事情中吸取教训，总结经验。
2. 今天的市场是一个大海，是一个以诚信为准则的市场经济的大海。
3. 今天的平安已经是大海里的一艘航空母舰，我们不仅是一艘守规则的航母，更是一艘抗风浪的航母。
4. 在当前情况下，我们一定要居安思危，一定要看到可能要出现的危机。
5. 华为公司老喊狼来了。喊多了，大家有些不信了，但狼真的会来。
6. This is a province that is leading in economic growth, with the Pearl River Delta being the fastest growing part of the fastest growing province in the fastest growing large economy in the world.
7. Two overall messages come through clearly.
8. There comes a point in the growth of any organization or region when future development cannot be secured simply by "more of the same".
9. The record has been a proud one, but now new engines of growth are needed for the future.
10. In preparing this plan, we listened to your ideas and expectations as well as those of other key clients, staff, partners and stakeholders—we thought about our environment and opportunities—and we translated this into specific directions and outcomes.

第14单元

交通与物流

Transportation & Logistics

1 Background Knowledge

Directions: Read the following English passages and then compare them with their Chinese equivalents.

Passage 1

What is logistics? Some people define it very generally and briefly, saying, e.g. "logistics is support"; others give extensively long and precise definitions, which run for pages. There are almost as many definitions of logistics as the number of books written on the subject. This, to some extent, is also reflecting the very characteristics of logistics, which is undergoing a constant evolution of itself during the recent decades. A widely adopted textbook defines logistics management as follows: "The process of planning, implementing and controlling the efficient, effective flow and storage of goods, services, and related information from point of origin to point of consumption for the purpose of conforming to customer requirements."

What is Supply Chain Management (SCM)? Starting from the late 1980s, logistics has been extended to cover a wider range of interest and activities. Such an enlarged concept and practice is called Supply Chain Management. A typical definition of Supply Chain Management is the following: "A supply chain is a network of facilities and distribution options that performs the functions of procurement of materials, transformation of these materials into intermediate and finished products, and the distribution of these finished products to customers."

什么是物流？ 有些人将"物流"一词界定得非常宽泛和简洁，比如说：

"物流即支持"。另外一些人给的定义精确却冗长,要用几页纸来说明。"物流"一词定义之多,几乎与讨论物流书籍的数量相当。在某种程度上,这种现象正好反映了物流的特点,即在最近几十年间一直在不断演变。在一本人们广泛使用的教材中,物流管理被定义为:"以满足客户需求为目的,为提高产品、服务和相关信息从起始点到消费点的流动和储存的效率和效益,而对其进行计划、执行和控制的过程。"

什么是供应链管理(SCM)? 从二十世纪八十年代末开始,物流的外延有所扩展,从而包含了一系列更为广泛的活动。这个延伸的理念与做法被称为供应链管理。供应链管理的典型定义如下:"供应链是执行采购原材料,将它们转换为中间产品和成品,并将成品销售到用户的设施与分配网络。"

Passage 2

Modern logistical activities are no longer limited to passive storage and transportation. It involves systemic operations, including transportation supports, warehousing, packaging, loading, distribution and processing, which will all contribute to the overall performance. After several years' effort, China has now seen significant developments in logistical infrastructure and equipment, such as traffic transportation, storage facilities, information communication, goods packaging and handling. This provides infrastructural foundations for developing logistical activities. Developments of distribution centers, merchandise supplier delivery and third-party logistics have all improved China's logistics industry in recent years. Governments of the largest cities, such as Beijing, Shanghai, Guangzhou, Shenzhen and Tianjin, are all keen to develop regional logistical industries, and most of them have already established corresponding planning and policies to promote local logistical development.

With the explosive growth in international investments and trades, as well as the increasing number of Chinese companies going overseas, there is enormous potential for China's logistics industry. In addition, development of e-commerce, the Development of the West Regions of China, demand from traditional industries and rural area development are all positive factors for China's logistics industry.

In light of the current situations, it is important to utilize and integrate the available resources in SMCs (Small and Medium Cities) of China. For example, individual proprietors in logistical businesses can be combined together into corporations of moderate sizes. Such specialized companies with larger-scale fleets can not only achieve scale economies, but also be capable of participating in packaging, loading, goods handling and distribution businesses. For those waterside cities, incorporated operators may even engage in freight shipping business. Cost minimization alone may not be sufficient to produce significant performance; information flow is also an important factor. Even many large logistics companies in China are facing this problem: failure of modernizing information. Of course, such informationalization projects will need substantial funding commitment, and there may not be any tangible results in the short term. But benefits to the bottom line should be relatively significant in the long term, and logistics in SMCs should also undertake such informationalization initiatives.

现代物流活动已不限于被动的储存和运输。它涉及到一系列系统化的操作，包括运输支持、仓储、包装、装货、分配和加工，所有这些都将影响物流的总体运行状况。经过几年的努力，中国的物流基础设施和设备状况有了显著改善，如交通运输、仓储设施、信息通讯、货物包装和处理。这在基础设施方面为物流活动的发展提供了基础。在最近几年，配送中心、商品供应商送货和第三方物流的发展都改善了中国物流业。北京、上海、广州、深圳和天津等大城市的政府都积极发展区域物流产业，其中大部分城市已经制定了相应的计划和政策，以促进当地物流业的发展。

随着国际投资和贸易爆炸性增长，以及越来越多的中国企业投身海外市场，中国的物流业发展面临着巨大的机会。此外，电子商务的发展、中国西部大开发、传统产业的需求和农村地区发展，这一切都构成了中国物流业发展的积极因素。

鉴于当前情况，利用和整合中国中小城市的现有资源十分重要。例如，物流行业的个体业主可以合并，组成中等规模企业。这种规模较大的专业公司不仅可以实现规模经济，而且还能够参与包装、装卸、货物处理和经销业务。而在那些滨水城市，已经合并的运营商甚至可以从事水上货物运输。仅仅减少成本可能不足以产生显著的成效，信息流通也是一个重要因素。即便是中国许多大型物流企业也都面临这样的问题：缺乏现代化的信息。当然，信息化工程将需要大量的资金，并在短期内可能不会有任何具体的成果。但是，从长远的角度看，最终的利润应该是相对显著的。中小型城市的物流产业也应该实施这种信息化的举措。

商务口译

II Warm-up

1 **Directions:** Give the English equivalents of the following Chinese expressions.

比雷埃夫斯港	港口腹地
联合国欧洲经济委员会	产业转移
传播和弘扬	大显身手
历史巨变	与国际接轨
集装箱吞吐量	班轮公司
标箱	挂靠中国港口
环境友好型	规划先行
资源节约型	适度超前
统筹规划	以港兴市
合理布局	以市促港
东部优先现代化	良性互动
西部大开发	中国—欧盟海运协定
中部崛起	金融资产缩水

2 **Directions:** Give the Chinese equivalents of the following English expressions.

logistical infrastructure	Modern Logistics and Freeport Development
distribution center	
third-party logistics	Bo'ao Forum for Asia (BFA)
SMCs (Small and Medium Cities)	a somber setting
cost minimization	globalization mandate
Canadian Transportation Agency	build-up of inventory
CILTNA	just-in-time
quasi-judicial tribunal	vast archipelago
federal jurisdiction	industrial powerhouse
ministerial advisory committee	center of economic gravity
deliver on our mandate	render obsolete the concept of...
hybrid organizational model	
caseload management efficiency	

第 14 单元　交通与物流

III Passages for Interpreting

Passage 1

Directions: Listen to the passage and interpret from Chinese into English at the end of each segment.

尊敬的希腊海运部部长帕帕里古拉斯先生，各位代表，各位嘉宾，女士们、先生们：//

上午好！//

非常高兴来到美丽的比雷埃夫斯港，参加在这里举行的联合国欧洲经济委员会的会议。首先，我要对会议主办单位的盛情邀请以及对东道主希腊政府为此次会议所作的周到安排，表示衷心的感谢。//

众所周知，北京刚刚举办了第 29 届奥运会，奥运会促进了中国与世界的交流，传播和弘扬了团结、友谊和公平竞争的奥林匹克精神。正如国际奥委会主席雅克·罗格所说，"通过本届奥运会，世界更多地了解了中国，中国更多地了解了世界。"// 许多到北京观看奥运比赛的国际友人亲眼目睹了中国的巨大变化，而这些巨变却是中国改革开放 30 年来尤其是过去 10 多年来发生的。// 在这历史巨变的进程中，中国的港口特别是沿海港口也不断发展壮大，取得了举世瞩目的成就，成为促使中国走向世界、世界走近中国的重要因素之一。在此，我愿应会议要求向各位介绍具有中国特色的港口业发展的情况和我们取得的经验。//

交通运输是中国重要的基础性产业之一，也是重要的服务业部门。中国 90% 以上的对外贸易货物是通过海运完成的。根据中国经济发展的需要，我们建立了以煤炭、石油、铁矿石和集装箱四大货类为主的专业化海港运输系统。// 在 1997 年到 2007 年的 10 年间，中国大陆港口集装箱吞吐量实现了从 1,000 万标箱增加到 1 亿标箱，年均增长 26%，包括上海港在内的 6 个港口已进入全球 20 大集装箱港口的行列。在港口吞吐量连续快速增长的过程中，中国港口的装卸效率也屡创世界记录，并且始终保持畅通，没有发生大的拥堵。//

目前，中国正在加快建设环境友好型、资源节约型社会。中国政府已把交通运输业列为优先发展的产业，按照统筹规划、合理布局的原则，建设便捷、畅通、高效、安全的综合运输体系。在未来一个时期，中国将进一步完善沿海沿江港口布局，扩大港口吞吐能力。// 同时，为推进"东部优先现代化"和"西部大开发"、"中部崛起"的战略，促进东部沿海地区与中西部地区的协调发展，我们将改善内河通航条件，积极推进江海联运。我们将更加重视港口物

商务口译

流效率和多式联运,特别是加强公路、铁路与港口的连接,实现促进港口腹地及更纵深内地经济发展的目标。//

回顾和审视中国港口发展的历程,我们感到积累了以下几点经验,愿与联合国欧经会各成员国的同事们分享://

一是坚持改革开放,努力驾驭经济全球化潮流,实现合作共赢。中国港口业和海运业的快速发展是经济全球化和中国改革开放的重要成果。// 一方面,经济全球化的深入发展促进了世界经济格局的调整和产业转移,中国迅速崛起为"世界工厂",中国经济的繁荣和对外贸易的长足发展,为中国港口和世界其他地方的港口提供了广阔的发展空间,当然也为世界海运业界提供了大显身手的舞台。// 另一方面,经过 30 年改革开放的实践,中国建立了符合中国国情、与国际接轨的具有中国特色的港口投融资和管理体制。中国政府鼓励民间资本和外资参与港口建设,并依法保护投资者的合法权益。我们履行加入世界贸易组织的承诺,不断扩大开放,大约有 60% 的沿海集装箱码头由外商参与投资和经营;全球前 20 大班轮公司均开辟了挂靠中国港口的国际航线,境外公司在中国海运市场的份额已经占到了 80%。//

二是坚持以需求为导向,规划先行,适度超前。// 中国的港口发展以国内国际的运输市场为导向,努力做到适应中国国民经济和社会的发展以及对外贸易的需要。我们制定了全国港口布局规划,以东部沿海和主要的内河——长江作为港口发展的重点,根据布局规划再制定出各个港口比较详细的总体规划。// 我们主张以港兴市、以市促港,大力发展临港产业;与此同时,坚持港口建设适度超前,达到与区域经济协调发展。//

三是充分发挥海港的桥梁纽带作用,实现沿海与内地经济良性互动。// 东部沿海港口既是中国对外开放的门户,也是中国沿海地区与中西部内陆地区经济发展的纽带和桥梁。中国政府按照已有规划正致力于建设长江三角洲、珠江三角洲、环渤海、东南沿海和西南沿海等五大沿海港口群,致力于发展煤炭、石油、铁矿石、集装箱、粮食、商品汽车、陆岛滚装和旅客运输等八大运输系统,覆盖中国东部和西南沿海地区并辐射所有中西部地区,为助推中西部经济社会发展、促进区域经济良性互动和平衡发展发挥着积极而有效的作用。//

四是坚持以科学发展观为指导,实现港航业健康可持续发展。// 中国政府鼓励采用节能减排技术,实现港口建设项目环境影响评价和节能评估,以促进港口与环境相协调,实现国际社会倡导的、也符合我们自身利益的可持续发展。中国鼓励先进科学技术在港口领域的应用,在港口装卸设备制造方面达到了国际领先水平。// 我们重视通过技术创新改善劳动者的工作条件,依法保护劳动者的合法权益。中国所有的国际航线港口都严格履行国际海事组织等有关

第 14 单元　交通与物流

国际组织制定的相关国际公约，确保港口安全运营，符合环保要求。//

女士们、先生们，本次会议的主题确定为"海港的作用——内陆与海运连接的桥梁"，这充分体现了联合国欧经委对海港在国际贸易运输及经济发展中所起重要作用的高度重视。// 欧洲大陆及附近海岛幅员辽阔，国家众多，而经济发展也像中国所在的远东地区一样并不十分平衡，但我们对海港在助推经济快速发展中不可替代的作用的认识是完全一致的。港口是许许多多国家走向海洋、走向世界的始发点，海运可以说是最先全球化的产业部门。// 中国政府十分重视并积极参与港口和海运领域的国际合作，我们与世界各主要海运国家和地区保持着良好的海运合作关系。中国—欧盟海运协定已于今年 3 月 1 日起正式生效，中方与希腊等欧洲国家已在海运、港口投资、造船、船舶检验等各个方面开展了实质性合作项目。//

我们清楚地看到，目前世界港口发展正共同面临气候变化加剧、世界经济增速放缓、全球金融资产缩水等严峻的挑战，各国单凭自己的智慧和力量不可能有效应对。// 我们希望通过这次会议能与各国充分交流和分享港口发展的经验，拓展并深化合作领域，共同迎接面临的挑战，为推动世界港口业的持续发展和全球经济的繁荣而不懈努力。// 同时，欢迎各位到中国去走走，去看看，为我们提出宝贵的意见。//

最后，预祝此次大会圆满成功。//

谢谢大家！//

Passage 2

Directions: Listen to the passage and interpret from English into Chinese at the end of each segment.

Good Evening, Ladies and Gentlemen. //

My name is John Scott and I have been a member of the Canadian Transportation Agency since this past spring. Just a few weeks ago, it was a great honour for me to be designated as the next Vice-Chair of the Agency, an appointment that will take effect when the term of my colleague, Gilles Dufault, ends early in the new year. //

Thank you for this opportunity to speak about the Agency—we very much believe that open and responsive communications, such as this presentation this evening, are critical to the Agency's success and to meeting our commitment to quality service. //

商务口译

In this fast-paced world, almost everyone—CILTNA members being a significant exception—takes transportation issues for granted. We hop on a plane to attend a meeting in another city. We take a train to work everyday. We drive a foreign-made car that was delivered to a Canadian port, then to a train, then to a truck and then to a dealer. All of this without a thought to how these transportation modes are managed for the public good. //

That's where the Canadian Transportation Agency comes in. And my comments this evening will be focused on two aspects of the Agency—who we are in 2007 and how some recent key legislative changes are impacting our direction into the future. // As you know, we are an independent, quasi-judicial tribunal that regulates air, marine and rail transport that fall under federal jurisdiction. The Agency oversees Canadian ownership and control requirements for the airline industry and is the federal licensing authority for air and rail carriers. We are also responsible for ensuring that undue obstacles to the mobility of persons with disabilities are removed from federally regulated transportation services and facilities. //

Being this country's most experienced tribunal of its kind, the Agency is of course well aware that change is never a finite matter, but rather a constant process—change is never-ending. As it has been, on several other occasions throughout its history, our organization is now at a crossroads, where we must imperatively choose the right path if we are to continue to effectively deliver on our mandate. // However, it is important to emphasize that whenever we undergo change, the Agency is always focused on a single strategic outcome, as enunciated in the Agency's 2006/2007 Performance Report tabled by the Minister of Transport, Infrastructure and Communities in the House of Commons on November 1, 2007. That stated outcome is "a fair and transparent economic regulatory regime that helps achieve a viable and accessible national transport system", and that is what we are evaluated against by Parliament. //

And to drive our achievement of that outcome in the years to come, there are new decision-makers and a new approach at the Agency. With the passage of amendments to the Canada Transportation Act this past summer, the Agency, on the decision-making side, will be made up of five, rather than seven, full-time members, now all being based in the National Capital Region. //

The new Chair and Chief Executive Officer, Geoffrey Hare, was appointed on January 25 of this year. Mr. Hare came to the Agency after a distinguished 25-year career in the Ontario public service in the areas of economic policy development and finance, including extensive experience in dealing with transportation issues. // Another new member, also appointed early this year, is Raymon Kaduck, an experienced air transportation economist who has served on ministerial advisory committees on trade policy and airline restructuring issues. //

As noted earlier I joined the Agency a few months ago and, shortly after that, Mark MacKeigan, most recently senior legal counsel with IATA and prior to that a lawyer with Nav Canada, was appointed to the Agency. // Our backgrounds are different but very complementary, and already, under the leadership of Geoff Hare, our collegiality and ability to be immediately accessible on the many issues facing the Agency has had an impact on our staff and the direction of the Agency. // And we, as new members are also very fortunate to have excellent transition guidance from former members, including the Agency's current Vice-Chair, Gilles Dufault, who will have spent a decade as a member of the Agency when he retires from the organization in early 2008, and also including Beaton Tulk, who has been an Agency member since 2002 and will also be leaving the Agency in 2008. //

As concerns the new approach to delivering on our mandate, a core internal change is being implemented by the Agency, namely a clear redefinition of our two primary business lines. One—Dispute Resolution and two—Industry Regulation and Determinations. // Of course, the Agency's specialized modal expertise in the air, rail and marine areas is still present in each of the two new branches within this hybrid organizational model. However, this more functional business delivery structure allows the Agency to make the best use of our people, our knowledge and our experience to respond to ever increasing and changing caseload demands. // Our intent is to make it easier for all our stakeholders to better understand the Agency and how we work. We want to facilitate their access to the Agency in a way which better assists us in processing their issues—which in the last year involved some 3,500 rulings across all transportation modes. //

The Agency's commitment to improving stakeholder access, achieving greater caseload management efficiencies and to faster rulings is a priority shared both by the Agency executive team and members. // As you can therefore well appreciate, "the times, they are a-changing" for transportation—one of the most dynamic sectors, CILTNA's sector, in our Canadian economy. Our Agency commitment and goal, as I have hopefully outlined in these comments, is to embrace those changes, while remaining true, in our regulatory role, to our core values of being responsive, effective, fair and transparent to help achieve an efficient and accessible transportation system for Canadians. //

Thank you. //

Passage 3

Directions: Listen to the passage and interpret from English into Chinese at the end of each segment.

Dear Friends, Distinguished Guests, Ladies and Gentlemen, //

I am delighted to add my welcome to those already expressed here for all the participants at this international seminar on "Modern Logistics and Freeport Development" sponsored jointly by the Bo'ao Forum for Asia, BFA, the Zhejiang Investment and Trade Symposium—with the full and active support of the Ningbo City government. //

As Chairman of the BFA, which was founded in February 2001 on the belief that our continent needed a Forum where Asians and their partners from other regions could discuss Asian concerns—economic and social, as well as political and cultural—in an Asian setting, indeed, I am proud to be part of this gathering of leaders in regional and global logistics cooperation. //

If interdependence is to develop to everyone's benefit, then it must be built on mutual trust, mutual support and mutual interests. The promotion of regional cooperation for mutually beneficial and sustained development is our principal reason for the establishment of the BFA. //

Our seminar takes place in a somber setting. All of China and much of the Asia-Pacific is still mourning the victims of last month's Sichuan Earthquake—this country's worst in 30 years. That great tragedy has naturally evoked worldwide compassion for the Chinese people. // I am sure we will in the course of our Seminar make a formal and collective gesture of sympathy and support. // Calamities and disasters are not unknown challenges to the people of Asia—historically, the crises caused by nature's destructive phenomena have helped to sharpen the spirit of caring, sharing and daring among Asians. //

And even sorrow leaves us with important object lessons. Certainly the Sichuan Earthquake—which impelled the Chinese government and the Chinese people to

第 14 单元　交通与物流

take heroic action to come to the aid of their stricken fellow citizens—should direct our priorities to the shared need to ensure that our national and regional logistics capabilities are equal to every contingency, whether natural or man-made. //

But I hope recalling the tragedy does not dim our appreciation of Ningbo—this evergreen and lovely city of Zhejiang Province—and one of the great logistics centers on China's eastern seaboard. // Ningbo—whose name translates into "calm waves"—is also an industrial powerhouse of the Yangtze River Delta and the whole East of China. //

At the 2008 BFA Annual Conference last 11-13 April, President Hu Jintao set a harmonious and optimistic tone by pledging China's continued reform and opening up, plus "interaction and cooperation among countries and business communities in Asia". The most dramatic happening that took place at the Annual Conference of the BFA was the highest level dialog between Chinese leader and Taiwan regional leader since 1949. // President Hu and Vincent Siew had a quiet, but highly publicized, one-on-one meeting at Bo'ao last 12 April, auguring better times for cross-straits relations—with anticipated economic and peace dividends for the Asia-Pacific region. //

Our seminar deals with the kind of day-to-day interdependence that globalization mandates—as well as the business opportunities opening up in our globalizing world. // As we know, logistics is that part of the supply chain that plans, controls, and carries out the efficient and effective forward and reverse flow and storage of goods, services, and related information between the point of origin and the point of consumption. // Balance and efficiency are the defining qualities of modern logistics management. On the one hand, factories must avoid crippling shortages of materials and components. On the other, factories must prevent costly build-up of inventories. //

The ideal solution to this industrial dilemma is the "just-in-time" (J-I-T) production and delivery system. // We all know that if a factory is to subsist on minimal inventories, it must rely on prompt, predictable and frequent deliveries of raw materials and components from suppliers arriving just before they become needed. //

Modernizing Ningbo's logistics facilities will mean greater assurances to its customers worldwide that they can rely on Ningbo's suppliers to deliver their goods at the strategic point in time of their need. Success in this effort will surely make this city a major link in the chain of economic strong points the East Asian states are building up. // What will work for Ningbo as a logistics center will equally work well for other similarly-endowed cities in the Philippines, Japan, India, Republic of

Korea, Ukraine, Europe, Africa and the Americas. //

At the macro-economic level, my own country—the Philippines—is investing a great deal of capital and human talent to link up the vast archipelago with regional markets and industrial powerhouses. // Only through these investments in logistics facilities and systems can the Philippines take advantage of its strategic location at the heart of East Asia—with easy and quick access to China, Japan, Republic of Korea, to the nine other Southeast Asian states, as well as to the rest of the world. //

Throughout East Asia, state-of-the-art logistics networks are being organized. The regional linkages that most of our port and hub cities are building will start to really pay off beginning in 2010 when China and the 10 ASEAN states complete consolidating their Free Trade Agreement (FTA)—which would become the world's largest in terms of markets and population. //

And the ASEAN-10 plus China FTA would only be the beginning. Certainly, Japan, India and the Republic of Korea—which are also negotiating a Free Trade Agreement with ASEAN—cannot resist joining such a huge potential market at their very doorstep. //

All our countries—from East to West, from North to South—should benefit from these investment, trade and networking opportunities that are emerging. //

Asians nowadays say that, more and more, the world's center of economic gravity is tilting to the Asia-Pacific region. I prefer to regard our world as now coming into balance—and in such a way as to make East and West so nearly equal as to render obsolete the concept of the two sides being in opposition or in conflict with each other. //

In our time, I have great hopes for the wave of economic interdependence and globalization to bring greater prosperity and social equity around the world. We must all regard seminars like this one as building bridges to link our respective countries and regions into effective logistic networks of mutual understanding and mutual prosperity. // This is the higher significance of this "International Seminar on Modern Logistics and Freeport Development". //

Thank you and Mabuhay—Best wishes to all! //

IV Guide to Interpreting

1. Passage 1 节选自 2008 年 9 月 17 日交通运输部副部长徐祖远在联合国欧

第 14 单元　交通与物流

洲经济委员会 (UNECE) 海港大会上的官方发言。译员在翻译之前应对交通和物流，尤其是中国港口业物流发展有一定的了解，要事先熟悉港口运输方面的词汇，比如"集装箱"、"吞吐量"、"船舶检验"等，以及地域方面的专有名词，比如"希腊比雷埃夫斯港"、"长三角"、"珠三角"、"环渤海"等，还要了解中国政府在优先发展交通运输业方面的有关政策。文章中讲话人通过回顾和审视中国港口发展的历程，向 UNECE 各成员国重点介绍我国在港口业发展方面的经验。在这篇练习材料中，可以针对性地训练第四段中的数字口译，也可以重点训练长段交传笔记，比如连续听译材料中有关中国经验的四个方面，从讲话人的分层讲述中抓核心信息，即"改革开放，合作共赢"、"以需求为导向，规划先行，适度超前"、"沿海与内地经济良性互动"、"科学发展，可持续发展"等，然后补充上其他辅助性信息。此外，还要针对性地对一些具有中国特色的用语进行翻译训练，比如"以港兴市，以市促港"、"科学发展观"、"环境友好型、资源节约型社会"等。

2. Passage 2 节选自 2007 年 11 月 26 日加拿大运输局官员约翰·斯科特 (John Scott) 在国际物流与运输学会（北美分会）(CILTNA) 上的演讲。作为刚刚被任命的副局长，讲话人向听众陈述了该局的战略决策和人事配置，承诺以开放和积极的态度完成管理任务，为客户提供一个"公平透明"、"高效率"和"无障碍"的管理机制。然后，他简要回顾了一下 2007 年度的工作状况，结合加拿大政府一些新的立法谈了如何调整该局的工作发展方向。本篇训练材料虽然专业性词汇不多，专业性难度不大，但是里面有许多与加拿大本土知识相关的内容，尤其是一些专有名词和人名。译员要很好地完成任务，最好事先上网浏览一下该组织的网站，收集相关的人事材料，熟悉其业务类型和核心价值观，以便达到"事半功倍"的效果。

3. 和 Passage 2 不同，Passage 3 虽是英文演讲，内容却与中国的交通物流密切相关。本篇节选自 2008 年 6 月 8 日菲律宾前总统、博鳌亚洲论坛（海南）理事长拉莫斯在博鳌亚洲论坛"现代物流与自由港发展"国际研讨会开幕式上的讲话。会议在浙江宁波召开，该讲话具有鲜明的时代特征。除了论及会议主题，讲话人还表现出了强烈的人文关怀，尤其是对会议召开不久前中国汶川大地震中的死难者表示了深切的哀悼和同情，因此译员在翻译时应注意语言风格的凝重与严肃。当然，事先收集博鳌亚洲论坛的有关知识，熟悉宁波的地理环境，了解大会的主题，进行充分的词汇热身等译前准备更是必不可少。

商务口译

Ⅴ Highlight for Interpreting

Directions: Interpret the following sentences from Chinese into English or vice versa.

1. 在此，我愿应会议要求向各位介绍具有中国特色的港口业发展的情况和我们取得的经验。
2. 在 1997 年到 2007 年的 10 年间，中国大陆港口集装箱吞吐量实现了从 1,000 万标箱增加到 1 亿标箱，年均增长 26%，包括上海港在内的 6 个港口已进入全球 20 大集装箱港口的行列。
3. 中国政府已把交通运输业列为优先发展的产业，按照统筹规划、合理布局的原则，建设便捷、畅通、高效、安全的综合运输体系。在未来一个时期，中国将进一步完善沿海沿江港口布局，扩大港口吞吐能力。
4. 我们履行加入世界贸易组织的承诺，不断扩大开放，大约有 60% 的沿海集装箱码头由外商参与投资和经营；全球前 20 大班轮公司均开辟了挂靠中国港口的国际航线，境外公司在中国海运市场的份额已经占到了 80%。
5. 我们主张以港兴市、以市促港，大力发展临港产业；与此同时，坚持港口建设适度超前，达到与区域经济协调发展。
6. 中国政府按照已有规划正致力于建设长江三角洲、珠江三角洲、环渤海、东南沿海和西南沿海等五大沿海港口群，致力于发展煤炭、石油、铁矿石、集装箱、粮食、商品汽车、陆岛滚装和旅客运输等八大运输系统，覆盖中国东部和西南沿海地区并辐射所有中西部地区，为助推中西部经济社会发展、促进区域经济良性互动和平衡发展发挥着积极而有效的作用。
7. Thank you for this opportunity to speak about the Agency—we very much believe that open and responsive communications, such as this presentation this evening, are critical to the Agency's success and to meeting our commitment to quality service.
8. As it has been, on several other occasions throughout its history, our organization is now at a crossroads, where we must imperatively choose the right path if we are to continue to effectively deliver on our mandate.
9. With the passage of amendments to the Canada Transportation Act this past summer, the Agency, on the decision-making side, will be made up of five, rather than seven, full-time members, now all being based in the National Capital Region.
10. As concerns the new approach to delivering on our mandate, a core internal

change is being implemented by the Agency, namely a clear redefinition of our two primary business lines.
11. Our Agency commitment and goal, as I have hopefully outlined in these comments, is to embrace those changes, while remaining true, in our regulatory role, to our core values of being responsive, effective, fair and transparent to help achieve an efficient and accessible transportation system for Canadians.
12. If interdependence is to develop to everyone's benefit, then it must be built on mutual trust, mutual support and mutual interests. The promotion of regional cooperation for mutually beneficial and sustained development is our principal reason for the establishment of the BFA.
13. Our seminar deals with the kind of day-to-day interdependence that globalization mandates—as well as the business opportunities opening up in our globalizing world.
14. The ideal solution to this industrial dilemma is the "just-in-time" (J-I-T) production and delivery system. We all know that if a factory is to subsist on minimal inventories, it must rely on prompt, predictable and frequent deliveries of raw materials and components from suppliers arriving just before they become needed.
15. Asians nowadays say that, more and more, the world's center of economic gravity is tilting to the Asia-Pacific region. I prefer to regard our world as now coming into balance—and in such a way as to make East and West so nearly equal as to render obsolete the concept of the two sides being in opposition or in conflict with each other.

第15单元

金融与证券

Finance & Securities

1 Background Knowledge

Directions: Read the following English passages and then compare them with their Chinese equivalents.

Passage 1

The field of finance refers to the concepts of time, money and risk and how they are interrelated. Banks are the main facilitators of funding through the provision of credit, although private equity, mutual funds, hedge funds, and other organizations have become important. Financial assets, known as investments, are financially managed with careful attention to financial risk management to control financial risk. Financial instruments allow many forms of securitized assets to be traded on securities exchanges such as stock exchanges, including debt such as bonds as well as equity in publicly-traded corporations.

An entity whose income exceeds its expenditure can lend or invest the excess income. On the other hand, an entity whose income is less than its expenditure can raise capital by borrowing or selling equity claims, decreasing its expenses, or increasing its income. The lender can find a borrower, through a financial intermediary such as a bank, or buy notes or bonds in the bond market. The lender receives interest, the borrower pays a higher interest than the lender receives, and the financial intermediary pockets the difference.

A bank aggregates the activities of many borrowers and lenders. A bank accepts deposits from lenders, on which it pays the interest. The bank then lends these deposits to borrowers. Banks allow borrowers and lenders of different sizes, to coordinate their activity. Banks are thus compensators of money flows in space.

Finance is used by individuals (personal finance), by governments (public finance), by businesses (corporate finance), as well as by a wide variety of organizations including schools and non-profit organizations. In general, the goals of each of the above activities are achieved through the use of appropriate financial instruments, with consideration to their institutional setting.

A specific example of corporate finance is the sale of stock by a company to institutional investors like investment banks, who in turn generally sell it to the public. The stock gives whoever owns it part ownership in that company. If you buy one share of XYZ Inc, and they have 100 shares outstanding (held by investors), you are 1/100 owner of that company. Of course, in return for the stock, the company receives cash, which it uses to expand its business in a process called "equity financing". Equity financing mixed with the sale of bonds (or any other debt financing) is called the company's capital structure.

Finance is one of the most important aspects of business management. Without proper financial planning a new enterprise is unlikely to be successful. Managing money (a liquid asset) is essential to ensure a secure future, both for the individual and an organization.

金融涵盖的领域包括时间、金钱和风险等概念以及它们之间的关系。贷款是主要的融资手段。因此，尽管私募资金、对冲基金、保值基金和其他的融资机构丰富了融资市场，银行仍然是融资的主要"推手"。金融资产，也称作投资，需要谨慎管理，规避金融风险。凭借一定金融工具，人们可以在证券交易所交易各种证券化的资产，例如股票交易，包括上市公司的各种债券和权益。

当一个公司的收入大于支出时，它可以选择把富余的资本贷出或者用作投资。相反，当其支出大于收入时，它可以选择多种方式筹集资金：借入资本、出售权益、降低成本或增加收益。拥有富足资本的贷方会通过金融中介机构，通常是银行，贷出资本；或者在债券市场上购买票据或债券。中介机构赚取贷方和借方的利息差。

银行是众多借方和贷方的中介机构。首先，银行吸纳存款，支付存款人一定的利息。这样所有的存款人都是贷方。银行把这些存款贷出给借方。大大小小的借贷双方通过银行协调其借贷行为。银行实际上是资金流动的变压器。

融资分为个人融资、公共融资和企业融资，融资的主体分别是个人、政府、企业和其他组织机构，包括学校和非赢利性组织。一般来说，只要根据其机构的特点采用了得当的金融工具，融资的目的通常就能实现。

下面举例说明什么是企业融资。公司把股票出售给投资机构，例如投资银行，投资银行再将股票转售给公众，这就是企业融资的一种。股票代表的是对该公司的部分拥有权。如果某家公司有100股已售股票（由投资者持有），你拥有其中一股，那么你就是该公司1%的拥有者。公司出售了产权，作为回报它得到了你买股票所支付的现金。公司用这些现金拓展业务，实现产权理财。产权理财和债券销售（或其他任何形式的债务资金筹措）一起构成该公司的资本结构。

融资是商业管理最重要的内容之一。一家新的企业如果没有进行正确的金融规划是很难获得成功的。无论是个人还是组织，要想拥有有保障的未来，就要对金钱（流动资产）进行管理。

Passage 2

A security is a fungible, negotiable instrument representing financial value. Securities are broadly categorized into debt securities (such as banknotes, bonds and debentures) and equity securities (e.g. common stocks). The company or other entity issuing the security is called the issuer. What specifically qualifies as a security is dependent on the regulatory structure in a country. For example, private investment pools may have some features of securities, but they may not be registered or regulated as such if they don't meet various restrictions.

Securities may be represented by a certificate or, more typically, by an electronic book entry. Certificates may be bearer, meaning they entitle the holder to rights under the security merely by holding the security, or registered, meaning they entitle the holder to rights only if he or she appears on a security register maintained by the issuer or an intermediary. They include shares of corporate stock or mutual funds, bonds issued by corporations or governmental agencies, stock options or other options, limited partnership units, and various other formal investment instruments that are negotiable and fungible.

证券是一种具有金融价值的可替换和转让的金融工具。证券大致可以分为两种：债务证券（如钞票、债券和退税凭单）和产权证券（如普通股）。发行证券的公司或者单位叫做发行机构。证券的界定因不同国家的不同管制结构而不同。比如，私人投资池和证券有相似之处，但是如果它有不符合证券管制条令的因素的话，则不能登记为证券。

商务口译

证券可以由一张证书代表。但是更常见的代表方式是电子账单条目。证书可以用作持票标记，证明持有人拥有票面所规定的权益；证书也可以用于登记，持有人只有在发行机构或者中介完成登记才能凭证书享受票面权益。证券包括各种可转让和替换的投资工具：公司股票、交互基金、公司债券、政府债券、股票期权和其他期权、有限合伙单位和其他投资工具。

Warm-up

1 **Directions:** Give the English equivalents of the following Chinese expressions.

招商证券论坛	网上交易
15周年华诞	资产管理
大喜之日	敦行致远
招商银行证券部	良好市场形象
综合类券商	思想的盛宴
银行间同业拆借市场	不容错过
自营	

2 **Directions:** Give the Chinese equivalents of the following English expressions.

private equity	OMX
mutual fund	exchange owner
hedge fund	clearing house
securitized assets	niche market
publicly-traded corporation	going through the roof
personal finance	the bubble finally burst
public finance	quick profit
corporate finance	jump onto the Internet bandwagon
institutional setting	the break-even point
outstanding share	brand awareness
fungible, negotiable instrument	phenomenal growth
common stock	rely on alternative yardsticks
stock option	audience reach
derivative	due a sell-off

第 15 单元　金融与证券

leveling out	general upward trend
roller-coaster ride	take off
breaking news	soar
million-dollar question	very strong recovery
consolidation activity	peak at
enter into a joint venture	collapse by 50%

III Passages for Interpreting

Passage 1

Directions: Listen to the passage and interpret from Chinese into English at the end of each segment.

尊敬的各位领导，亲爱的各位嘉宾，现场的各位朋友：

大家下午好！//

感谢各位光临首届招商证券论坛。今天我们的主题是挑战和超越。我们将共同关注在全流通背景之下中国证券市场的机会。// 这是我们首届招商证券论坛举办的日子，同时还有一个好消息要告诉各位，这也是我们招商证券 15 周年华诞的一个大喜之日，所以在这里我首先要建议我们各位把我们最美好的祝福融在我们热烈的掌声当中送给我们的招商证券，生日快乐！//

我想，提到招商证券，在座的各位对它一定都不会陌生。各位马上能够联想到的就是 1991 年 7 月招商银行证券部的成立。作为招商证券的前身，从那一刻开始，他们就开始了在中国证券市场跋涉的日子。//

在 15 年发展的历程当中，招商证券在中国证券市场发展当中留下了一串串坚实的足迹。目前他们无论是综合实力，或者是各项指标的排名，都已经位列全国的 10 强当中。而且 15 年当中，他们创下了很多的国内第一。//

我愿意在这样一个特别的日子和大家来分享这些第一：他们是我国证券交易所第一批的会员，也是第一批经核准的综合类的券商；第一批的主承销商，也是全国银行间同业拆借市场第一批成员；以及第一批具有自营、网上交易和资产管理业务资格的券商。很多很多的荣誉都写在了昨天。//

其实在这样的一个特别的日子当中，我们更能够感受到招商证券的一份深厚的社会责任。因为在 15 年的历程当中"敦行致远"的价值观始终在影响着他

199

们和我们。这 15 年当中，招商证券也已经成功地树立起了规范经营、创新发展、高速成长的一个良好的市场形象。我想他们的社会责任可以从今天这样一个思想的盛宴，我们这样一个盛大的论坛看出来他们身上的这份责任。因为他们始终都在关注着资本市场的热点，始终都愿意以推动证券市场的规范发展作为自己的己任，所以这样的一个思想盛宴应该是我们大家都不容错过的。//

Passage 2

Directions: Listen to the passage and interpret from English into Chinese at the end of each segment.

Thank you very much. It's a true honor to be here today and speak at this third annual conference. I will talk about some of the financial trends in the industry that we all see globally and that it certainly will impact the China market as well. //

In this presentation I will talk about first three things. I will start by an overview of some main mega trends in the world. I will talk about the huge potential of stock options and derivatives as such for Asia Pacific and finally I will give you an example of an exchange that started a stock option market from scraps to be the world No. 1 (in the financial market, and it) did that in only three years. //

So, let's see, first of all, who am I? Where do I come from? I come from a company called OMX. We are a company that was founded (in) 1984. We are from Stockholm, Sweden. Today we are a very global company. We are present all over the world. We consist of two main divisions. One is exchange owner. We are an exchange owner and operator in Nordic region of Europe. We are the owner of seven stock exchanges and derivatives markets and three clearing houses. We also deliver and build technology for exchanges and clearing houses. We have more than 65 exchanges as our customers around the world. This is a list of the markets where we work. These are exchanges in marketplaces around the world that uses [use] our technology. Today (there are) more than 65 and we will add another five or six within the next couple of months. Working in this industry in a very niche market, delivering technology for trading technology, and clearing and settlement and risk management technologies for exchanges gives us a unique insight in the market. It's that insight that I would like to share with you together today. //

So looking at the financial industry and especially the exchanges and clearing houses, what trends are impacting the world we live in? Well, there are many trends that have impact in different parts of the world. We see that there are maybe three mega trends that have significant impact in... and will impact all the exchanges around the world. That is globalization, consolidation and market revitalization. //

And what do we mean by those? Globalization and consolidation is [are] are something that is definitely ongoing and we are very much part of that...all...exchanges around the world. Market revitalization very much comes from the mutualization process and creating exchanges as full profit companies. And I will come back to that a little bit later. There are other trends as well in this industry. And maybe some of them will become mega trends and impact all of us. Of course the growth of the China market is something that impacts a large part of the world but we feel that, as for now, maybe it is not a mega trend in the same concept as the three previous. //

Passage 3

Directions: Listen to the following interview and interpret from English into Chinese at the end of each segment.

R = Richard   K = Katy

R: Now, Internet stock. They were going through the roof earlier this year until they ran into their recent difficulties. So the question is, has the bubble finally burst? Our technology correspondent, Katy Johnson, joins me in the studio. So Katy, first of all, what drove these prices up so high in the first place? //

K: Well, all the hype about the Internet would have attracted some investors looking for a quick profit. But I think the real driving force has been the fact that demand has far exceeded the limited supply. There were only a handful of Internet shares offered last year. So opportunities to jump onto the Internet bandwagon have been limited. //

R: And all this is despite the fact they're far from what you'd called the safe investment. //

K: Absolutely yes. //

R: But what about good old profit? Do they match the performance of the share prices? //

K: Well, this is what's so fascinating. Take Amazon.com for example, the Internet bookseller. They have a market value of $18 billion, turnover in excess of

$1 billion, and yet they haven't reached the break-even point. // Apart from a couple of companies, such as Yahoo and America Online, most of them are a long long way away from making any kind of profit whatsoever, never mind the huge profit everyone is hoping for. //

R: So why on earth is everyone so keen to invest in them? //

K: Well, they're very trendy. And of course, there's always the brand factor, which is another reason. Companies like Yahoo and America Online now enjoy incredibly high brand awareness. But the real attraction is the tremendous potential for future revenue, particularly from advertising. Yahoo already has 144 million page hits a day and nearly 200 advertisers. And with Internet usages expected to double within five years, advertising spending is bound to increase. //

R: But then how do analysts value these companies? //

K: Well, it's not easy. They have few assets in the traditional sense and they all show phenomenal growth in terms of turnover, so analysts are having to rely on alternative yardsticks to compare them. //

R: Such as? //

K: Such as things like audience reach. Lycos, another search engine like Yahoo, saw its shares jump by more than a third recently when figures came out saying it reached 45% of all home Internet users. //

R: So, let's turn to the recent collapse in these share prices. Has the bubble finally burst? //

K: Well, we were due a sell-off. So it's not surprising that shareholders took advantage of the recent sharp prices. But I think, what's really depressed prices is the flow of Internet companies that floated recently and saturated the market with their shares. // It seems that supply and demand are now leveling out. In fact, several companies have even seen their shares slightly below the offer prices. So, yes, enthusiasm does seem to be cooling. //

R: Well, it seems to me that everyone investing in Internet shares is in for a bit of roller-coaster ride. So just why is the market so volatile? //

K: Well, it's a very young market, don't forget. And many companies have been listed for only a couple of months. Also, a lot of people investing in their stocks actually use the Internet to trade on-line. // Without the broker's commission, they can afford to buy in and out of stocks several times a day. This makes the market very sensitive to any breaking news. And I think it's this responsiveness which makes it so volatile. //

R: So, Katy, the big question—what's the market going to do next? //

K: Well, Richard, that's the million-dollar question, isn't it? Some of the prices being paid do reflect the value of these companies. So I can't really see prices falling much more. And although confidence will return, enthusiasm is cooling. So don't expect to see prices soaring in the near future. //

R: So how do you see the future of companies in this sector? //

K: Well, I think the sector is going to see lots of consolidation activity as the bigger players look to buy talent and market share. Lycos, for example, has just acquired HotBot, one of its rivals. We'll also see one or two large established non-Internet companies looking to enter the market. // The giant German publisher Bertelsmann, for example, has just entered into a joint venture with US bookseller Barns and Noble to challenge Amazon's dominance on the Net. And if the Internet continues to grow like this, then a few of these companies are about to see substantial returns on their investments. //

R: Now, earlier you mentioned Amazon.com, the Internet bookseller, and I believe you're going to show us a graph illustrating what's been happening to their shares over the last 12 months. //

K: Yes, and here it is. Now this example really is typical of what's been happening throughout this whole sector. As you can see, there was a general upward trend in the first six months, with shares going from just $14 to over $100 a share by December last year. But then in January this year, they really took off, soaring to almost $200. // Predictably enough, I suppose, investors took advantage of these sharp gains. And we saw a sell-off, which was made by February, Amazon's shares had fallen back to their December level again. //

R: So, we've seen one sell-off this year already, then? //

K: Yes, and that's why I don't think there's real need to panic about current losses, because as we can see here, there was a very strong recovery and by May, they'd more than doubled in value again, peaking at nearly $220. So I think the recent losses were predictable. But having said that the price has collapsed by 50% in the last four weeks. And finally, there we have today's price, down almost $6 at just over $111. //

IV Guide to Interpreting

1. Passage 1 是一篇主持人的讲话，语言听起来很流畅、连贯，但是仔细思考后会发现讲话者的中式思维很明显，译员需要根据受众的文化特点做深加工：把冗余的信息撇去，重组散乱的信息。在这篇讲话中还有些华丽的表达，如"思想盛宴"，在笔译中会比较讲究，但是在以信息传递为主要任务的口译中可以略去不译。
2. Passage 2 是一篇有幻灯片的演讲，因此有些内容需要结合投影片才能得到更好的理解。对于译员来说，这种专业性质浓厚的演讲比较难以翻译，事先要做大量的准备，比如事先了解 OMX 的历史、它和 Nasdaq 的合作及市场地位等。译员要主动缩小演讲者与听众之间的专业背景差异。否则，听众理解的生成会过于依赖演讲者的语言，译员就很被动。
3. Passage 3 的这个访谈乍一看像个扫盲性质的对话。作为证券分析师，凯蒂用生动形象的语言描述了各种股票的走势，谈话中充满地道的英语习语，比如"jump onto the Internet bandwagon"（赶网络股大流）、"a bit of roller-coaster ride"（如同坐过山车）等。因此，本练习的重点就是让译员理解对话中主题知识的重要意义。当然，译员还应该注意口语的特征，在练习之前先熟悉一下词汇热身中的英语习语与描述股票走势的常用词汇，熟悉它们的用法。

V Highlight for Interpreting

Directions: Interpret the following sentences from Chinese into English or vice versa.

1. 今天我们的主题是挑战和超越。我们将共同关注在全流通背景之下中国证券市场的机会。
2. 作为招商证券的前身，从那一刻开始，他们就开始了他们在中国证券市场跋涉的日子。
3. 而且 15 年当中，他们创下了很多的国内第一。我愿意在这样一个特别的日子里和大家来分享这些第一：他们是我国证券交易所第一批的会员，也是第一批经核准的综合类的券商；第一批的主承销商，也是全国银行间同业拆借市场第一批成员；以及第一批具有自营、网上交易和资产管理业务资格的券商。

4. I will talk about the huge potential of stock options and derivatives as such for Asia Pacific and finally I will give you an example of an exchange that started a stock option market from scraps to be the world No. 1 (in the financial market, and it) did that in only three years.

5. We are the owner of seven stock exchanges and derivatives markets and three clearing houses. We also deliver and build technology for exchanges and clearing houses.

6. We see that there are maybe three mega trends that have significant impact in... and will impact all the exchanges around the world. That is globalization, consolidation and market revitalization.

7. Of course the growth of the China market is something that impacts a large part of the world but we feel that, as for now, maybe it is not a mega trend in the same concept as the three previous.

8. But I think the real driving force has been the fact that demand has far exceeded the limited supply. There were only a handful of Internet shares offered last year. So opportunities to jump onto the Internet bandwagon have been limited.

9. Take Amazon.com for example, the Internet bookseller. They have a market value of $18 billion, turnover in excess of $1 billion, and yet they haven't reached the break-even point.

10. They have few assets in the traditional sense and they all show phenomenal growth in terms of turnover, so analysts are having to rely on alternative yardsticks to compare them.

11. Well, we were due a sell-off. So it's not surprising that shareholders took advantage of the recent sharp prices. But I think, what's really depressed prices is the flow of Internet companies that floated recently and saturated the market with their shares.

12. The giant German publisher Bertelsmann, for example, has just entered into a joint venture with US bookseller Barns and Noble to challenge Amazon's dominance on the Net. And if the Internet continues to grow like this, then a few of these companies are about to see substantial returns on their investments.

第16单元
会计与税收

Accounting & Taxations

I Background Knowledge

Directions: Read the following English passages and then compare them with their Chinese equivalents.

Passage 1

Accounting is an information system necessitated by the great complexity of modern business. One of the most important functions of accounting is to accumulate and report financial information that shows an organization's financial position and the results of its operations to its interested users. These users include managers, stockholders, banks and other creditors, government agencies, investment advisors, and general public. For example, stock holders must have an organization's financial information in order to hold the share; banks and other creditors must consider the financial strength of a business before permitting it to borrow funds. Potential investors need financial data in order to compare prospective investments.

Many laws require that extensive financial information should be reported to the various levels of government. Businesses usually publish such reports at least annually. To meet the needs of the external users, a framework of accounting standards, principles and procedures known as "generally accepted principles" have been developed to insure the relevance and reliability of the accounting information contained in these external financial reports. The subdivision of the accounting process that produces these external reports is referred to as financial accounting.

会计是一个相当复杂的现代企业所必须的信息系统。会计一个最重要的功能就是合计和报告财务信息,借以向与某个机构有利害关系的用户显示这个机构的经济地位和运营成果。这些用户包括管理者、股东、银行和其他贷款人、政府机构、投资顾问人和公众。例如:股东持有股票必须有该机构的财务信息;银行和其他贷款人在给企业贷款之前必须考虑其经济实力。潜在的投资人需要财务数据来比较预期投资。

许多法律规定财务信息必须上报到政府的各级机构。企业通常至少每年一次公布这样的财务报告。为了满足外部用户的需求,一个包含会计标准、原则和程序的会计标准框架(即人们所熟知的"公认会计原则")已经发展成为用于保证这些外部财务报告中会计信息切适性和可靠性的工具。提出这些外部报告的会计过程分支就是我们所指的财务会计。

Passage 2

Taxation is a national way to obtain revenue by compulsorily distributing part of social products by virtue of political power and law.

Compared to other revenues, taxation has three major characteristics in form: mandatory, free and fixed, which is the most important difference from other revenues. "Mandatory" means that tax law is formulated through certain legislative process, so taxpayers must fulfil their obligation to pay tax in accordance with law. If they disobey, the state is entitled to levy according to law enforcement. "Free" means that taxation is made by the state to taxpayers for free, once tax is collected, it will belong to the state and will never return to taxpayers. "Fixed" means that tax is levied by the state according to the standard stipulated in law, and this standard can't be changed by any taxpayer or tax authority.

Taxation embraces three basic functions: first, raising revenue; second, adjusting economy; third, supervising economy.

税收是国家凭借政治权力、运用法律手段,对一部分社会产品进行强制性的分配从而无偿取得财政收入的一种形式。

税收与其他财政收入相比,在形式上有三项主要特征:强制性、无偿性和固定性,这是区别于其他财政收入的最重要标志。"强制性"指税法是通过一定的立法程序制定的,纳税人有依法纳税的义务。如果纳税人不依法履行纳税义务,国家就要依法强制征收。"无偿性"指税收是国家向纳税人的一种无偿征收,税款一经征收,即转归国家所有,不再归还给纳税人。"固定性"指税收是国家按照法律规定的标准向纳税人征收的,任何纳税人和征收机关都无权改变法律规定的征税标准。

税收的基本职能有三项：第一，筹集财政收入；第二，调节经济；第三，监督经济。

II Warm-up

1 **Directions:** Give the English equivalents of the following Chinese expressions.

特许会计师协会	流通市值	市场法律框架
注册会计师	金融债券	证券投资基金法
资本市场	主板市场	行政法规
中国经济体制改革	创业板	转型阶段
市场经济体制	社会保障基金	债权人
国有企业	金融机构	职业操守
上市公司	投资理念	

2 **Directions:** Give the Chinese equivalents of the following English expressions.

Accounting Student Society	Corporate Tax Association (CTA)
inauguration ceremony	public company
accountancy sector	tax reform
acountancy profession	tax system
future career path	tax collection
meet deadline	business tax
accountancy firm	Treasury Minister
qualified accountant	corporate governance
HKICPA	audit reform
financial management	corporate disclosure
regulatory measure	corporate regulation
life-long learning	tax risk
burgeoning economy	tax return
harsh working environment	opening offer
future pillar	Commissioner of Taxation

商务口译

tax compliance
Board of Taxation
short-sighted approach
tax community

national interest
tax design
short-term project

III Passages for Interpreting

Passage 1

Directions: Listen to the passage and interpret from Chinese into English at the end of each segment.

尊敬的主席,先生们、女士们:

我很高兴出席英格兰和威尔士特许会计师协会成立125周年举行的首场系列性国际活动。// 中国注册会计师协会与英格兰和威尔士特许会计师协会有着长期稳定的合作关系。因此,我代表中国注册会计师协会对大会的召开向英格兰和威尔士特许会计师协会表示热烈的祝贺。//

本次大会以"全球资本市场:对商业、政府及各行业的挑战"为主题,这是一个全球关注的问题。我将借此机会来谈论一下中国资本市场的发展和中国会计行业的建设。//

随着中国经济体制改革的发展,中国资本市场取得了巨大进步,现已成为中国社会主义市场经济体制的重要组成部分。// 资本市场的迅速发展在改革国有企业和金融市场、优化资源配置和促进经济发展和结构调整方面起着重要作用。//

由于起步较晚,中国资本市场在市场规模和交易量上始终落后于发达的资本市场。但是,随着十几年的发展,中国资本市场在规模和投资种类上已经得到了发展壮大。//

截止到2004年底,中国的上市公司达1,337家(包括A股和B股),总市值达3.71万亿(元)人民币,其中1.17万亿(元)为流通市值,投资开户数达7,211万家。另外,共有111家公司在海外上市。//

政府债券和金融债券占中国债券市场的主导地位,公司债券只占一小部分。随着主板市场的逐步扩大,创业板也取得了巨大进步。//

近几年中国资本市场的一个显著变化就是金融机构投资者的壮大。我们已经放宽了对社会保障基金、企业年金和商业保险基金的市场准入限制。// 合格境外金融机构投资者制度自 2002 年 12 月试行以来发展迅速,许多境外金融机构投资者获得了这种许可。// 通过鼓励这些金融机构投资者进入中国资本市场,中国的金融机构投资群体迅速增加,从而改变了过去中小投资者占主体的资本组合,一定程度上促进了投资理念的改革,提高了效率,促进了市场的规范性和稳定性。//

中国在积极促进资本市场发展的同时,高度关注市场法律框架的建设。目前,中国资本市场的一个初步法律框架已基本形成。// 除了像公司法、证券法、证券投资基金法这些关键法律外,此框架也包括一系列的行政法规、部门规则和标准文件,涵盖了证券、期货和证券投资基金等多个领域。// 对于依法实施规范市场的指导思想,规范市场主体的行为,防止和化解市场风险,有效保护投资者的合法权益,特别是那些公共投资者的权益,这样一个法律框架的建立将会起到一个很重要的作用。//

中国在加快其经济体制改革的同时,资本市场的运行环境也经历了深刻变化。在这一重大历史转型阶段,中国资本市场面临前所未有的机遇和挑战。中国经济的持续快速发展表明中国资本市场会有一个光明的前景。//

资本市场的健康发展是中国在促进社会主义市场经济的过程中必须实现的战略要素,也是努力改善金融体制的重要组成部分。// 中国已经建立了在本世纪头 20 年使国民生产总值翻两番,全面建设小康社会的战略目标。在这一点上,资本市场的发展意义重大。//

考虑到目前形势和参照海外成熟市场的做法,中国正积极提出一系列措施来加强资本市场的基础结构建设,建立和完善资本市场发展的各项体制,为资本市场的稳定健康发展创造有利环境。//

资本市场的发展已经改变了传统的会计概念,这就要求使用适合的资本市场运作技术和方法来处理会计信息,并且要求这些会计信息要有更高的质量。// 因此,会计行业的发展就成为了确保会计信息的真实性和可靠性,保护投资者及债权人的利益,保证市场公平平等必不可少的一个因素。//

中国在 1980 年恢复了注册会计师制度。中国政府和中国注册会计师协会实施了一系列改革措施来提高该行业的规范性,整顿会计市场秩序,促进该行业专业操守的发展,提高公众信誉。//

中国会计市场的发展与会计行业的改革和发展息息相关。会计市场的自由化程度越来越高。目前,7 家中外联合的会计公司、27 家国际会计公司的成员公司、7 家国际会计公司的联络公司和 20 家国际会计公司代表处设在中国。// 几百名海外考生已经通过了中国注册会计师考试,其中有 30 多名已经成功申请到了中国注册会计师资格。//

今后我们将继续关注职业操守的发展，平等对待职业建设，改善职业环境，开放国内市场，同时，进入国际市场，推动机构创新和技术创新，全面提高会计行业的信誉和竞争性。// 作为中国会计师的法定专业组织，中国会计师协会将积极促进会计市场和会计行业的发展。//

本次大会为我们提供了一个相互学习、共同探讨相关问题的机会。会计服务是相互的，会计本身是一个国际性商业语言。// 我们中国会计界很高兴与国际同仁一道共同努力来面对资本市场的全球化，抓住机遇，迎接挑战。//

我祝愿本次大会取得圆满成功。//

谢谢！//

Passage 2

Directions: Listen to the passage and interpret from English into Chinese at the end of each segment.

President John Leung, Professors, Fellow Students, Ladies and Gentlemen,

Good evening! // Today is your big day, the day to start your mission, and make your dream come true by becoming core members of the Accounting Student Society. //

It is my great pleasure to be invited here, to witness your inauguration ceremony, share your happiness and say a few words to you as a lawmaker representing the accountancy sector of Hong Kong. //

I believe most of you will choose the accounting profession as your future career. Am I correct? Could you please raise your hands if you aspire to be an accountant or auditor after graduation? Yes, many of you have decided your future career path. //

But I would like to give you a warning here—as an accountant, the job is very tough and stressful. Working hours are very long and you have to meet countless working deadlines. //

Even if you make a lot of money, you may not have time to spend it and enjoy your life. Is this acceptable to you? I hope you will reflect carefully and make sure you really want to involve yourself in accountancy profession. Maybe I sound scary, but this is the fact. // The path to becoming an accountant is not an easy one. There are many challenges along the way before you become a successful accountant. But there are also learning opportunities. If you love to face challenges and can solve problems involving figures, then the road to accounting and taxation practice is surely for you. //

The accountancy profession currently enjoys its most thriving time ever. There are over 1, 300 accountancy firms in Hong Kong, compared with 1,040 in 1999. Now, we have over 26,000 qualified accountants who are registered in HKICPA, compared with only 13,000 ten years ago. // With the globalization of economic trade and the closer relationship between the economies of Hong Kong and the Chinese Mainland, the prospect for accountancy profession is certainly boundless and exciting. There are enormous opportunities for local accountants working here and on the mainland. //

I heard from many accounting friends that accountants are actively engaged as information providers for local or overseas enterprises targeting the Chinese Mainland market. // Accountants are also expected to provide expert advice about financial management, taxation, and even some operational or managerial solutions to their clients. //

Hence, you have to prepare yourself well for these duties. You have to familiarize yourself with the systems and regulatory measures across different industries and different geographical locations. // Many friends told me that we are seriously lacking talent and new blood in the accountancy profession given the fast-growing business and huge demand for personnel. //

Hence, my advice to you is to keep enhancing your knowledge, not only in the accounting field but also in the fields of finance and management. Don't simply view "Life-Long Learning" as a slogan advocated by the government, but a motto inside your heart. Always get ready to absorb new knowledge. Adding value to yourself will be a key to success. //

Meanwhile, a successful accountant usually possesses good communication skills. If you work on the Chinese Mainland, you need to deal with people from a different culture, you have to be flexible enough to embrace change and learn new things as the system in China advances rapidly with the burgeoning economy. //

To sum up, you have to learn to deal with stress, as well as to face frustration and failure. You must work hard and adapt well to a sometimes-harsh working environment. //

Dear students, don't be frightened by my remarks. The road ahead of you is bright and wide; opportunities are plentiful and golden. // Remember what I said in the early part of my speech? Accountancy is now enjoying its most flourishing time ever, we expect that this trend will keep growing rather than declining. Dear students, you will be the future pillars of our society, so seize every learning opportunity to upgrade yourself. //

Finally, I wish all of you a happy university life and a fruitful career in accountancy. Thank you very much. //

Passage 3

Directions: Listen to the passage and interpret from English into Chinese at the end of each segment.

Ladies and Gentlemen, //

I am delighted to be here today to open the 2004 Corporate Tax Association (CTA) Convention. The Convention provides an opportunity for tax experts from many of Australia's leading public companies to reflect on some important issues in tax reform. // There are not a lot of opportunities to talk constructively about tax reform—it is an emotive subject for most of us—so I am eager to utilize this opportunity to the full! //

An efficient and competitive tax system is part of the architecture of the modern economy. And tax reform is about removing the barriers to productivity that will enable economic prosperity and keep Australia in the enviable economic position we currently find ourselves enjoying. //

I welcome Frank Drenth's recent assessment that Australia has undoubtedly experienced a prolonged period of economic growth that has significantly exceeded rates achieved by other developed countries, because of the government's strong economic management. // Obviously Frank was commenting in the context of improved company profits and the resulting increase in corporate tax collection. Whatever the context, the strength in company tax contribution to revenue can be attributed to sustained economic expansion which has become a hallmark of the Howard government. //

In discussing tax reform I endorse the view of a US Treasury official who said almost 30 years ago that the blueprint for tax reform should be "that a tax system looks like someone designed it on purpose". Certainly, from my perspective, I vouch that the government has taken this sentiment on board. //

I am rightly proud of the Howard government's achievements in tax reform, particularly in the area of business tax reform. It is not an overstatement that these reforms represent the most far-reaching and dramatic tax reforms ever attempted in Australia's history. //

During a lunch I attended recently I was told that extensive tax reform would not occur unless accompanied by "real political will". // As a Treasury Minister in the Australian government that has been at the helm during the implementation of business tax reforms, the government has the right to feel incredulous at the suggestion that political will is lacking when it comes to tax reform. //

The sweeping tax reforms undertaken over the past few years have underpinned Australia's sustained economic performance, a fact underscored by the OECD[1] view that a key economic reform in Australia has been the reform of our tax system. An internationally competitive and structurally sound business tax system is now a reality. //

The government has listened and been responsive to industry calls for specific tax initiatives to remove impediments to business investment. Recent reforms are delivering significant economic benefits to Australia by contributing to a faster-growing and more dynamic Australian economy. //

The International Monetary Fund in its April 2004 World Economic Outlook expects [expected] that Australia's strong economic performance will [would] continue. We understand that creating an environment in which business can prosper is essential. // A strong corporate sector creates jobs, secures critical investment and trade for Australia, all of which are fundamental to our continuing economic prosperity. //

The government has also made the same commitment to a robust, modern and flexible regulatory framework for corporate governance. The drive to improve corporate governance is another part of the government's ongoing program to modernize business regulation in Australia. // The government's Corporate Law Economic Reform Program (CLERP) is designed to ensure that we improve productivity, promote business activity and confidence in our corporate culture. //

The object of recent reforms dealing with audit reform and corporate disclosure is to improve the operation of the market by promoting transparency, accountability and shareholders' rights. // CLERP 9 takes a balanced approach to corporate regulation

---

1 The Organization for Economic Cooperation and Development.

without over-burdening business with unnecessary regulation nor being overly prescriptive. //

It is self-evident that good corporate governance also includes managing risk in respect of taxation. As someone once said: "A tax return is not an opening offer." // The Commissioner of Taxation recently wrote to the boards of large Australian companies highlighting the need for boards to be actively involved in assessing tax-related decisions. // I note there has been some concern about the Commissioner's approach and some concerns about the capacity of boards to get across the technical details that determine those risks. //

However, despite these concerns I do not think anyone denies that tax decisions can pose a risk to the reputation of a company and the returns it can make to shareholders. I share the Commissioner's view that company boards have a responsibility to ensure that tax laws are properly applied. // Recent surveys indicate a high percentage of company directors agree that tax is a real corporate governance risk area. Judgments about tax compliance should be part of the corporate governance processes of every company and board. //

At a practical level, I do note concerns remain about the Commissioner's access to this kind of risk management information in the event of an audit.// While the position here is a work in progress, I understand that there are ongoing discussions with the ATO[1] that will ensure that an appropriate balance can be struck between the Commissioner and corporate Australia in managing this issue. // I will continue to carefully monitor an acceptable solution between governance and tax risk requirements. //

We are also changing the way we undertake the tax reform process. Crucial to that change has been the integration of the tax policy and tax law design functions, and the new community consultation arrangements for the development of new tax law. // The resulting closer engagement between government, the Board of Taxation and the business community has been evident in the valuable and constructive consultative role played by the Corporate Tax Association and its members. // It's gratifying to see business endorsement for the quality and effectiveness of the recent consultation process for the Review of International Tax Arrangements (RITA) legislation. //

I welcome and endorse comments made by Frank Drenth in a recent article where he said this new consultation environment also carries with it enhanced responsi-

---

[1] Australian Taxation Office.

bilities for business participants. // These responsibilities extend to ensuring integrity issues are appropriately identified by participants in the consultation process up front, rather than taking a short-sighted approach and cherry picking the benefits from consultation. // The government must be able to trust that consultation is occurring in an honest and frank environment. If that trust is breached then the consultation process ultimately fails. //

You will have noticed that consultation with the tax community has been a consistent theme across each of the tax reform issues I have canvassed today. // Through engagement with stakeholders, the government has been able to draw on the experiences and knowledge of tax professionals, and others, to improve the tax system for the community more broadly. //

A continuing challenge for the government is to build on the collaborative working relationships. These relationships will form the foundation for sharing the government's continuing vision for improving the tax system. // I will have an opportunity to elaborate on that vision, in more detail, later in the year. //

We have come a very long way from the shambolic tax system we had to endure before the Coalition came to government. // We are a government that will not shirk the political risk of making tough decisions in the national interest. Nowhere has this political will been more evident than in reform of the tax system. // I invite the CTA to continue this journey by working with the government on tax design and developing a more principles-based statement of the law. This is not a short-term project, but one for the benefit of future generations of Australians. //

Thank you! //

IV Guide to Interpreting

1. Passage 1 节选自原财政部部长以及中国注册会计师协会会长刘仲藜在英国的一篇演讲稿，专业性较强。译员在做口译前有必要了解如下一些专题知识。比如，中国注册会计师协会是依据《注册会计师法》和《社会团体登记条例》的有关规定设立的社会团体法人，是中国注册会计师行业的自律管理组织，成立于 1988 年 11 月。而 "accounting" 指的是会计学、会计制度，涉及经济交往中财会记录的制作和准备有关财产、债务和企业运行结果的报告的制作方法；而 "accountancy" 指的是会计工作，即会计的职位。翻译时要注意这两个词的区别。A 股 (A shares) 的正式名称是人民币普通股票。它是由我国境内的公司发行，供境内机构、组织或个人（不含台、港、澳投资者）以人民币认购和交易的普通股股票；B 股（B shares）是指以人民币为股票面值，以外币为认购和交易币种的股票，它是境外投资者和国内投资者向我国的股份有限公司投资而形成的股份，在上海证券交易所或深圳证券交易所上市流通。市值是指上市公司在股票市场上的价值，一家上市公司每股股票的价格乘以发行总股数即为这家公司的市值，市值的英语翻译为 "market capitalization" 或 "market cap"，有时也翻作 "market capitalization value"；流通市值指的是在特定时间内当时可交易的流通股股数乘以当时股价所得出的流通股票总价值，英语为 "negotiable market capitalization"。另外，在翻译时，汉语在结构上多用主动语态，而英语在结构上多用被动语态，在翻译时要注意英汉两种语言在结构上的区别。例如，在 "我们已经放宽了对社会保障基金、企业年金和商业保险基金的市场准入限制" 这句话的翻译中，译员就应使用被动句 "Limitation has been relaxed on..." 来强调该句的主干部分；又如句子 "……，这样一个法律框架的建立将会起到一个很重要的作用"，在处理时要分清层次，抓住句子的主干部分。此句的重点应是后面一句，所以在翻译时应先翻译主句，前面五个分句作为补充成分。口译时还要注意倍数的表达：两倍（double）、三倍（treble/triple）、四倍（quadruple）、五倍（quintuple）、六倍（sextuple）、七倍（septuple）、八倍（octuple）、九倍（nonuple）、十倍（decuple）。文中 "翻两番" 实际是原来的四倍，所以翻译时应用 "quadruple"。

2. Passage 2 节选自某位资深会计师在 2007 年 4 月 14 日香港公开大学会计学会就职典礼上的演讲，风格较为正式，译员要注意根据具体的语境选择合适的用词。例如，"say a few words to you" 就不能够直接译为 "给你们讲几句话"，在这里译为 "与你们一起交流" 更为正式。在 "I hope you will reflect carefully and make sure you really want to involve yourself in accountancy profession." 这句话中，连词 "and" 在此并不是表示并列关系，根据上文应该是展示一种先后的关系，所以将它译为 "然后" 更符合讲话人的意思。汉语中通常喜欢用四字成语，在英译汉的口译中，特别是在较正式的场合中也要注意成语的恰当使用。例如，"Maybe I sound scary, but this is the fact. The path to becoming an accountant is not an easy one." 在翻译这两句话时，译员就可以把 "scary" 和 "not an easy one" 翻译为 "危言耸听" 和 "一帆风顺"。另外，在口译时，为了使意思表达更加清楚，避免产生误解，通常要求译得具体明了。例如，"...for local or overseas enterprises..." 中的 "local" 指 "香港当地企业"；"You have to familiarize

yourself with the systems"中的"the system"指"会计制度"。但在"The road ahead of you is bright and wide; opportunities are plentiful and golden."的翻译中，"bright"和"wide"以及"plentiful"和"golden"就没必要全部翻译出来，大概译出意思就行。
3. Passage 3 节选自澳大利亚原国税局长及财务部副部长海伦·库南 (Helen Coonan) 在开启"2004年企业所得税协会公约"时的讲话。语篇行文正式，是针对英语国家专业人士而做的演讲，讲述的是政府的会计政策和税收改革。翻译时应注意一些长句表达的处理，例如，"I welcome Frank Drenth's recent assessment that Australia has undoubtedly experienced a prolonged period of economic growth that has significantly exceeded rates achieved by other developed countries, because of the government's strong economic management."这句话结构比较复杂，从句里面套从句，处理这样的句子应先理清句子的逻辑关系，然后按照汉语先因后果、先表达事实再表达意见的习惯进行翻译。因此，这句话应采取由后往前的翻译方法，把"welcome"放在最后作为对这个评价的看法。翻译中还要注意肯定句与否定句之间的相互转换。例如，"We are a government that will not shirk the political risk of making tough decisions in the national interest."在这句话的翻译中，译员可以把"not shirk the political risk"译为"敢冒政治风险"；同样，"This is not a short-term project"也可以译为"这是一个长期的工程"。

V Highlight for Interpreting

Directions: Interpret the following sentences from Chinese into English or vice versa.

1. 资本市场的迅速发展在改革国有企业和金融市场、优化资源配置和促进经济发展和结构调整方面起着重要作用。
2. 由于起步较晚，中国资本市场在市场规模和交易量上始终落后于发达的资本市场。但是，随着十几年的发展，中国资本市场在规模和投资种类上已经得到了发展壮大。
3. 通过鼓励这些金融机构投资者进入中国资本市场，中国的金融机构投资群体迅速增加，从而改变了过去中小投资者占主体的资本组合，一定程度上促进了投资理念的改革，提高了效率，促进了市场的规范性和稳定性。
4. 除了像公司法、证券法、证券投资基金法这些关键法律外，此框架也包括一系列的行政法规、部门规则和标准文件，涵盖了证券、期货和证券投基金等多个领域。

5. 对于依法实施规范市场的指导思想，规范市场主体的行为，防止和化解市场风险，有效保护投资者的合法权益，特别是那些公共投资者的权益，这样一个法律框架的建立将会起到一个很重要的作用。

6. 今后我们将继续关注职业操守的发展，平等对待职业建设，改善职业环境，开放国内市场，同时，进入国际市场，推动机构创新和技术创新，全面提高会计行业的信誉和竞争性。

7. With the globalization of economic trade and the closer relationship between the economies of Hong Kong and the Chinese Mainland, the prospect for accountancy profession is certainly boundless and exciting.

8. I heard from many accounting friends that accountants are actively engaged as information providers for local or overseas enterprises targeting the Chinese Mainland market.

9. You have to familiarize yourself with the systems and regulatory measures across different industries and different geographical locations.

10. Don't simply view "Life-Long Learning" as a slogan advocated by the government, but a motto inside your heart. Always get ready to absorb new knowledge. Adding value to yourself will be a key to success.

11. And tax reform is about removing the barriers to productivity that will enable economic prosperity and keep Australia in the enviable economic position we currently find ourselves enjoying.

12. I welcome Frank Drenth's recent assessment that Australia has undoubtedly experienced a prolonged period of economic growth that has significantly exceeded rates achieved by other developed countries, because of the government's strong economic management.

13. As a Treasury Minister in the Australian government that has been at the helm during the implementation of business tax reforms, the government has the right to feel incredulous at the suggestion that political will is lacking when it comes to tax reform.

14. The object of recent reforms dealing with audit reform and corporate disclosure is to improve the operation of the market by promoting transparency, accountability and shareholders' rights.

15. These responsibilities extend to ensuring integrity issues are appropriately identified by participants in the consultation process up front, rather than taking a short-sighted approach and cherry picking the benefits from consultation.

第17单元

国际经济组织

International Business Organization

I Background Knowledge

Directions: Read the following English passages and then compare them with their Chinese equivalents.

Passage 1

What is the World Trade Organization (WTO)? The World Trade Organization was formed in 1995 to administer existing multilateral trade agreements among its 153 member, support ongoing negotiations for new trade agreements, and handle trade disputes. Why WTO membership is important? WTO membership means that the economy automatically receives Most Favored Nation status. Basically, all 153 WTO members are "most favored", which means they must all treat each other the same, and give no preferential trade preference to any one partner without giving that preference to all. WTO members trade with lower trade barriers, including tariffs, import quotas and excessive regulations. This allows them a larger market for their goods, leading to greater sales, more jobs and faster economic growth.

Over 75% of WTO members are developing countries. WTO membership allows them access to developed markets at the lower tariffs, while taking time to remove reciprocal tariffs in their own markets. This gives them an opportunity to "catch up" to sophisticated multinational corporations and their mature industries before opening their markets to overwhelming competitive pressure.

世界贸易组织是什么？世界贸易组织成立于1995年，执行其153个成员之间现有的多边贸易协议，支持持续的新贸易协议的谈判，处理贸易冲突。

商务口译

世界贸易组织成员地位为什么很重要？成为世贸组织成员就意味着自动享受最惠国待遇。基本上所有 153 个世贸成员都是"最惠"的，意即它们必须同等对待所有成员，给予任何一个成员的优惠待遇必须同时给予其他所有成员。世贸成员之间诸如关税、进口配额和过度管制这样的贸易壁垒都要少些。这使得成员的货物市场更大，带来更多销售和工作机会，从而加快经济增长。

75% 以上的世贸组织成员属发展中国家。世贸组织成员地位使得他们能够以更低的关税进入发达国家市场，同时有时间逐渐取消自身市场的互惠关税。这样他们有机会赶上成熟的跨国企业以及发达国家成熟的产业，避免市场开放面对过于激烈的竞争压力。

Passage 2

Upon entering the 21st century, the Chinese government made timely diplomatic strategy readjustments and started to push for better relations with its neighboring countries, seeking mutual trust politically and co-prosperity economically. As part of the effort, the process of bringing about a China-ASEAN Free Trade Area (FTA) is being driven ahead. In November 2002, the Chinese and ASEAN leaders signed the Framework Agreement on Comprehensive Economic Cooperation between China and ASEAN and decided that a China-ASEAN FTA would be set up in 10 years. The process of establishing the China-ASEAN FTA was thus set in motion. Starting on January 1, 2004, the two parties began implementing an Early Harvest Plan (EHP), cutting tariffs on more than 500 products, as part of the effort to facilitate the birth of the FTA.

The Chinese and ASEAN economies complement one another as shown by the results of the EHP. ASEAN's tropical fruits and China's apples, pears, cabbages and potatoes are competitive respectively. The China-ASEAN FTA plan has already produced good initial results. At the 8th China-ASEAN Summit convened on November 29, 2004 in Vientiane, capital of Laos, the two parties signed a package of agreements on trade in goods and dispute settlement, laying down foundations for standardizing tariff cutting and resolving disputes. Starting from July 20, 2005, China and ASEAN began to cut tariffs on more than 7,000 products, which marked the coming of the phase of substantial tariff reduction between China and ASEAN in the run-up to the establishment of the FTA.

The Framework Agreement on Comprehensive Economic Cooperation between China and ASEAN has helped advance bilateral trade, with the China-ASEAN trade volume crossing the threshold of US$100 billion for the first time in 2004 and hitting US$130.37 billion the next year. In addition, the two sides have been cooperating closely in direct investment, services and technology, which has also yielded significant results. From the point of view of regional economic integration, the future Asian economic integration should be based on a more extensive and more economically powerful regional cooperative entity, of which the China-ASEAN FTA is a vitally important component. //

Once founded, China-ASEAN FTA will be the largest FTA in Asia, the most populous FTA in the world and the biggest FTA in the developing world. The China-ASEAN FTA is expected to accelerate the trend of regional integration in Asia and, in turn, will have positive impacts on the world economy.

进入21世纪，中国政府及时进行了外交战略调整，追求睦邻友好关系，寻求政治互信、经济共同繁荣。其中包括努力建设中国—东盟自由贸易区。2002年11月，中国和东盟领导人签署了《中国东盟全面经济合作框架协议》，决定以10年的时间建设中国—东盟自由贸易区。就此，中国—东盟自由贸易区的建设正式启动。2004年1月1日起，双方开始执行"早期收获计划"，减让500多种产品的关税，促进中国—东盟自由贸易区的建设。

早期收获计划证明，中国和东盟各国经济互补。东盟的热带水果、中国的苹果、梨、白菜以及土豆各有竞争力。收获计划早期效果良好。2004年11月29日，在老挝首都万象召开的第八次中国东盟峰会上，双方签署了一揽子货物贸易和争端解决协议，为关税减让和争端解决奠定了基础。2005年7月20日起，中国和东盟就7,000多种产品进行关税减让，标志着中国和东盟进入实质性关税减让阶段，为中国—东盟自由贸易区的成立铺平道路。

《中国东盟全面经济合作框架协议》促进了中国与东盟双边贸易的发展，双边贸易额于2004年首次突破1,000亿美元，2005年达1,303.7亿美元。此外，双方还在直接投资、服务和技术上进行紧密合作，并取得了显著成效。从区域经济一体化的角度来看，未来亚洲经济一体化应当建立在更广泛、经济更强大的区域合作实体基础之上，而中国—东盟自由贸易区是其中不可或缺的组成部分。

一经成立，中国—东盟自由贸易区将成为亚洲最大、世界人口最多、发展中世界最大的自由贸易区。中国—东盟自由贸易区有望加速亚洲一体化进程，并最终对世界经济产生积极的影响。

商务口译

Warm-up

1 **Directions:** Give the English equivalents of the following Chinese expressions.

贸易体制	计划调节	缔约方
入世谈判	市场调节	让步
市场经济	企业运行机制	市场准入
关贸总协定	中央党校	双边谈判
成员国贸易协议	社会主义市场经济	多边谈判
商品经济体制	十四大	减税

2 **Directions:** Give the Chinese equivalents of the following English expressions.

multilateral trade agreement	dispute settlement
trade dispute	bilateral trade
Most Favored Nation status	economic integration
trade preference	China-ASEAN Expo
trade barrier	Organization of Islamic Countries (OIC)
import quota	
reciprocal tariff	Ministry of Culture, Arts & Tourism
ASEAN	
Free Trade Area (FTA)	Visit Malaysia Year
Early Harvest Plan (EHP)	

Passages for Interpreting

Passage 1

Directions: Listen to the passage and interpret from English into Chinese at the end of each segment.

It is a pleasure for me to be invited to attend this auspicious event—"Forum on Tourism Cooperation between China (Guangxi) and ASEAN" in this beautiful city of Nanning. On behalf of Malaysia, I would like to congratulate the organizer for taking this initiative in organizing this Forum, which is being hosted in conjunction with the 1st ASEAN-China Expo, by gathering all ASEAN countries under one roof. //

Tourism Malaysia had agreed to participate without hesitation in this forum as well as the Expo, as we are well aware that China is a market of vast potential and more importantly, we would like to lend support to our friendly neighbor, that is China. //

Malaysia has been a very close and serious partner with China in many fields and for at least 600 years. Some of you may be aware that Malaysia is the largest trading partner for China in Southeast Asia, accounting for 25% of China's trade with the ASEAN countries, and the 2nd largest in Asia, after Japan. As such, Malaysia is very much in a position to serve China as its gateway to Southeast Asia with its 550 million population and a market size of over US$320 billion. Beyond ASEAN, Malaysia is also well affiliated with the Organization of Islamic Countries, in short we call it OIC, and therefore would be a good strategy [strategic] alliance partner for Chinese investors looking further. //

With regard to the diplomatic ties between Malaysia and China, these were officially established on 31 May, 1974 when Malaysia's second Prime Minister visited China. Malaysia was thus the first nation in ASEAN to have established such ties. This year, we are celebrating our 30th year of good relationship and friendship with China. The relationship has since grown to be very cordial and warm with exchange of visits between high-level leaders and the general public for business and tourism. //

On the home front, Malaysia has been developing its tourism industry since the inception of its Tourism Board in 1972. Nevertheless, the industry was then not given much priority due to our other abundant primary base resources. At that time, we were agricultural and primary base, as I said, such as the cultivation of rubber, palm oil and tin mining. Malaysia was the largest producer of tin and rubber in the 1960s and (19)70s. //

However, when the economic recession struck Malaysia in the mid-1980s, we embarked on our diversify [diversification] plan. Tourism was identified as one of the industries that could provide us with very quick returns. This plan led to the establishment of our Ministry of Culture, Arts & Tourism in 1987, and followed by the very first, we call it, Visit Malaysia Year campaign in 1990. Building on the success of

商务口译

the 1st campaign in 1990, a second Visit Malaysia Year campaign again was marketed in the year 1994. // These campaigns, together with other promotional efforts has [have] helped raise our tourism profile in the international markets. The development has also created confidence for the government to allocate bigger budget for our tourism development and promotion. (The) 1997 Asian financial crisis, for example, saw the government providing us with the funding to launch our Malaysia—Truly Asia campaign. //

Through these concerted efforts, tourists arrival figures have shown very encouraging increase: from 5.55 million in the year 1998 to 13.29 million in the year 2002. The year 2003 figure of course saw a plunge to only 10.3 million, due to the SARS epidemic and Iraq war crisis. Correspondingly, we also recorded growth in tourism receipts: from RM[1] 9.7 billion or US$2.6 billion in 1998 to RM25.8 billion or US$6.9 billion in the year 2002. (In) 2003, however, the receipt was reduced to RM21.3 billion, or in US is US$5.6 billion. //

Passage 2

Directions: Listen to the passage and interpret from Chinese into English at the end of each segment.

那么，今天应学校的邀请，就中国和多边贸易体制的关系做一个简单的报告。中国和多边贸易体制的关系是非常复杂的，所以在你们学校给我的要求中就希望我谈一谈中国加入WTO的历程及入世以后中国经济发展前景的展望。因为在座都是很年轻的同志，对中国当年入世谈判的经历呢，不是很了解，那么今天我就想介绍一下我们中国谈判的历史的回顾。//

中国入世三年以后，我们越来越感觉到我们中国入世谈判的15年特别是最后的10年是一个相当艰苦的历程，因为它从一个层面反映了我们改革开放的那种复杂性，那种艰苦性。也反映了整个中国在改革开放中所具有的那种政治勇气和政治魄力，也反映了全世界怎么适应和接受一个崛起的大国。所以中国入世谈判的回顾确实从很多方面反映了我们中国一些重大的历史的侧面。//

那么关于我们中国从1986年到2001年结束的15年的谈判，我想主要是分三个阶段，这三个阶段都给了我们许多重要的启示。我们中国入世谈判的第

---

1 马来西亚货币令吉（Ringgit）的官方符号。

第17单元　国际经济组织

一个阶段就是从1986年到1992年底，这六年时间里面，我在入世谈判结束以后作的报告中讲过我们中国谈判的前六年其实是解决四个字——市场经济。// 今天，市场经济对于我们大家来讲都是一个司空见惯的、大家都可以接受的概念。但是在（19）92年以前，市场经济对我们来讲完全就是一个禁区，可以说，市场经济对于当时来讲等同于资本主义，谁讲市场经济，谁搞市场经济，谁就是搞资本主义。//

但是大家知道关贸总协定，当时的关贸总协定和现在的世界贸易组织是一个所谓的市场经济俱乐部，那么你参加世界贸易组织一个最重要的条件就是必须承认搞市场经济。我们恰恰在这个最关键的问题上没法满足当时关贸总协定各个契约方的要求，所以谈判进行地非常地艰苦。// 大家都知道当时我们对中国经济体制的描述是什么呢？是所谓"计划调节和市场调节相结合的商品经济体制"，非常复杂。当时我们的谈判对手首先就不知道什么是商品经济体制，他们好像觉得是百货大楼商品堆积起来的一个体制。所以，对这个体制，他们不熟悉，不了解，虽然我们做了很大的努力来解释什么叫做商品经济体制，可是他们还是不能够接受这样一个概念。//

另外呢，他们认为市场调节和计划调节是不能够结合的。他们认为市场调节是客观范畴的东西，它反映客观的经济规律，就像水从高处向低处流一样。而计划调节是属于主观范畴的东西，它是由政府来做出的一些决策、制定的一套政策，所以他们认为计划调节和市场调节，一个客观范畴的东西和一个主观范畴的东西是很难结合的。// 当然，我们解释在中国计划调节和市场调节是可以结合的而且结合得很好。那么，他们说，我们承认市场调节和计划调节是可以结合的，但是市场调节和计划调节相结合的结果就使得中国的经济体制变得不透明、不稳定、不具有可预见性。为什么呢？因为他们认为，你们一会儿用市场调节一会儿用计划调节，不知道什么时候用计划调节什么时候用市场调节，什么时候市场调节的力度大，什么时候计划调节的力度大。这样就使得整个经济体制是不透明的、不稳定的。所以在这样一种情况下，中国的入世谈判确实碰到了很大的困难。//

难就难在我们当时不接受市场经济这样一个基本的概念。后来我记得从这样一个宏观的层面上来研究中国的经济体制碰到很大的困难的时候，我们就开始从微观的层面，也就是从企业的运作来研究市场经济体制。// 大家知道，企业是一个国家经济的细胞，一个国家经济的健康会从企业的健康得到反映。一个国家的整个经济运行的体制会从企业的运行中得到体现。所以当时从宏观层面上来审查中国的经济体制遇到困难的时候，我们就开始从微观的层面来审查中国的经济体制。//

商务口译

当时在日内瓦谈判的时候,我们很多驻中国的外交官也参加了,他们对中国的情况非常了解。这次日内瓦会议上,一个很资深的美国驻华外交官提出来,他说,请问中国代表团,我最近在报纸上看到在谈到企业的运行机制的时候,你们讲,厂长是中心,书记是核心,两心变一心,请问中国代表团,你们这个两心是怎么变成一心的?当时我们代表团很多同志感到很愤怒,就觉得中国复关的谈判是一个关于经济问题的谈判,为什么会涉及到政治的问题呢?!// 在我们的企业建立党委书记制是我们中国的内政,我们不允许外国干涉我们的内政,所以当时,大家是感到很不理解为什么美国代表提出这样一个问题。所以我们当时坚决跟他顶了回去。//

后来这位美国代表感到很委屈,他下来的时候就找我们谈,他说,龙先生,我们并没有什么恶意,他说,你们在过去几年当中谈这个市场调节和计划调节相结合的市场经济体制,一直没讲清楚,我们想让你们从一个企业的运行机制来讲清楚这个计划调节和市场调节是怎么结合的。那么这个老外,当时有点形而上学了,他认为这个书记是上面派的,可能就代表你们讲的计划调节,那么厂长是代表企业的利益,他是管怎样挣钱的,他是代表你们所讲的这个市场调节,那么你们把这个"两心变一心"讲清楚了是不是就把市场调节和计划调节讲清楚了呢。当时我们一听,这个美国人也没什么特别的恶意,所以就觉得好,总算找到了一个突破口,就来大讲一下两心变一心。// 所以回到中国以后,我们把很多关于企业管理的专家都请到日内瓦来给大家讲两心变一心的问题,最后是越讲越复杂,越讲越讲不清楚,把自己也给绕进去了。因为大家知道,我们书记、厂长都是上面派的,目标都是一致的。所以在整个谈判的过程中我们当时确实就绕不开这样一个很大的困难,就是中国的计划经济体制怎么样来适应多边贸易体制的以市场经济为基础的这样一套国际规则体系。//

我记得当时我们的谈判很困难的时候,李岚清同志当时是我们的部长,他思想比较解放,就把我叫去说,我们能不能提出来中国的经济是有计划的市场经济体制?我觉得这可能是一个出路。// 所以我们当时就把美国和其他一些西方国家的代表请到一起,告诉他们说如果我们承诺中国是有计划的市场经济,你们看行不行?这些外国代表说,可以啊,只要你们承认是市场经济,有计划也没关系嘛,很多市场经济国家也是有计划的。所以我们喜出望外,回到国内之后马上就给上面打报告。// 哪知道这个报告还没走到一半,就被退了回来。因为当时大家都认为,计划调节和市场调节相结合的商品经济体制,这是我们中国经济的一个基本描述,不可能为了一场国际贸易谈判来改变这个基本的提法。所以这样一条路又没有走通。//

所以,一直到 1992 年小平同志南巡讲话,提出了在社会主义条件下也可

第 17 单元　国际经济组织

以搞市场经济。也就是市场经济和社会主义不是矛盾的。从现在来看，小平同志这句话好像很一般。但是对当时整个中国经济体制的改革，对我们的谈判，却是一次重大的突破。大家觉得豁然开朗。后来到了那年的 6 月份，江泽民同志到中央党校讲话，提出了关于社会主义市场经济的问题。后来又到了十四大，正式提出了我们中国经济体制改革的目标就是建立社会主义市场经济，这样第一次在党的文件里面为市场经济正了名。// 所以当时我们记得，在十四大开完以后没有多久就到日内瓦参加了一次中国工作组的会议，就是在日内瓦召开的当时关贸总协定缔约方的会议。我记得当时我们中国代表团在会议上宣布，我们中国是搞市场经济的，我们搞的是社会主义市场经济！当时全场鼓掌，鼓了三分钟，好像这帮老兄比我们还激动。因为他们逼了中国人那么多年，总算逼出个市场经济出来。// 所以，从此，中国的经济、改革也好，还有我们在日内瓦的谈判也好，就迈出了一个全新的阶段。我们从 1986 年到 1992 年谈了六年，总算是过了这个坎——就是承诺了搞市场经济。这对我们中国整个参与国际经济，特别是参与经济全球化奠定了最重要的理论基础。//

Passage 3

Directions: Listen to the passage and interpret from Chinese into English at the end of each segment.

那么我们中国入世谈判的第二个阶段就是从 1993 年到 1999 年 11 月份和美国达成协议。这是我们中国加入世界贸易组织的第二个阶段。这个阶段也是解决了四个字——开放市场。// 开放市场对于任何一个国家来讲都是极为敏感的事情。不仅仅对于中国，对于世界上所有的国家，开放自己本土的市场，让外国的产品和外国的服务进入自己的国土，始终是一件非常敏感的事情，至今还是一件敏感的事情。// 但是中国经过了六年的谈判，认识到开放市场并不是一味的让步。开放市场在某种意义上不是让步，而是进步。这是我们用了六年艰苦的谈判最后才摸索出来的一个道理。入世的谈判，特别是在开放市场方面的谈判是非常复杂的也是很艰苦的。//

它的复杂性就在于，从理论上来讲，如果中国要加入世界贸易组织，中国必须和一百多个世贸成员就市场准入的问题一个一个达成协议。它是通过双边谈判来解决的，而不是通过多边谈判来解决的。// 因为每个国家的经济结构不一样，产品结构不一样，所以每个国家所关心的问题也不一样。所以你必须通过双边谈判一个一个地解决每个国家所关心的个案问题，反映它特殊（性）的

商务口译

问题。所以同每个国家的谈判，有些国家就比较简单，有些国家就相当复杂。// 比如说冰岛，它没有什么汽车产业，也没有什么制造业，冰岛的主要支柱产业就是捕鱼。因为它在北冰洋，它最重要的产业就是在北冰洋打鱼。所以我们和冰岛的谈判比较简单。当时冰岛代表团提出来，很简单，如果你能把北冰洋捕回来的鱼的进口关税降下来，我们就可以达成协议。所以我们当时分析了一下，我们离北冰洋那么远，而且北冰洋捕鱼也是成本非常昂贵的，所以我们就想，这个对我们的产业没有什么大的影响。// 所以当时我记得我们和冰岛的谈判进行得非常轻松。我记得那天是日内瓦非常明媚的一个早晨，我们坐在咖啡厅里面，心情也很愉快，因为当时中央已经给了我完全的授权，冰岛要求的鱼的关税可以全部答应，不需要谈判。但是也不能坐下来就说，"好，你们的五条我们全部同意"，三分钟就结束这样的谈判。所以我花了很多时间谈谈冰岛的情况，谈谈日内瓦的天气，一直到最后，15分钟进入主题，很快就达成协议，握手言和，非常高兴。//

其他很多国家也是比较容易的。比如说哥伦比亚，它关心的主要就是两种（商品），一个就是咖啡，大家都知道哥伦比亚的咖啡是很有名的，我也不知道你们云山咖啡屋的咖啡是哪个国家的，反正哥伦比亚的咖啡是很有名的，产量也很高。另外一个就是鲜花，它生产的鲜花非常好。// 所以当时我们想这两个东西也不是很复杂，咖啡我们中国就是海南和云南生产一点点，多进口一点哥伦比亚的咖啡也没什么了不起，再加上我们中国人虽然喝了那么多年咖啡，但是愿意喝咖啡的人也不是很多，可能你们这些将来的"洋务派人物"可能会愿意喝点咖啡，像我这样搞了一辈子洋务的至今仍不喝咖啡。// 对很多人来讲，喝咖啡就像喝刷锅水一样，索然无味。所以中国人还是要喝点绿茶，喝点乌龙茶。所以我觉得对我们的产业也没什么太大的影响。// 哥伦比亚的鲜花再具有竞争能力，哥伦比亚远在拉丁美洲，等你把鲜花千山万水地运到中国来，可能也鲜不到哪儿去了。所以我们考虑也没什么了不起。所以和哥伦比亚的谈判也非常顺利。唉呀，回顾跟每个国家的谈判都是非常有意思的经历。//

当然，最困难的就是和美国的谈判。美国这个国家，在关贸总协定，在世界贸易组织确实是财大气粗，说一不二。和美国人谈判开始的时候，我们都有个适应的过程，美国人也有个适应的过程，因为美国人那么多年谈判，常常是坐下来就说，我们美利坚合众国的要求是一二三四五，这一二三四五没有什么谈判的余地。一上来就是这样子，当时我们中国代表团开始和它谈的时候美国人也用这种态度对待我们。// 我们觉得从心理上根本就接受不了这种态度——既然是一二三四五统统接受，我还谈判什么呢？干脆你拿个单子出来我们写个"YES"就完了。所以开始和美国的谈判可以说不是实质性的谈判，而是一种

230

所谓"打态度"的谈判。我这个湖南人脾气也是很暴躁的,看了美国人的这些态度以后,我们当时是根本不可能接受他们这种态度的。// 所以当时我是拍了不少桌子。我记得后来美国的一个商务部长见到吴仪同志说:"希望你们这位代表少拍点桌子。"我心想,如果不给你们拍桌子,美国人不知道跟中国人谈判得采取另外一种方式。所以和美国人谈了两三年之后,美国人逐渐知道中国人不是那么容易啃的。//

而且他们在很多问题上确实是相当霸道的。比如说我们谈判商品减税方案的问题,刚才我们也讲了,哥伦比亚、冰岛也就那么几项。美国人,那就不一样了。我们整个中国的关税表上有6,000多种商品,也就是中国要解决6,000多种商品进口(关税)下降的问题。当时美国人一上来就说,我们可不是冰岛啊,我们这6,000多种商品,我们美国人要和你谈4,800多种。那一下来气势很大的。// 我们一想,要和美国人谈4,800种产品的话,这个压力是很大的。所以后来我们咨询了一些世界贸易组织的专家,他们说美国人要求和你们谈4,800多种是完全没有道理的。// 因为根据世界贸易组织的规定,如果你要谈这样一个商品,比如哥伦比亚要和我们谈咖啡这个商品,你必须满足两个条件:第一,你必须是这项商品最大的三个生产国(之一);第二,你必须是这个产品最大的三个出口国(之一)。两者至少要其一。所以我们和美国的谈判,开始它讲谈4,800多种,后来我们很好地研究了美国提出的这个单子,发现其中很多的产品(美国)既不是前三名的生产国,也不是前三名的出口国。// 所以我们一个产品一个产品给它刷掉。后来美国人一看,中国人也懂点了,才开始认认真真地和你谈判。所以这个美国人,和他谈判你必须懂点东西。不懂它就唬你的,因为它唬惯了。所以和美国人的谈判确实是进行得非常艰苦。//

可以说,从1993年起,1994、1995、1996、1997、1998,一直没有任何进展。双方都在打太极拳。但是美国人可以和我们打太极拳,而我们实在是耗不起这个时间啊。所以当时和美国的谈判没有进展,一方面是由于美国的霸道,但你也必须承认,在我们国内对于市场开放有很多的争论。// 可以说这些争论也许是当时制约谈判的更重要的一些因素,因为各个部门不可能对很多问题达成共识。//

经过了1993、1994、1995和那么多年的磨合,大家对对外开放,对中国加入世界贸易组织市场的开放问题开始逐步形成了很多重要的共识。在这个方面我觉得朱镕基总理起了很多重要的作用。// 所以1998年以后我们中国的对美谈判加速进行,特别是决定了朱总理在1999年4月份要访美的时候,我们中美的谈判开始进行密集型的谈判。美国的谈判代表团到中国,我们到华盛顿去,一个月当中可以来回一两次、两三次。到了朱总理1999年4月份访美的

时候，我和美国就很多重大的问题已经基本上达成协议。//

IV Guide to Interpreting

1. Passage 1 节选自马来西亚国家旅游局国际合作司处长钟玉霞在 2004 年 10 月中国（广西）—东盟国际旅游合作论坛上的专题发言。东盟，即东南亚国家联盟（Association of Southeast Asian Nations），简称 ASEAN，成立于 1967 年，迄今已有 10 个成员国。在这篇英文演讲稿中，讲话人代表马来西亚国家旅游局做主题发言，回顾了马来西亚与中国之间的传统友谊和外交往来，详细介绍了马来西亚的多元化产业发展战略，尤其是旅游业的发展情况。这篇练习材料是个较好的数字训练篇章，口译时可进行针对性的数字翻译技巧训练。此外，在口译之前，要上网查阅马来西亚的旅游业发展概况，当然，还要做关于马来西亚人文地理的背景知识准备。

2. Passage 2 和 Passage 3 两篇汉译英练习材料节选自原中国对外贸易经济合作部副部长、现博鳌论坛秘书长龙永图 2004 年 10 月在广东外语外贸大学的讲座。龙部长是中国加入世界贸易组织谈判的主要领导和参与者，讲座中他用生动的语言详细回顾了那段漫长曲折的历史，再现了诸多精彩激烈的唇枪舌剑的交锋。讲话人用词幽默风趣、富有感染力、口语风格显著，用了许多通俗的表达。比如，"两心变一心"、"四个字——市场经济"、"司空见惯"、"这帮老兄"、"过了这个坎"、"洋务派人物"、"拍了不少桌子"、"这个老外，当时有点形而上学了"等，口译训练时应注意讲话人的语言风格，注意如何处理汉语口语表达，如何从中提取核心信息，滤掉一些冗余的表达，译出符合英语习惯的表达来。此外，在口译之前应该充分了解关税与贸易总协定和世贸组织的原则以及中国改革开放以来经济政策的相应调整，比如从计划经济向市场经济转化的承诺与加入世贸的关系。

V Highlight for Interpreting

Directions: Interpret the following sentences from Chinese into English or vice versa.

1. Some of you may be aware that Malaysia is the largest trading partner for China in Southeast Asia, accounting for 25% of China's trade with the ASEAN

countries, and the 2nd largest in Asia, after Japan.

2. As such, Malaysia is very much in a position to serve China as its gateway to Southeast Asia with its 550 million population and a market size of over US$320 billion.

3. The relationship has since grown to be very cordial and warm with exchange of visits between high-level leaders and the general public for business and tourism.

4. However, when the economic recession struck Malaysia in the mid-1980s, we embarked on our diversification plan. Tourism was identified as one of the industries that could provide us with very quick returns.

5. These campaigns, together with other promotional efforts have helped raise our tourism profile in the international markets. The development has also created confidence for the government to allocate bigger budget for our tourism development and promotion.

6. The 1997 Asian financial crisis, for example, saw the government providing us with the funding to launch our Malaysia—Truly Asia campaign.

7. 中国入世三年以后，我们越来越感觉到我们中国入世谈判的15年特别是最后的10年是一个相当艰苦的历程，因为它从一个层面反映了我们改革开放的那种复杂性，那种艰苦性。

8. 但是，在1992年以前，市场经济对我们来讲完全就是一个禁区，可以说，市场经济对于当时来讲等同于资本主义，谁讲市场经济，谁搞市场经济，谁就是搞资本主义。

9. 大家都知道当时我们对中国经济体制的描述是什么呢？是所谓"计划调节和市场调节相结合的商品经济体制"，非常复杂。

10. 大家知道，企业是一个国家经济的细胞，一个国家经济的健康会从企业的健康得到反映。一个国家的整个经济运行的体制会从企业的运行中得到体现。

11. 那么这个老外，当时有点形而上学了，他认为这个书记是上面派的，可能就代表你们讲的计划调节，那么厂长是代表企业的利益，他是管怎样挣钱的，他是代表你们所讲的这个市场调节，那么你们把这个"两心变一心"讲清楚了是不是就把市场调节和计划调节讲清楚了呢。

12. 所以在整个谈判的过程中我们当时确实就绕不开这样一个很大的困难，就是中国的计划经济体制怎么样来适应多边贸易体制的以市场经济为基础的这样一套国际规则体系。

13. 所以开始和美国的谈判可以说不是实质性的谈判，而是一种所谓"打态度"的谈判。我这个湖南人脾气也是很暴躁的，看了美国人的这些态度以后，我们当时是根本不可能接受他们这种态度的。

第18单元

IT产业

IT Industry

I Background Knowledge

Directions: Read the following English passages and then compare them with their Chinese equivalents.

Passage 1

Generally speaking, Information Technology (IT) or infotech is the "marrying-up" of products from several key industries: computers, telephones, television, and satellites. It means using micro-electronics, telecommunication networks, and fiber optics to help produce, store, obtain and send information by way of words, numbers, pictures and sound more quickly and efficiently than ever before.

The impact infotech is having, and is going to have on our lives and work is tremendous. It is already linking the skills of the space industry with those of cable television so programs can be beamed directly into our homes from all over the world. Armies of "steel collar" workers, the robots, will soon be working in factories doing the boring, complex and unpleasant jobs which are at present still done by man. In some areas such as the car industry this has already started. Television will also be used to enable customers to shop from the comfort of their homes by simply ordering via the TV screen, payment being made by direct debit of their credit cards. Home banking and the automatic booking of tickets will also be done through the television screen. Cable television which in many countries now gives a choice of dozens of channels will soon be used to protect our homes by operating burglar and fire alarms linked to police and fire stations. Computers will run our homes, controlling the heating, air conditioning and cooking systems while robots will cope with the housework. The friendly postman will be a thing of the past as the postal service and letters disappear with the electronic mail received via viewdata screen.

All these things are coming very fast and their effects will be as far-reaching as those of the industrial revolution. Infotech is part of the technological revolution and it is with us now.

一般而言，信息技术是若干骨干工业产品，如计算机、电话、电视和卫星的"嫁接品"。它是指使用微电子产品、通信网络和光纤技术来帮助生产、储存、获取信息，并以文字、数字、画面以及声音的形式比以前更快捷、更高效地传送信息。

信息技术正在并将会对我们的生活和工作产生巨大的影响。它已把空间工业技术与有线电视技术结合，让电视节目能从世界各地直接传送到千家万户。在工厂，目前由人做的一些枯燥、繁杂及无趣的工作也很快将会由成批的"钢领"工人——机器人来进行。在一些领域，如汽车工业，已经开始这样做了。电视也将用来帮助顾客在舒适的家中购物，只需通过电视屏幕订货并使用信用卡付款结账就行。家庭银行业务及自动订票也将可以通过电视屏幕进行。目前在许多国家，可为人们提供众多电视频道选择的有线电视也将很快通过操作与警察局和消防站相连的防盗及防火警报来保护我们的家产。计算机将管理我们的家，控制取暖、空调及烹饪系统，而机器人则处理家务。友好的邮递员将随着邮政服务和信件的消失以及邮件在计算机数据显示屏上的接收而成为历史。

所有这一切来势迅猛，而且其影响也将犹如工业革命一样意义深远。信息技术是科技革命的一部分，它已与我们密不可分。

Passage 2

E-commerce refers to trade or transactions concluded through networks by communication accesses that provided by the Internet. In a broad sense, it means e-business which includes various business activities in an electronic environment. Business practices such as market analyzing, client management, production management, resource distribution, virtual shop management, and decision making all fall into this category.

Nowadays, there are mainly three major e-commerce models in terms of party differentiation, namely, the B-to-C Model (or B2C Model), the B-to-B Model (or B2B Model) and the C-to-C Model (C2C Model). To elaborate, the B2C pattern is more commonly applied to retailing and service businesses than to other industries, which involves more than two crucial parties, i.e., business and customer. They also require certification authentication (CA) and banks offering online service (e-bank). Companies have claimed significant success in conducting B-to-C businesses in various fields such as stock exchanges, finance, PCs, modems, intermediaries, flowers and gifts. The B-to-B model is deployed in business-to-business transactions and is especially popular among business firms dealing in machinery, bidding, electrical components, security, and IT solutions. This is so far the most engaging "cake" for the numerous dot-coms. The third model, the C-to-C model, refers to the trade between customers themselves in which e-commerce web sites provide a platform. It is very much like a "second-hand market" or a "flea market".

电子商务指的是用通过因特网所提供的通讯网络而完成的贸易或业务交易。从广义上讲，电子商务涵盖了几乎所有电子环境下的商务活动，包括市场分析、客户管理、生产管理、资源配置、网上商店管理和决策等。

从参与者的不同来分，目前电子商务可以分成三种类型：B2C模式、B2B模式和C2C模式。具体来说，B2C模式更多地用于零售业和服务业，而不是其他的行业。这种模式不仅牵涉到两个关键的因素——商家和消费者，而且还涉及到证书认证（CA）和提供网上服务的电子银行（e-bank）。在诸如股票交易、金融、个人电脑、调制解调器、中介服务和鲜花礼品等行业，这种模式运作地相当成功。B2B模式存在于商家之间的业务往来，尤其是普遍存在于经营机械、招标、电子配件、保安和IT决策的商家之间。该模式目前是许多网络公司趋之若鹜的美味"蛋糕"。第三种模式——C2C模式，是指消费者之间进行的电子商务活动，消费者利用因特网所提供的平台进行交易，这种模式与"二手货市场"或"跳蚤市场"极为相似。

Warm-up

1 **Directions:** Give the English equivalents of the following Chinese expressions.

国信办	信息和知识相对密集
信息产业部	客户关系管理
发改委	先天优势
商务部	第三方电子商务服务
国家信息化专家咨询委员会	中国国家统计局

商务口译

教育部	新农村商网
高交会	农副产品网上购销对接会
网上产品博览会	亚太经合组织
网上投资贸易洽谈会	亚欧会议
网上消费品博览会	上海合作组织

2 **Directions:** Give the Chinese equivalents of the following English expressions.

fiber optics	encryption product
"steel collar" worker	competitive advantage
communication access	Developers Conference
virtual shop management	exponential increase
party differentiation	gigabyte of storage
certification authentication (CA)	multiple-processor machine
CeBIT	SMP
after the splash and promises	Digital Nervous System (DNS)
old issue in new dimension	vertical application
economic landscape	SAP
discriminatory tax policy	business application
stifle	Unix
OECD	

III Passages for Interpreting

Passage 1

Directions: Listen to the passage and interpret from Chinese into English at the end of each segment.

尊敬的各位领导、各位来宾：//

国信办、信息产业部、发改委、商务部、国家信息化专家咨询委员会共同主办的"2007中国信息化推进大会"今天开幕了。这是中国信息界的一次盛

会，将对推进我国信息化事业的健康、快速、持续发展起到积极促进作用，我代表商务部对本次大会的召开表示热烈的祝贺！//

今天，我就"加快电子商务发展，促进现代服务业成长"谈一谈自己的看法。//

一、现代服务业在国民经济中突显重要地位 //

十六大以来，党中央提出了科学发展观，要求全面协调可持续发展。发展现代服务业，正是适应对外开放新形势、实现全面协调可持续发展的有效途径。//

国务院于今年3月19日印发了《国务院关于加快发展服务业的若干意见》，明确指出服务是国民经济的重要组成部分，提出了服务业发展的具体目标。到2010年，服务业增加值占国内生产总值的比重比2005年提高3%，服务业从业人员占全社会从业人员的比重比2005年提高4%，服务贸易总额达到4,000亿美元。//

二、电子商务的广泛应用促进了现代服务业成长 //

现代服务业是指信息和知识相对密集的服务业，它依托现代化的新技术和新的服务方式，向社会提供高附加值、高层次的生产服务和生活服务。电子商务作为信息技术在经济活动中的一个典型应用，越来越成为现代服务业成长的一个不可或缺的重要环节。//

（一）电子商务提高了服务业的服务能力 //

电子商务促进了服务企业的营销范围扩大，促进了企业的客户关系管理。生产性服务业利用电子商务可以向生产者提供更加全面服务，使其能在生产前更深入地了解市场供求状况，经过充分的信息交换，从而降低企业生产成本，提高生产效率。//

（二）电子商务提高了服务业的服务效率 //

电子商务的应用可以大大节约交易成本，为客户提供更好的服务，从整体上提高运营效率。特别是在金融、物流、旅游、咨询等传统服务业领域，电子商务的应用具有先天优势。//

（三）电子商务开辟了新的服务业领域 //

电子商务在不断提高传统服务业服务能力的同时，还开辟了新的服务业领域，形成更多新兴行业和就业机会。如网上商店、网上银行、信息技术支持以及第三方电子商务服务提供商等等。以阿里巴巴为代表的第三方电子商务服务平台，为中小企业提供电子商务服务，既节省了中小企业自己开发和管理电子商务平台的费用，又可为中小企业提供大量买家信息及产品的进出口服务。//

三、商务部在推进电子商务方面所做的努力 //

多年来，商务部一直致力推动电子商务的应用与发展，主要开展了以下工作：//

（一）为改善我国网上交易发展的外部环境，防范网上交易风险，推动网上交易健康有序发展，商务部在今年3月6日发布了《关于网上交易的指导意见（暂行）》。目前正与中国国家统计局联合开展电子商务统计，第一批统计数据预计在2007年年底前可正式对外发布，中国第一个权威的电子商务统计指标体系正在逐步形成。//

（二）商务部自2003年起每年组织撰写《中国电子商务发展报告》。报告从宏观上分析了我国电子商务的发展状况，并对外贸、国内流通、网上零售等方面进行了重点分析，对引领中国电子商务的发展发挥了积极的作用。//

（三）为推广电子商务应用，商务部与教育部自2005年开始联合组织有关高等院校，开展了电子商务案例调研和理论研究。到目前为止，共完成了200多个电子商务案例调研。//

（四）在中国进出口商品交易会（广交会）、中国国际高新技术成果交易会（高交会）等大型展会上，商务部积极推动电子商务应用工作。每届广交会为超过8,000家参展商会员提供电子商务服务。商务部还支持和推动福建省举办中小企业"网上产品博览会"和"网上投资贸易洽谈会"，推动宁波市举办"网上消费品博览会"。//

（五）为提高地方和企业应用电子商务的能力，商务部组织了多期地方商务主管部门领导参加的"电子商务培训高级研究班"。//

（六）商务部启动了"农村商务信息服务"工程。在农业部、信息产业部和国信办等单位支持下于2006年8月25日开通了"新农村商网"。举办了三次"农副产品网上购销对接会"，共促成交易金额40.66亿元。//

（七）商务部积极组织参与电子商务领域的国际合作和交流，与13个国家和地区建立了电子商务交流合作机制。从2004年开始，商务部与部分国外政府商务主管部门合作建立并开通了"中国俄罗斯经贸合作网站"、"中国新加坡经贸合作网站"等九个经贸合作网站，利用信息技术为国内外企业开拓市场、开展业务提供了全面、及时、权威的商务信息服务。//

商务部还积极组织参与亚太经合组织、亚欧会议、上海合作组织等国际与地区组织中的电子商务工作，分别于2004年、2005年、2006年主办了"APEC电子商务博览会"、"APEC无纸贸易高级别研讨会"和"亚欧会议电子商务论坛"。//

最后，预祝大会获得圆满成功！//

第 18 单元　IT 产业

Passage 2

Directions: Listen to the passage and interpret from English into Chinese at the end of each segment.

Good evening. I have been looking forward to this evening for a long time, because I have known for many years how important CeBIT is to the global Information Technology industry. So before I go any further I want to thank you very much for inviting me to participate in this important forum. //

Now I have given a lot of thoughts as to what I would say to you this evening. On the one hand, I am here as a representative of the Information Technology industry on the event that is bigger by orders of magnitude than any other technology exhibit. That's quite a statement in an industry that's good at many things, especially celebrating its own creations. // On the other hand, like most of you, I've spent most of my professional life as a customer of this industry. So I know that after the splash and promises comes the harsh light of morning and often the customer is left standing alone wondering what happened, or as the head of one of our most important German customers put it, "Yours is an industry that is very good at weddings and not so good at marriages." // So tonight, while I will talk about the power and potential of Information Technology, I hope the temper of my remarks with the perspective I had when I came to IBM five years ago, the perspective of a customer. //

Now I started out this evening saying I hope to represent the voice of the customer. And as we project the benefit of this network world, the hundreds of millions of people may be even a billion. // It's clear that the Information Technology industry has a lot of work to do. We have got to make this technology easier to use and more natural. And that video you saw some of the things we and others are doing and working on ease of use today. We have got our rich agreement on standards, standards for communications, for security, for software development. // And I am asking you as customers to keep the heat on this industry—demand that we deliver open standards, everybody's software running on everybody's hardware over everybody's network. //

There is another set of issues that extend beyond the Information Technology industry—there are public policy issues. Some have been around for ever, like privacy. Some we recognize as old issues in new dimensions, like security and taxation in the global market place of the Internet. // Resolving these issues is gonna require

241

a new level of international cooperation. And I think the nations of the European Union have set a real leadership example in preparing for the common currency—perhaps the most important change since European integration and the treaty of your own. // IBM has been pleased, being involved in helping a number of you prepare for this, which will fundamentally alter the economic landscape and make it easier for all our companies to grow in Europe. But because the nature of the network world is just global—it has to be global, agreements to these critical policy issues are going to take this issue of cooperation to a new level. We are going to have to have a global public policy. //

First, people must have inexpensive access to the telecommunication services they need to participate, meaning governments have to encourage competition and end monopoly structures. And the news from Europe is very encouraging recently here. // It's also clear that the discriminatory tax policies can stifle this very nascent, early forming economic engine. We have to insure that electronic business is taxed the same way as the physical business world, no more, no less. // And the OECD has taken on this work, and we hardly support their efforts. We also support the move to keep the Internet a tariff free zone. This will be a big fight, but it's one we have to win together. //

Next, security. The domains of customers for strong encryption, and governments' legitimate concerns about their ability to provide public safety and enforce laws don't have to be neutrally exclusive. // IBM is working with the US government, with the European Union, and governments around the world to support an unrestricted market for encryption products that can interoperate globally. We are not anywhere near as for along on this as we need to be, but I am confident we will get there. We have to get there, there is too much of stake. //

Finally, privacy. How can we continue to strike the balance, the right balance between respect for the individuals' privacy and the benefits, on the other hand, of information flow in a connected world. The solution here must start with the private sector, not government. And a reaffirmation of a few proven principles by all businesses (is) that consumers get fair notice about information that is used, that is theirs, and an opportunity to control, and confirm its use. And a number of companies are moving in this direction. // IBM has recently adopted a global privacy policy for managing information online and it is posted on all of our websites around the world. With global agreement and cooperation and understanding, the Information

第 18 单元　IT 产业

Technology industry, government and our customers will go forward. I believe and insure that this global market place grows boldly, safely, and delivers on a real promise. That's important to every one. //

As we look ahead to the next millennium, I don't think there is any question any longer about the profound power of this technology. In an incredibly short span of time, it is developed to the point where it can, we can talk about it in the same context as any of the other great technologies that had transformed our world. // We are watching, we are participating in the emergence of something much bigger than the new computing model, much different than just a new channel for human interaction. // Information Technology, and specifically network technology, represents the most powerful tool we have ever had for change. It's a new engine for economic growth, a new medium that will redefine the nature of our relationships among governments and institutions and businesses of all kinds, and the people they serve now, and they might serve tomorrow. // This powerful tool is here for all of us today. Each of us will have to decide how will it (be) exploited, and how soon. But in any case, the nations, the government agencies, the public sector and commercial institutions, that do theirs most effectively, will create enormous competitive advantage into the 21 century. //

Thank you very much, and I hope you have the most successful CeBIT ever. //

Passage 3

Directions: Listen to the passage and interpret from English into Chinese at the end of each segment.

Good morning. It's a great pleasure to be here. // Today is a major milestone for Microsoft as our first Developers Conference here in China. The key partnerships we build with software developers around the world are central not only to the success of Windows but also to realize the great possibilities that PC technology provides. It's through applications of every variety that businesses will be using the personal computer as the tool of the information age. //

It's rather amazing how fast this innovation is moving. Even to people like myself that are deeply involved in the industry to go and see the improvements and every element (that are) taking place on a yearly basis is quite fantastic. // Of course one of the driving factors of this business is the exponential increase in processor performance. There is no doubt that the magic of chip capabilities as delivered through the advance in top microprocessors really are allowing us to think of applications that never would have been possible before. //

The PC industry is one of the few industries that can deliver both lower price equipment at the same time as improving the capabilities. The storage systems are now delivering gigabyte of storage as the standard capability. Over 80 million PCs are being sold a year. And the server market, the higher performance machines that these PCs networked with—that's the fastest growing part of this business. // The performance of those servers is increasing not only because the individual processors are faster, but also because we are using multiple-processor machines, so called SMP designs and clustering nodes together. //

We are also improving the high-end software on the server level. So a year ago, the fastest transaction benchmarks using PC technology, was about 6,000 transactions a minute. Today that's more than double to over 14,000 transactions a minute. And I can say with great confidence that during the next year we'll more than double that again. //

It's fair to say that even the most demanding applications now can be handled with PC technology. At the same time as we have this power, we also need to improve the simplicity of the machine and to make interface easier to work with. And I will talk today at the end of my presentation about some of the research that we are doing, in areas like handwriting and vision and linguistics. These are gonna make the machines far more natural than they are today, and make it clear to everyone these tools of the information age are for everyone, not just people with particular expertise in computer technology. //

Microsoft has a vision for where the PC is going. And that vision says that PCs will become a central element of how companies share information. The name of that vision is the so called Digital Nervous System (DNS), allowing companies to reduce paper work and make better decisions. // The Digital Nervous System means that not only do you have the PCs that are connected together, and not only do you have standard elements like electronic mail but also you really thought [think] carefully about what information is important—and so all of the processes, order taking, sales planning, personnel management, project management—all of those have been set up to take full advantage of the capabilities of the computer. //

By empowering every one in the company to have the information they need and allowing them to focus in on what really counts, not only will customer service improve, but the ability to collaborate with partners around the world will be very straightforward. // It's fair to say that the key platform for the Digital Nervous System is the combination of the Internet with the PC. The benefit of this kind of system is even clearer when you are dealing with surprises. //

And in this economy when there is [are] all kinds of surprises whether it's new regulations or customer who wants a product in a different way or something the competitor is doing. These systems are particularly good at allowing one company to do better than other companies in dealing with these unplanned events. // So truly saying that the modern companies will not only have the technology but use it in a very deep fashion for competitive advantage. //

The building blocks that allow company to have the world's best Digital Nervous System are very simple. In fact, most companies are investing in these things today. The up-to-date computer, the productivity tools, the e-mail which I think will become very standard. Today when you get business cards, it's not that common to have no electronic mail address. // I think in five to ten years here in China, most business people will have an electronic mail address. It won't just be simple messages that would be exchanged. All the things that are done on paper forms today where you have to fill out information, those will shift over into the electronic form. //

Since every business has particular means—why business applications are important to fill out the picture. These are not applications that Microsoft will be building. We will lie on other companies to do the vertical applications. // On a global basis, that includes companies like SAP, or Bond or Peoplesoft. And I think there is [are] incredible opportunities for lots of new companies in this area. In fact, one of our big big priorities here in China is to help companies build these new business applications. // In some cases these are applications that in the past would have been built on Unix, and are now moving into Windows NT. In other cases, these are new applications that are being built from the very beginning to take advantage of NT and its rich server capabilities. //

IV Guide to Interpreting

1. Passage 1 节选自商务部部长助理陈健在"2007 中国信息化推进大会"上

的发言。这篇讲话比较正式，谈论的主要是商务部有关"加快电子商务发展，促进现代服务业成长"的政策，内容涉及许多政府出台的文件和政策，以及各种商务活动的专有名词。在口译之前必须对这些专有名词做好准备，同时也要充分了解有关主题知识。比如，信息技术（Information Technology，简称 IT）是主要用于管理和处理信息所采用的各种技术的总称。它主要是应用计算机科学和通信技术来设计、开发、安装和实施信息系统及应用软件，也常被称为信息和通信技术（Information and Communications Technology, ICT）。电子商务 (electronic commerce) 通常是指在全球各地广泛的商业贸易活动中，在因特网开放的网络环境下，基于浏览器/服务器应用方式，买卖双方不谋面地进行各种商贸活动，实现消费者的网上购物、商户之间的网上交易和在线电子支付以及各种商务活动、交易活动、金融活动和相关的综合服务活动的一种新型的商业运营模式。此外，在口译训练时要针对中国领导人讲话的特点：有时说是谈一点看法，却分条列举许多分门别类的信息；有时说主要有三大条，第二条又有三小条内容，而第三条又有七小条细节。口译时一定要注意做针对性的笔记练习，段落小标题涵盖的通常是主要的信息点，翻译时不可错过。

2. Passage 2 节选自前 IBM 公司董事长兼首席执行官路易斯·格斯特纳先生（Mr. Louis Gerstner）2001 年在 CeBIT 论坛上的讲话录音。讲话人用轻松幽默的方式娓娓道来，不时博得阵阵笑声和热烈的掌声。口译时要注意讲话人的语气，译出的汉语尽量不要显得太干涩无味。此外，值得提醒的是，讲话人谈到 IT 产业所面临的三个问题，即"公众政策"、"安全性"以及"隐私权"，并将它们作为三个核心信息点来展开，口译时不妨按这三点做长交传的笔记训练。需要指出的是，CeBIT 是"办公及信息技术中心"的缩写，又称"CeBIT 信息及通信技术博览会"，是一个国际性的以信息技术（IT 业）和信息工程（IE 业）为主的大型展览会，自 1986 年起的每年春季在德国汉诺威举行，是全球最大的信息和通信工程类展览会。展览会的组织者是德意志展览股份公司（Deutsche Messe AG，简称 DMAG）。

3. Passage 3 节选自 IT 界鼎鼎大名的微软公司创办者比尔·盖茨 10 年前在北京的一次经典演讲，所讲的内容和涉及的专题知识今天已成为司空见惯的科技现实。作为全球最大的软件公司，微软公司一直是新技术变革的领导者。对于这样一个知名人物所作的经典演讲进行口译，充分的专题知识的准备必不可少，否则就会"卡壳"。

第 18 单元　IT 产业

V　Highlight for Interpreting

Directions: Interpret the following sentences from Chinese into English or vice versa.

1. 这是中国信息界的一次盛会，将对推进我国信息化事业的健康、快速、持续发展起到积极促进作用，我代表商务部对本次大会的召开表示热烈的祝贺！
2. 现代服务业是指信息和知识相对密集的服务业，它依托现代化的新技术和新的服务方式，向社会提供高附加值、高层次的生产服务和生活服务。电子商务作为信息技术在经济活动中的一个典型应用，越来越成为现代服务业成长的一个不可或缺的重要环节。
3. 电子商务的应用可以大大节约交易成本，为客户提供更好的服务，从整体上提高运营效率。特别是在金融、物流、旅游、咨询等传统服务业领域，电子商务的应用具有先天优势。
4. 以阿里巴巴为代表的第三方电子商务服务平台，为中小企业提供电子商务服务，既节省了中小企业自己开发和管理电子商务平台的费用，又可为中小企业提供大量买家信息及产品的进出口服务。
5. 每届广交会为超过 8,000 家参展商会员提供电子商务服务。商务部还支持和推动福建省举办中小企业"网上产品博览会"和"网上投资贸易洽谈会"，推动宁波市举办"网上消费品博览会"。
6. 商务部还积极组织参与亚太经合组织、亚欧会议、上海合作组织等国际与地区组织中的电子商务工作，分别于 2004 年、2005 年、2006 年主办了"APEC 电子商务博览会"、"APEC 无纸贸易高级别研讨会"和"亚欧会议电子商务论坛"。
7. So I know that after the splash and promises comes the harsh light of morning and often the customer is left standing alone wondering what happened, or as the head of one of our most important German customers put it, "Yours is an industry that is very good at weddings and not so good at marriages."
8. IBM has been pleased, being involved in helping a number of you prepare for this, which will fundamentally alter the economic landscape and make it easier for all our companies to grow in Europe.
9. IBM has recently adopted a global privacy policy for managing information online and it is posted on all of our websites around the world. With global agreement and cooperation and understanding, the Information Technology

industry, government and our customers will go forward.
10. Information technology, and specifically network technology, represents the most powerful tool we have ever had for change. It is a new engine for economic growth, a new medium that will redefine the nature of our relationships among governments and institutions and businesses of all kinds, and the people they serve now, and they might serve tomorrow.
11. It's rather amazing how fast this innovation is moving. Even to people like myself that are deeply involved in the industry to go and see the improvements and every element (that are) taking place on a yearly basis is quite fantastic.
12. The performance of those servers is increasing not only because the individual processors are faster, but also because we are using multiple-processor machines, so called SMP designs and clustering nodes together.
13. Microsoft has a vision for where the PC is going. And that vision says that PCs will become a central element of how companies share information. The name of that vision is the so called Digital Nervous System (DNS), allowing companies to reduce paper work and make better decisions.
14. By empowering every one in the company to have the information they need and allowing them to focus in on what really counts, not only will customer service improve, but the ability to collaborate with partners around the world will be very straightforward.
15. In some cases these are applications that in the past would have been built on Unix, and now we are now moving into Windows NT. In other cases, these are new applications that are being built from the very beginning to take advantage of NT and its rich server capabilities.

附录一

参考词汇表

第一单元 礼仪致词
Ceremonial Speeches

II Warm-up

1.

坦诚交流	candid exchange of ideas
集思广益	pool the wisdom of the masses
以……的名义	in the name of
论坛	forum
时代华纳集团	Time Warner Inc.
源远流长	of long standing
博大精深	greatness and profound richness
自强不息	to strive continuously to make new progress
顽强奋进	pioneering spirit
壮阔历程	great history
丧权辱国	humiliate the nation and forfeit its sovereignty; humiliating defeat
民不聊生	the people languished in poverty and starvation
内忧外患	be faced with troubles at home and agression from abroad
小康社会	moderately prosperous society
资源节约型	resource-effective
环境友好型	environment-friendly
值此……之际	on the occasion of
欢迎宴会	welcome banquet

商务口译

便宴	informal dinner
午宴	luncheon
便餐	refection
工作午餐	work lunch
自助餐	buffet dinner
答谢宴会	thank-you banquet
告别宴会	farewell banquet
庆功宴	celebration banquet
招待会	reception
鸡尾酒会	cocktail lounge
茶话会	tea party
欢聚一堂	enjoy a happy get-together
分论坛	parallel session
赞助人	sponsor
主办人	organizer
承办	organized by
协办	supported by
主持人	moderator
和谐社会	harmonious society
科学发展观	the scientific approach in achieving development/the scientific outlook on development

2.

commencement	毕业典礼
connecting the dots	一种小游戏，即把标有序列号的点连起来，就构成一幅图画
serif	衬线字体
san serif	无衬线字体
typeface	字体
typography	凸版印刷术
Macintosh	麦金塔电脑，苹果电脑
David Packard	戴维·帕卡德（普惠创始人之一）
Bob Noyce	鲍勃·诺伊斯（英特尔创始人之一）
NeXT	公司名，该公司由乔布斯于1985年创办
Pixar	皮克斯公司，它制作了世界上第一部全电

250

	脑动画电影《玩具总动员》
pancreas	胰腺
biopsy	切片检查
endoscope	内诊镜
dogma	教条
The Whole Earth Catalog	《全球目录》
Stewart Brand	斯图尔特·布兰德（《全球目录》杂志创始人）
Menlo Park	门洛帕克（市）
Stay Hungry, Stay Foolish	求知若饥，虚心若愚

第二单元　商务谈判
Business Negotiation

Warm-up

1.

提案	proposal
发盘	offer
反提案	counter proposal
还盘	counter offer
让步	make concession
掌握主动	be strong in a negotiation
多听少说	listen more and talk less
筹码	odds (for)
开放式问题	open-ended question

2.

common interest	共同利益
competing interest	冲突利益
complimentary interest	互补性利益
distributive negotiation	分配式谈判
integrative negotiation	整合式谈判
tax benefit	税项利益

251

telephone sales	电话销售
interest-based thinking	利益为基础的思维
barter deal	实物交易
forward foreign exchange contract	远期外汇合同
economic turmoil	经济动荡
raw material supplier	原料供货商
political analyst	政治分析师
cultural differences	文化差异
broker	经纪人
liaison	联络
best alternative to an agreement	达成协议的最佳选择

第三单元 商务访谈
Business Interview

Warm-up

1.

万有引力	gravitation
灵感	inspiration
最高成就	the highest achievement
尖锐	sharp
无聊	frivolity
创意产业	creative industry
传统产业	traditional industry
点石成金	turn the stone into gold
大力发展	greatly develop
优势	advantage
劣势	disadvantage
成本控制	cost control

2.

get preoccupied	全神贯注
equilibrium	均衡

information asymmetry	信息不对称
Information Technology	信息技术
gain some insight	洞察
Silicon Valley	硅谷
Internet bubble	互联网泡沫
venture capitalist	风险资本家
recruit faculty	招聘员工
computer animation	电脑动画
put the photograph on end	把照片竖着摆放
R&D	研究与开发
conventional service	传统服务
mind-set	思想
Hollywood studio	好莱坞电影工作室
bailout program	（金融）救援计划
distressed mortgage	不良按揭
American International Group	美国国际集团
Bear Stearns	贝尔斯登
JPMorgan Chase	摩根大通
Fannie Mae	房利美
Freddie Mac	房地美
soybean futures	大豆期货
Capitol Hill	国会山
foreclosure	丧失抵押品赎回权
savings portfolio	储蓄组合

第四单元　广告宣传
Advertising & Publicity

‖ Warm-up

1.

广交会	China Import and Export Fair; the Canton Fair
一地一馆两期	one location, one complex and two phases
琶洲一期展馆	Phase I Project of Pazhou Complex

商务口译

两地两馆两期	two locations, two complexes and two phases
专业展区	specialized exhibition section
采购商	buyer
重要平台	important platform
历史见证	witness of history
友谊纽带	road to friendship
贸易桥梁	bridge to trade
合作共赢	win-win cooperation
共同发展	common development
新闻发布会	press conference
各界朋友	friends from different communities
万商云集	great number of participants
亲身体验	experience by yourself
勃勃生机	vigor and vitality
建言献策	contribute ideas and suggestions

2.

Ultra HVDC	特高压直流输电技术
corporate activity	公司活动
self-drive	自主独立的精神
various restraints	各种制约
groundwork	基础
diversification of products	产品多元化
technological innovation	技术革新
business affair	商务活动
research institute	研究所
push forward	推进
cutting-edge	先进的
joint research	共同研究
industry-university cooperation	产学合作
intellectual property strategy	知识产权战略
creative cooperation	协创活动，创意合作
business operation	商业运作
hard disk drive	硬盘驱动器
automotive equipment	自动化设备

business collaboration	商业合作
semiconductor	半导体
personnel training	人员培训
in-house education system	企业内教育
invention incentive system	发明奖励机制
perpendicular magnetic disk	垂直磁记录式硬盘
finger vein authentication	手指静脉认证
μ-chip	微型芯片
energy saving technology	节能技术
social value	社会价值

第五单元 商务陈述
Business Presentation

Warm-up

1.

天津滨海新区	Tianjin Binhai New Area
"共赢奥运、传播奥运"	Beijing Olympics Games: Sharing the Success, Sharing the News
夏季达沃斯世界经济论坛	Summer Davos World Economic Forum
"10+3 媒体合作研讨会"	10+3 Media Cooperation Forum
亚欧大陆桥	Euro-Asia continental bridge
服务外包	service outsourcing
保税港区	bonded port
综合保税区	comprehensive bonded zone
保税物流园区	bonded logistics park
天津经济技术开发区	Tianjin Economic and Technological Development Area (TEDA)
首问负责	initial consultation
全程代办	whole charge d'affaires
一站式服务	one-stop service
人才支撑	personnel support
摩托罗拉	Motorola

商务口译

奥的斯电梯	Otis Elevator
丰田汽车	Toyota Motor
三星电子	Samsung Electronics
盐碱荒地	saline or alkaline land
天然气储量	natural gas reserve
开采	extract
地热	geothermal resource

2.

corporate entity	法人实体
etymology	词源学
agribusiness	农业综合企业
pompous	夸张的
bullet point	大纲，重点
confidence booster	信心提升手段
Transrapid	磁悬浮列车
portfolio	（产品）组合
megatrend	大趋势
cross-functional business unit	跨职能业务部门
high-end market	高端市场
sandwich of innovation	三明治创新（战略）
leapfrogging technologies	重点跨越技术
S.M.A.R.T. innovation	聪明的创新(西门子公司重点发展的特点)
Green Village Program	（西门子）绿色农村项目
innovation-driven economy	创新驱动的经济体
critical engine	重要引擎
low-end processing	低端加工
high-quality talent pool	高素质人才库
management know-how	管理技术
legal framework	法律体制
winning combination	双赢合作

第六单元 新闻发布会
Press Conference

Ⅱ Warm-up

1.

收支平衡	balance of payment
贸易顺差	trade surplus
外汇投资	foreign exchange investment
存款准备金率	deposit-reserve ratio
再贷款利率	refinancing rate
外包	outsource
扩大内需	boost domestic demand
发展服务业	develop the service/tertiary/industry
监管机构	supervisory institution
"三农"	(issues concerning) agriculture, peasant and rural areas
支付清算系统	account settlement system
残旧币	destroyed note
反洗钱	cracking down on transmission of illegal money
走私	smuggle
贩毒	narcotic traffic
贪污受贿	corruption and bribery
金融诈骗	financial fraud
逃税漏税	tax evasion
代理国库	acting agent of national treasury
拆借市场	fund lending market
债券市场	security market
中国外汇交易中心	China Foreign Exchange Trade Centre
农村信用社	Rural Credit Cooperative
中国银监会	China Banking Regulatory Commission
邮政储蓄	postal deposit business
抵押担保	mortgage guarantee
权威性	authoritativeness
股份制改革	reform of shareholding system
趋势性变化	change of trend
财政赤字	fiscal deficit
适当收缩	appropriate contracting

257

流动性过剩	liquidity surplus
股权分置	list non-tradable shares of listed companies
商务部	Ministry of Commerce
外交部	Ministry of Foreign Affairs
发改委	National Development and Reform Committee
工业和信息化部	Ministry of Industry and Information Technology
公安部	Ministry of Public Security
财政部	Ministry of Finance
人力资源和社会保障部	Ministry of Human Resources and Social Security
农业部	Ministry of Agriculture
中国海关总署	General Administration of Customs of the People's Republic of China
质检总局（国家质量监督检验检疫总局）	General Administration of Quality Supervision, Inspection and Quarantine of the People's Republic of China
民航总局	Civil Aviation Administration of China
食品药品监督管理局	State Food and Drug Administration
进出口银行	The Export-Import Bank of China
互利双赢	mutual benefit and win-win
贸易摩擦	trade conflict

2.

stock market	股票市场
average Chinese investor	普通中国股民
cool down	冷静下来
diversification	多元化
foreign exchange reserves	外汇储备
JCCT (Joint Commission of Commerce and Trade)	商贸联委会
comment on	就……发表评论
civilian nuclear cooperation	民用核能合作
military trade	军品贸易

第七单元　企业社会责任
Corporate Social Responsibility

Warm-up

1.

企业社会责任	corporate social responsibility (CSR)
非政府组织	non-governmental organization
认证	certification
技术标准	technical standard
消费者群体	consumer community
利益相关人	stakeholder
《关于企业社会责任合作的谅解备忘录》	Memorandum of Understanding (MOU) on Cooperation in CSR
投资者	investor
重要法宝	a vital source of
赠人玫瑰，手有余香。	The rose is in her hand and the fragrance in mine.
《劳动合同法》	Labor Contract Law
增长方式	growth mode
贯穿"一条主线"	follow through "one main thread"
突出"三个结合"	focus on "three alignments"
实现"四个和谐"	achieve "four harmonies"
以点带面，循序渐进	start with small steps, build on existing experience, and gradually enhance the overall performance

2.

sound-bite	言简意赅地说
corporate strategy	企业战略
World Business Council for Sustainable Development	世界可持续发展工商理事会

International Labour Organization	国际劳工组织
occupational health and safety	职业健康与安全
buyer	采购商
contractor	承包商
local community	当地社区
labor right	劳工权利
ethical issue	伦理问题
animal testing	动物试验
annual report	年度报告
labor standard	劳工标准
anti-corruption effort	反腐败努力
supply chain	供应链
global sourcing	全球采购
conflict prevention	防止冲突
International Standard Organization	国际标准组织
labor right	劳工权利
compliance	合规
Fair Labor Association (FLA)	公平劳工协会
external audit	外部审计
transparency	透明
Universal Declaration of Human Rights	《国际人权宣言》
industrial relation	劳资关系
capacity building	能力建设
worker representative	员工代表
secret ballot	不记名投票
worker retention	员工留用
worker turnover	工人流动

第八单元　企业文化
Corporate Culture

II Warm-up

1.

企业竞争力	corporate competitiveness
精神支柱	spiritual support
企业管理	corporate management
市场竞争力	competitiveness in the market
社会主义先进文化	socialist advanced culture
企业价值观	corporate value
企业精神	enterprising spirit
以人为本	people-oriented
公平竞争，诚信共赢的精神	win-win spirit of fair competition and credibility
诚信互利	mutual trust and mutual benefits
市场规则	market rule
讲究信用	pay attention to credit
假冒伪劣（产品）	counterfeit goods; fake and shoddy commodities
经济效益	economic benefit
文明经营	civilized operation
可持续性	sustainability
伦理规范	social ethics
公益事业	public welfare
义无反顾	without turning back
中国特色	Chinese characteristic

2.

corporate culture	企业文化
managing director	执行董事
core value	核心价值观
cost-consciousness	成本节约意识
real bond	真正的纽带

store concept	开店理念
Walking the Talk	《起而行》
retail skill	零售技巧
career development	事业发展
management introduction	管理入门
affordable product	买得起的产品
in situ	在原地，维持不变
institution set-up	制度安排
manufacturing company	制造企业
public sector	公共部门
innovative culture	创新型文化
boundary-breaking	打破常规的
CLSA	里昂证券
novel technology	新奇技术
economic tie	经济关系
closed innovation	封闭式创新
open innovation	开放式创新
internal capability	内部能力
do it alone	单独行动
start-up	创业型企业
open-source community	开源社区
spin-off	剥离企业
business model	商业模式
market presence	市场地位
innovation move	创新举措
core business	核心业务
ever-accelerating	不断加速的
strategic agility	战略灵活性
go-to-market agility	投入市场的灵活性
strategic partner	战略伙伴
ever-widening	更广泛的
mobile communications	移动通信
significant break from established thinking	不拘泥于既定思维

附录一

第九单元　国际会展
International Exhibitions

Warm-up

1.

会展城市	city for C&E
相关产业拉动效应	pull effect realized with neighboring industries
集聚效应	agglomeration effect
政府主导、政府主体	government being both the leader and the subject
展场面积	exhibition area
中国会展经济国际合作论坛	China Expo Forum for International Cooperation (CEFCO)
中国国际贸易促进委员会	China Council for the Promotion of International Trade (CCPIT)
国际展览业协会	Global Association of the Exhibition Industry (UFI)
国际展览与项目协会	International Association of Exhibitions and Events (IAEE)
独立组展商协会	Society of Independent Show Organizers (SISO)
"汇聚成长的力量"	Joining up with Growing Forces
中国国际展览会议展示会（展中展）	China International Trade Show for Exhibition and Conference Industry (InterExpo)
中国—东盟博览会	China-ASEAN Expo (CAEXPO)
中国—东盟商务与投资峰会	China-ASEAN Business and Investment Summit (CABIS)
市场准入	market access
大湄公河（次区域）	Greater Mekong Subregion
东盟东部增长区	East ASEAN Growth Area
次区域经济合作	subregional economic cooperation
山水相连	be connected by the same mountains

263

	and rivers
文化相通	share similar cultures
经济互补	mutual complements in economy; have much to offer each other economically
北部湾经济区	Beibu Bay Economic Zone
增长极	growth pole; area of growth
抗震救灾	battle against the (devastating Wenchuan) earthquake
坚定不移	remain committed to
始终不渝	steadfast; continue to

2.

entry promise	入世承诺
convention and exhibition industry	会展行业
MICE (meeting, incentive, conference and exhibition)	综合的旅游服务形式（包括集体会议、奖励旅游、大型会议和展览）
sunrise industry	朝阳产业
Shanghai World Expo	上海世博会
Munich International Trade Fairs (MMI)	慕尼黑国际博览集团
China International Exhibition Corporation (CIEC)	中国国际展览公司
Deutsche Messe Hanover	德国博览会集团公司
Messe Düsseldorf	德国杜塞尔多夫展览中心
Shanghai New International Expo Centre (SNIEC)	上海新国际博览中心

第十单元 政治与经济
Political & Economic Issues

Ⅱ Warm-up

1.

高层互访	exchange of high-level visits
双边贸易额	bilateral trade volume
同比增长	up by...year on year
组团旅游	group travel
通胀压力	inflationary pressure
趋利避害	draw on advantages and avert hazards
部长级会议	Ministerial Conference
零关税待遇	duty exemption on imports
投资兴业	invest and conduct business
商业融资	business financing
美中关系全国委员会	National Committee on US-China Relations
美中贸易全国委员会	US-China Business Council
美国对外关系委员会	US Council on Foreign Relations
亚洲协会	Asia Society
美国商会	American Chamber of Commerce
美国中国总商会	China General Chamber of Commerce—USA
百人会	Committee of 100
美中政策基金会	US-China Policy Foundation
美国中国论坛	US Forum on China
商业圆桌会议	the Business Roundtable
华美协进社	China Institute in America
共叙情谊	brings together...for a delightful gathering
合则两利，斗则俱伤	gain from peaceful coexistence, and lose from conflicts
战略对话机制	strategic dialog mechanism
执教	coach
花样游泳队	synchronized swimming team
金融动荡	financial volatility
能源紧张、粮食短缺	energy and food shortage

2.

NYSE	纽约证券交易所
NASDAQ	全美证券交易商自动报价系统协会（纳斯达克）
AMEX	美国证券交易所
NYMEX	纽约商业交易所
NYBOT	纽约期货交易所
subprime mortgage crisis	次贷危机
contracted liquidity	流动性紧缩
regulatory framework	监管机构
high default rates	高按揭款违约率
refinance	再融资
initial terms	首付款
defaults and foreclosure	（次级房贷借款人）违约和房产被没收
financial recovery plan	金融复兴计划
defining moment	决定性的时刻
Great Depression	大萧条
rescue effort	拯救努力
get oversight over	监督
final verdict	最终裁决
shred regulation	撕碎规章制度
trickle down	涓滴（财富从富人滴向穷人）
fair shake	公平待遇
work out a solution	得出解决方案
Wall Street	华尔街
Main Street	缅因街（村镇或小城市主要零售街道的通标）
come up with a package	拿出一揽子方案
subprime lending mess	次贷混乱
lax regulation	松散管理
Secretary of the Treasury	财政部长
stakeholder	利益相关者
economic philosophy	经济哲学

第十一单元 营销与全球采购
Marketing & Global Sourcing

Warm-up

1.

销售代表	sales representative
年度会议	annual meeting
开场白	opening remarks
销售老手	veteran salesman
纷扰不断	disturbances from time to time
变幻莫测	confusing; capricious
无人能及	unsurpassed
思维敏捷	have a quick, sharp mind
经年累月	over the years
行之有效	prove fruitful
重演	repeat

2.

marketing mix	营销组合
human rights movement	人权运动
consumerism	用户至上主义
threat and opportunity	风险和机遇
potential threat	潜在风险
product-market entry	产品市场进入
corporate and business-level strategy	公司和企业层面的战略
look further afield	高瞻远瞩
catalyst	催化剂
key criteria	重要的标准
island hop	转移
negative publicity	负面形象
weigh up	权衡
prospective partner	未来的伙伴
extract maximum value	实现最大价值
complete ownership	百分百股权

strategic alliance	战略联盟
buy the market	收购
prequalified vendor	合格的供货商
bidding process	招标流程
vulnerable to fluctuation	易受波动左右
availability	可获得性
primary ingredient	基本原料
short-term saving	短期收益
venture capital	风险资本

第十二单元　人力资源管理
Human Resources Management

Ⅱ Warm-up

1.

就业市场	employment market
人力资源	human resource
工作和生活平衡	work-life balance
有效措施	effective measure
人才竞争	competition of talents
人员更替	employee; staff turnover
职位空缺率	rate of job vacancy
薪酬制度	remuneration package
附加福利	fringe benefit; traditional welfare
员工留用	staff retention
收益递减规律	law of diminishing return
双赢局面	win-win scenario/situation
咨询服务	counseling service
开明就业	enlightened employment
大力推广	greatly popularize; vigorously promote
共同携手	join hands with

2.

legislative proposal	立法提案
SHRM (Society for Human Resource Management)	人力资源管理学会
snapshot	简介
rippling effect	波及效应
strong resiliency	强劲反弹
unemployment rate	失业率
payroll employment	非农业就业人口
purchasing power	购买力
wage earner	工薪族
knowledge-based economy	知识经济
post-secondary education	高中后教育；高等教育
healthcare provider	医护人员
technical specialist	技术专家
thoughtful comment	深思熟虑的评价
routine process	惯例
one-size-fits-all	一刀切
beacon of opportunity	充满机遇的灯塔
recruitment and staffing	人员征聘及其编制
Public Service Modernization Act (PSMA)	《公共服务现代化法案》
tight labor market	紧俏的劳动力市场
multiple objectives	多重目标
fast-paced environment	快速变化的环境
Auditor General	审计长
rules-driven	规则驱动的
staffing system	编制体系
externally and internally	里里外外
deputy head	常务次长
PSC (Public Service Commission)	公共服务委员会
Public Service Employment Act (PSEA)	《公共服务员工法案》
exclusive authority	独有的权威
oversight capacity	监督能力
values-based	以价值为基础的
assessment process	评估过程
oversight function	监督功能

商务口译

accountability instrument	问责工具
Staffing Management Accountability Framework	员工管理问责框架
Commission for Public Complaints Against the RCMP (Royal Canadian Mounted Police)	公共投诉皇家骑警委员会
audit plan	审计计划
external staffing	外部编制
political partisanship	政治伙伴
Public Service Staffing Tribunal	公共服务人员编制法庭
at arm's length	近在咫尺

第十三单元 战略管理
Strategic Management

Warm-up

1.

百年老店	centennial shop; shop of a century's standing
诚信	integrity
第一个吃螃蟹的人	the first person to try tomato
内控体系	internal control system
标准普尔	Standard Poor
茁壮成长	grow ever stronger
创业之本	root of business
诚信为基	hold integrity as sole principle
危机感	sense of crisis
措手不及	be caught totally unprepared
居安思危	be prepared for adversity
东山再起	revive some time in the future
喊狼来了	(the shepherd who is always) crying wolf for fun

2.

mission, vision and objective	使命、远景和目标
balanced scorecard	平衡记分卡
strategic alignment	战略协同

strategic consistency	战略一致性
SWOT analysis	公司内部（优势、弱势、机会和风险）分析
BP (British Petroleum)	英国石油公司
Advisory Board	顾问团；咨询委员会
"more of the same"	规模效应
reach the limit of one's capacity	尽其所能
oil and gas field	油气田
complex social and economic organism	复杂的社会和经济有机体
IPIC Annual Meeting	加拿大知识产权协会年会
CIPO (Canadian Intellectual Property Office)	加拿大知识产权局
Five-Year Strategic Plan	五年战略规划
dual mandate	双重任务
fine-tuning performance measure	细微的绩效调节措施
outreach	外围服务
average total pendency	平均总搁置时间
accessibility	接触便利性
turnaround time	周转时间
performance metric	绩效参数

第十四单元 交通与物流
Transportation & Logistics

Warm-up

1.

比雷埃夫斯港	Port of Piraeus
联合国欧洲经济委员会	United Nations Economic Commission for Europe (UNECE)
传播和弘扬	carry forward and disseminate
历史巨变	the great changes
集装箱吞吐量	container throughput
标箱	TEU (twenty-foot equivalent unit)

商务口译

环境友好型	environment-friendly
资源节约型	resource-saving
统筹规划	unified planning
合理布局	rational distribution
东部优先现代化	the precedent modernization of the east China
西部大开发	the development of the west China
中部崛起	the rise of the middle China
港口腹地	the port hinterland
产业转移	industrial transfer
大显身手	strut one's stuff
与国际接轨	in accordance with the international standard
班轮公司	shipping service company
挂靠中国港口	connected with Chinese ports
规划先行	prepare advanced plans
适度超前	moderately go further than the need of the development
以港兴市	prosper the cities with the ports
以市促港	develop the ports with the cities
良性互动	realize a positive interaction
中国—欧盟海运协定	China-EU maritime transport agreement
金融资产缩水	the world's financial assets shrinking

2.

logistical infrastructure	物流基础设施
distribution center	配送中心
third-party logistics	第三方物流
SMCs (Small and Medium Cities)	中国中小城市
cost minimization	成本最小化
Canadian Transportation Agency	加拿大运输局
CILTNA (the Chartered Institute of Logistics and Transport in North America)	国际物流与运输协会（北美分会）
quasi-judicial tribunal	准司法法庭
federal jurisdiction	联邦法律体制
ministerial advisory committee	部长级顾问委员会
deliver on our mandate	履行职责

hybrid organizational model	混合组织模式
caseload management efficiency	个案管理效率
Modern Logistics and Freeport Development	现代物流与自由港发展
Bo'ao Forum for Asia (BFA)	博鳌亚洲论坛
a somber setting	气氛沉重
globalization mandate	全球化任务
build-up of inventory	库存积压
just-in-time	及时制（零库存）
vast archipelago	群岛
industrial powerhouse	产业基地
center of economic gravity	经济中心
render obsolete the concept of...	摒弃以往的观念

第十五单元　金融与证券
Finance & Securities

Ⅱ Warm-up

1.

招商证券论坛	China Merchants Securities Forum
15周年华诞	the 15th anniversary
大喜之日	big day
招商银行证券部	Division of Securities in China Merchants Bank
综合类券商	synthetic securities trader
银行间同业拆借市场	interbank borrowing market
自营	brokerage
网上交易	online trading
资产管理	asset management
敦行致远	responsibility for the present and the future
良好市场形象	sound image in the market
思想的盛宴	nourishment of thought
不容错过	can not be missed

2.

private equity	私募资金
mutual fund	对冲基金
hedge fund	保值基金
securitized assets	证券化资产
publicly-traded corporation	上市公司
personal finance	个人融资/理财
public finance	公共融资/理财
corporate finance	公司融资/理财
institutional setting	机构性背景
outstanding share	已发行股票
fungible, negotiable instrument	可替换和转让的金融工具
common stock	普通股
stock option	股票期权
derivative	衍生产品
OMX	北欧证券交易商瑞典OMX公司
exchange owner	交易所所有者
clearing house	清算公司
niche market	利基市场，瞄准机会的市场
going through the roof	居高不下，飞涨
the bubble finally burst	泡沫终于爆裂
quick profit	快速盈利
jump onto the Internet bandwagon	赶网络股大流
the break-even point	盈亏持平
brand awareness	品牌意识
phenomenal growth	惊人增长
rely on alternative yardsticks	依赖于其他标准
audience reach	受众接触面
due a sell-off	要抛售
leveling out	持平
roller-coaster ride	坐过山车
breaking news	突发新闻
million-dollar question	关键的问题
consolidation activity	联合，并购活动
enter into a joint venture	建立合资企业

general upward trend	总体上升趋势
take off	起动
soar	飙升
very strong recovery	强劲反弹
peak at	最高点在
collapse by 50%	跌了五成

第十六单元　会计与税收
Accounting & Taxations

Warm-up

1.

特许会计师协会	Institute of Chartered Accountants
注册会计师	Certified Public Accountant (CPA)
资本市场	capital market
中国经济体制改革	Chinese economic structural reform
市场经济体制	market economy system
国有企业	state-owned enterprise (SOE)
上市公司	listed company
流通市值	negotiable market capitalization
金融债券	financial bond
主板市场	Main Board
创业板	GEM Board（Growth Enterprise Market Board）
社会保障基金	social security fund
金融机构	financial institution
投资理念	investment philosophy
市场法律框架	legal framework of the market
证券投资基金法	Law on Securities Investment Funds
行政法规	administrative regulation
转型阶段	transition stage
债权人	creditor
职业操守	professional integrity

2.

Accounting Student Society	会计学生协会
inauguration ceremony	就职典礼
accountancy sector	会计行业
accountancy profession	会计职业
future career path	未来职业道路
meet deadline	按期完成
accountancy firm	会计事务所
qualified accountant	认证合格的会计
HKICPA (The Hong Kong Institute of Certified Public Accountants)	香港会计师公会
financial management	财务管理
regulatory measure	管制措施
life-long learning	终生学习
burgeoning economy	新兴经济
harsh working environment	艰苦的工作环境
future pillar	未来的支柱
Corporate Tax Association (CTA)	企业所得税协会
public company	上市公司
tax reform	税收改革
tax system	税收体制
tax collection	征税
business tax	营业税
Treasury Minister	财政部长
corporate governance	公司治理
audit reform	审计改革
corporate disclosure	公司披露
corporate regulation	企业管制
tax risk	税收风险
tax return	税单，纳税申报单
opening offer	公开报价
Commissioner of Taxation	税务专员
tax compliance	守法纳税
Board of Taxation	税收委员会
short-sighted approach	短视行为

tax community	税务部门
national interest	国家利益
tax design	税收设计
short-term project	短期计划

第十七单元　国际经济组织
International Business Organization

Warm-up

1.

贸易体制	trade system
入世谈判	WTO entry negotiation
市场经济	market economy
关贸总协定	GATT (General Agreement on Tariff and Trade)
成员国贸易协议	trade agreement between member countries
商品经济体制	commodity economic system
计划调节	planned regulation
市场调节	market regulation
企业运行机制	corporate operational mechanism
中央党校	Party School of the CPC Central Commitee
社会主义市场经济	socialist market economy
十四大	14th CPC Congress
缔约方	signatory party
让步	make concession
市场准入	market access
双边谈判	bilateral negotiation
多边谈判	multilateral negotiation
减税	tax reduction

2.

multilateral trade agreement	多边贸易协定
trade dispute	贸易争端
Most Favored Nation status	最惠国待遇

trade preference	贸易优惠
trade barrier	贸易壁垒
import quota	进口配额
reciprocal tariff	互利性关税
ASEAN (Association of Southeast Asian Nations)	东盟
Free Trade Area (FTA)	自由贸易区
Early Harvest Plan (EHP)	早期收获计划
dispute settlement	争端解决
bilateral trade	双边贸易
economic integration	经济一体化
China-ASEAN Expo	中国—东盟博览会
Organization of Islamic Countries (OIC)	伊斯兰国家组织
Ministry of Culture, Arts & Tourism	文化艺术和旅游部
Visit Malaysia Year	马来西亚观光年

第十八单元　IT产业
IT Industry

Warm-up

1.

国信办	State Council Informatization Office
信息产业部	Ministry of Information Industry
发改委	National Development and Reform Commission
商务部	Ministry of Commerce (MOFCOM)
国家信息化专家咨询委员会	Advisory Committee for State Informatization
信息和知识相对密集	relatively information- and knowledge-intensive
客户关系管理	customer relations management
先天优势	inborn advantage
第三方电子商务服务	third-party e-commerce service
中国国家统计局	National Bureau of Statistics
教育部	Ministry of Education

高交会	China Hi-tech Fair
网上产品博览会	Online Fair
网上投资贸易洽谈会	Online Investment & Trade Symposium
网上消费品博览会	Online Consumer Goods Fair
新农村商网	New Rural Business Network
农副产品网上购销对接会	online fairs for agricultural by-products
亚太经合组织	APEC (Asia-Pacific Economic Cooperation)
亚欧会议	ASEM (Asia-Europe Meeting)
上海合作组织	Shanghai Cooperation Organization (SCO)

2.

fiber optics	光纤
"steel collar" worker	"钢领"工人（机器人）
communication access	通信入口
virtual shop management	网上商店管理
party differentiation	参与者的不同
certification authentication (CA)	证书认证
CeBIT (Centrum der Büro- und Informationstechnik)	信息及通信技术博览会
after the splash and promises	一通承诺之后
old issue in new dimension	老问题，新视角
economic landscape	经济形势
discriminatory tax policy	歧视性税收政策
stifle	压制
OECD (Organization for Economic Cooperation and Development)	经济合作与发展组织
encryption product	加密产品
competitive advantage	竞争优势
Developers Conference	专业开发者会议
exponential increase	呈指数倍数增长
gigabyte of storage	以千兆字节作为储量标准
multiple-processor machine	多处理器
SMP (Symmetrical Multi-Processing)	对称多处理技术
Digital Nervous System (DNS)	数字神经系统
vertical application	纵向应用

商务口译

SAP　　　　　　　　　　　　　公司名，欧洲最大的软件企业，总部设于德国沃尔多夫

business application　　　　　　商务应用

Unix　　　　　　　　　　　　　电脑操作系统，是美国AT&T公司1971年在PDP-II上运行的操作系统

附录二
主要参考书目

Frishberg, N. 1986. *Interpreting: an introduction*. Rockville: RID Publications.

Gile, Daniel. 1995. *Basic Concepts and Models for Interpreter and Translator Training*. Amsterdam/Philadelphia: John Benjamins.

Jones, R. 1998. *Conference Interpreting Explained*. Manchester: St. Jerome Publishing.

Phelan, M. 2001. *The Interpreter's Resource*. Clevedon: Multilingual Matters Ltd.

Pöchhacker, Franz. 2004. *Introducing Interpreting Studies*. London: Routeldge.

Seleskovitch, D. 1978. *Interpreting for International Conferences*. Washington: Pen Booth.

钟述孔，1999，《实用口译手册（增订版）》，北京：中国对外翻译出版公司。

梅德明，2000，《高级口译教程（第二版）》，上海：上海外语教育出版社。

徐亚南，1998，《外事翻译：口译和笔译技巧》，北京：世界知识出版社。

鲍刚，1998，《口译理论概述》，北京：旅游教育出版社。

柴明颎，2007，口译职业化带来的口译专业化，《广东外语外贸大学学报》，2007 (2)。

刘和平，2001，《口译技巧：思维科学与口译推理教学法》，北京：中国对外翻译出版公司。

张维为，1999，《英汉同声传译》，北京：中国对外翻译出版公司。

仲伟合，2001，英汉同声传译技巧与训练，《中国翻译》，2001 (5)。

仲伟合，2007，专业口译教学的原则与方法，《中国翻译》，2007 (3)。

仲伟合，2006，《英语口译教程》，北京：高等教育出版社。

仲伟合，2008，《英语同声传译教程》，北京：高等教育出版社。

赵军峰，1997，论口译中的语体识别与对等转换，《中国科技翻译》，1997 (3)。

赵军峰，1998，论口译者的跨文化意识，《中国科技翻译》，1998 (2)。

赵军峰，2005，论口译的翻译单位，《中国科技翻译》，2005 (2)。

赵军峰，2000，《新编经贸英语口译教程》，北京：中国社会科学出版社。

赵军峰，2003，《商务英语口译》，北京：高等教育出版社。

全国翻译硕士专业学位（MTI）系列教材

国内第一套专门针对MTI学生编写的专业教材

本系列教材由笔译、口译、理论、通识和工具书五大板块组成，具有专业化、实践性、应用型的鲜明特色。整套教材以职业翻译技能训练为核心，以适当的应用型翻译理论为指导，配合不同学科领域的专题训练，旨在完善学生翻译学科知识结构，提高学生口笔译实践能力。

MTI系列教材总主编：

何其莘　全国翻译专业学位研究生教育指导委员会副主任委员，北京外国语大学教授
仲伟合　全国翻译专业学位研究生教育指导委员会副主任委员，广东外语外贸大学校长
许　钧　全国翻译专业学位研究生教育指导委员会副主任委员，南京大学教授

笔译

高级英汉翻译	孙致礼　周晔
高级汉英翻译	陈宏薇
笔译理论与技巧	何刚强
高级文学翻译	胡显耀　李力
非文学翻译	李长栓
中国文化典籍英译	王宏印
世界文化典籍汉译	王宏印
外事翻译	姜秋霞
科技翻译	傅勇林　唐跃勤
计算机辅助翻译	钱多秀

理论

翻译概论	许钧
翻译研究方法概论	穆雷
中西翻译简史	谢天振　等
当代西方翻译研究原典选读	廖七一

口译

基础口译	仲伟合　王斌华
同声传译	仲伟合　詹成
交替传译（第二版）	任文
专题口译	柴明颎　张爱玲
英汉视译	秦亚青　何群
商务口译	赵军峰
外交口译	何群　李春怡

通识

翻译与跨文化交际	陈建平
英汉比较与翻译	秦洪武　王克非

工具书

翻译实用手册	文军　等
MTI毕业论文写作指南	黄国文